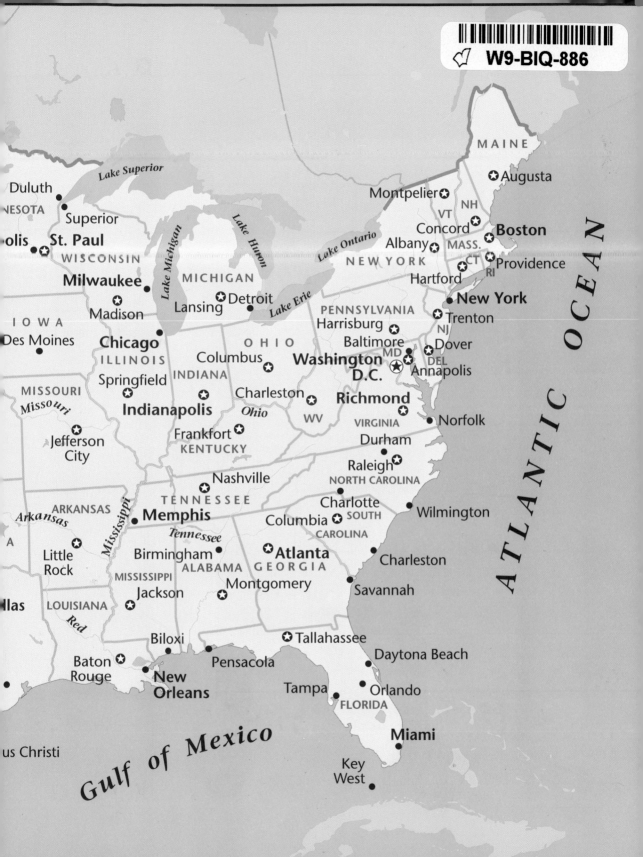

W9-BIQ-886

MAINE

Lake Superior

Duluth
Superior
MINNESOTA
 St. Paul
olis
WISCONSIN

Milwaukee
Madison
IOWA
Des Moines
Chicago
ILLINOIS
Springfield
INDIANA
MISSOURI
Indianapolis
Missouri
Jefferson
City
KENTUCKY
Frankfort

ARKANSAS
Arkansas
Memphis
Little
Rock
MISSISSIPPI

Jackson

LOUISIANA
Red
Biloxi
Baton
Rouge
New
Orleans
Pensacola

Lake Michigan
MICHIGAN
Lansing
Detroit
Lake Erie
OHIO
Columbus

Charleston
Ohio
WV

Nashville
TENNESSEE
Tennessee
Birmingham
ALABAMA
Montgomery

Lake Huron

Lake Ontario

Montpelier

Augusta

NH
VT
Concord
Albany
MASS.
Hartford
CT
RI

Boston
Providence

NEW YORK

PENNSYLVANIA
Harrisburg
Baltimore
Washington
D.C.
MD
Richmond
VIRGINIA
Durham
Raleigh
NORTH CAROLINA

New York
Trenton
NJ
Dover
DEL
Annapolis

Norfolk

Charlotte
Columbia SOUTH
CAROLINA
Atlanta GEORGIA

Wilmington

Charleston

Savannah

Tallahassee
Daytona Beach

Tampa
FLORIDA
Orlando

Miami

us Christi

Gulf of Mexico

Key
West

ATLANTIC OCEAN

Dallas

R
973.03
JUN
Junior Worldmark encyclopedia
of the states

DATE DUE	BORROWER'S NAME	

Junior Worldmark Encyclopedia of the States

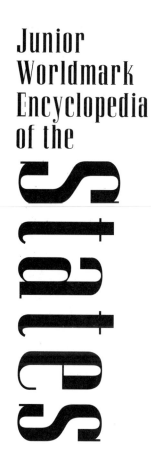

Junior Worldmark Encyclopedia of the

States

Third Edition

GALE GROUP

THOMSON LEARNING

Detroit • New York • San Diego • San Francisco
Boston • New Haven, Conn. • Waterville, Maine
London • Munich

Alabama to Illinois

JUNIOR WORLDMARK ENCYCLOPEDIA OF THE STATES, THIRD EDITION

Timothy L. Gall and Susan Bevan Gall, *Editors*
Karen Hanson, *Associate Editor*
Barbara Dickinson, Jennifer Jackson, Sarah Kunz, and Jennifer Wallace, *Assistant Editors*
Brian Rajewski, Deborah Rutti, and Bram Lambrecht, *Graphics and Layout*
Janet Fenn and Matthew Markovich, *Proofreaders*
University of Akron Laboratory for Cartographic and
    Spatial Analysis, Joseph W. Stoll, Supervisor;
    Scott Raypholtz, Mike Meger, *Cartographers*

U•X•L Staff

Allison McNeill, *U•X•L Senior Editor*
Carol DeKane Nagel, *U•X•L Managing Editor*
Thomas L. Romig, *U•X•L Publisher*
Evi Seoud, *Assistant Manager, Composition Purchasing and Electronic Prepress*
Rita Wimberley, *Senior Buyer*
Mary Krzewinski, *Art Director*
Mike Logusz, *Graphic Artist*

Library of Congress Cataloging-in-Publication Data

Junior Worldmark encyclopedia of the states / [Timothy L. Gall and Susan Bevan Gall, editors]. -- 3rd ed.
    p. cm.
  Includes bibliographical references and index.
  Contents : v. 1. Alabama to Illinois -- v. 2. Indiana to Nebraska -- v. 3. Nevada to South Dakota -- v. 4. Tennessee to Wyoming
  ISBN 0-7876-5376-4 (set) -- ISBN 0-7876-5377-2 (v. l) -- ISBN 0-7876-5378-0 (v. 2) -- ISBN 0-7876-5379-9 (v. 3) -- ISBN 0-7876-5380-2 (v. 4)
  1. United States--Encyclopedias, Juvenile. 2. U.S. states--Encyclopedias, Juvenile. [1. United States--Encyclopedias.] I. Gall, Timothy L. II. Gall, Susan B.

E156.J86 2001
973'.03--dc21
                                          2010041056

CONTENTS

READER'S GUIDE

Junior Worldmark Encyclopedia of the States, Third Edition, presents profiles of the 50 states of the nation, the District of Columbia, Puerto Rico, and the U.S. dependencies, arranged alphabetically in four volumes. *Junior Worldmark* is based on the fifth edition of the reference work, *Worldmark Encyclopedia of the States.* The *Worldmark* design organizes facts and data about every state in a common structure. Every profile contains a map, showing the state and its location in the nation.

For this third edition of *Junior Worldmark,* facts were updated and many new photographs were added. While the second edition photographs were chosen to illustrate economic activity in the state, new photographs for this edition were selected to feature notable citizens. In addition, a Population Profile was added to each state entry giving the breakdown of the state's population by race as enumerated by Census 2000. For the first time in history, respondents to Census 2000 were given the opportunity to select one or more race categories to indicate their racial identity. The U.S. Census Bureau reported data for each state in seven race categories: White *alone;* Black or African American *alone;* American Indian and Alaska Native *alone;* Asian *alone;* Native Hawaiian and Other Pacific Islander *alone;* Some other race *alone;* and Two or more races. About 98% of all respondents reported only one race. The population

profile gives users of *Junior Worldmark* access to the latest population data for the states.

Each state's political history is documented in the updated table listing the governors who have served the state since the founding of the nation. As with the first and second editions, recognition is due to the many professional photographers, tourist bureaus, convention centers, press offices, and state agencies that contributed the photographs that illustrate this encyclopedia.

Web sites listed at the end of the Bibliography for each state article have been verified and updated. An extensive survey of available sites was undertaken in May 2001 and only those with information relevant to the needs of students were chosen for inclusion.

Attention is also drawn to the many article reviewers listed at the end of this Reader's Guide. The reviewers contributed insights, updates, and substantive additions that were instrumental to the creation of this work. The editors are extremely grateful for the time and effort these distinguished reviewers devoted to improving the quality of this encyclopedia.

Sources

Due to the broad scope of this encyclopedia many sources were consulted in compiling the information and statistics presented in these volumes. Of primary importance were the publications of the U.S. Bureau of the Census. The most recent agricultural statistics on crops and livestock were obtained from files posted by the U.S. Department of Agriculture on its gopher server and its world-wide web site at http://www.econ.ag.gov. Finally, many fact sheets, booklets, and state statistical abstracts were used to update data not collected by the federal government.

Profile Features

The *Junior Worldmark* structure—40 numbered headings—allows student researchers to compare two or more states in a variety of ways.

Each state profile begins by listing the origin of the state name, its nickname, the capital, the date it entered the union, the state song and motto, and a description of the state coat of arms. The profile also presents a picture and textual description of both the state seal and the state flag (a key to the flag color symbols appears on page xii of each volume). Next, a listing of the official state animal, bird, fish, flower, tree, gem, etc. is given. The introductory information ends with the standard time given by time zone in relation to Greenwich mean time (GMT). The world is divided into 24 time zones, each one hour apart. The Greenwich meridian, which is 0 degrees, passes through Greenwich, England, a suburb of London. Greenwich is at the center of the initial time zone, known as Greenwich mean time (GMT). All times given are converted from noon in this zone. The time reported for the state is the official time zone.

The body of each country's profile is arranged in 40 numbered headings as follows:

1 LOCATION AND SIZE. The state is located on the North American continent. Statistics are given on area and boundary length. Size comparisons are made to the other 50 states of the United States.

2 TOPOGRAPHY. Dominant geographic features including terrain and major rivers and lakes are described.

3 CLIMATE. Temperature and rainfall are given for the various regions of the state in both English and metric units.

4 PLANTS AND ANIMALS. Described here are the plants and animals native to the state.

5 ENVIRONMENTAL PROTECTION. Destruction of natural resources—forests, water supply, air—is described here. Statistics on solid waste production, hazardous waste sites, and endangered and extinct species are also included.

6 POPULATION. Census 2000 statistics, including the seven categories identifying race introduced with the 2000 census of population, are provided. Population density and major urban populations are summarized.

7 ETHNIC GROUPS. The major ethnic groups are ranked in percentages. Where appropriate, some description of the influence or history of ethnicity is provided.

8 LANGUAGES. The regional dialects of the state are summarized as well as the number of people speaking languages other than English at home.

9 RELIGIONS. The population is broken down according to religion and/or denominations.

10 TRANSPORTATION. Statistics on roads, railways, waterways, and air traffic, along with a listing of key ports for trade and travel, are provided.

11 HISTORY. Includes a concise summary of the state's history from ancient times (where appropriate) to the present.

12 STATE GOVERNMENT. The form of government is described, and the process of governing is summarized. A table listing the state governors, updated to 2000, accompanies each entry.

13 POLITICAL PARTIES. Describes the significant political parties through history, where appropriate, and the influential parties in the mid-1990s.

14 LOCAL GOVERNMENT. The system of local government structure is summarized.

15 JUDICIAL SYSTEM. Structure of the court system and the jurisdiction of courts in each category is provided. Crime rates as reported by the Federal Bureau of Investigation (FBI) are also included.

16 MIGRATION. Population shifts since the end of World War II are summarized.

17 ECONOMY. This section presents the key elements of the economy. Major industries and employment figures are also summarized.

18 INCOME. Personal income and the poverty level are given as is the state's ranking among the 50 states in per person income.

19 INDUSTRY. Key industries are listed, and important aspects of industrial development are described.

20 LABOR. Statistics are given on the civilian labor force, including numbers of workers, leading areas of employment, and unemployment figures.

21 AGRICULTURE. Statistics on key agricultural crops, market share, and total farm income are provided.

22 DOMESTICATED ANIMALS. Statistics on livestock—cattle, hogs, sheep, etc.—and the land area devoted to raising them are given.

23 FISHING. The relative significance of fishing to the state is provided, with statistics on fish and seafood products.

24 FORESTRY. Land area classified as forest is given, along with a listing of key forest products and a description of government policy toward forest land.

25 MINING. Description of mineral deposits and statistics on related mining activity and export are provided.

26 ENERGY AND POWER. Description of the state's power resources, including electricity produced and oil reserves and production, are provided.

27 COMMERCE. A summary of the amount of wholesale trade, retail trade, and receipts of service establishments is given.

28 **PUBLIC FINANCE.** Revenues, expenditures, and total and per person debt are provided.

29 **TAXATION.** The state's tax system is explained.

30 **HEALTH.** Statistics on and description of such public health factors as disease and suicide rates, principal causes of death, numbers of hospitals and medical facilities appear here. Information is also provided on the percentage of citizens without health insurance within each state.

31 **HOUSING.** Housing shortages and government programs to build housing are described. Statistics on numbers of dwellings and median home values are provided.

32 **EDUCATION.** Statistical data on educational achievement and primary and secondary schools is given. Per person state spending on primary and secondary education is also given. Major universities are listed, and government programs to foster education are described.

33 **ARTS.** A summary of the state's major cultural institutions is provided together with the amount of federal and state funds designated to the arts.

34 **LIBRARIES AND MUSEUMS.** The number of libraries, their holdings, and their yearly circulation is provided. Major museums are listed.

35 **COMMUNICATIONS.** The state of telecommunications (television, radio, and telephone) is summarized. Activity related to the Internet is reported where available.

36 **PRESS.** Major daily and Sunday newspapers are listed together with data on their circulations.

37 **TOURISM, TRAVEL, AND RECREATION.** Under this heading, the student will find a summary of the importance of tourism to the state, and factors affecting the tourism industry. Key tourist attractions are listed.

38 **SPORTS.** The major sports teams in the state, both professional and collegiate, are summarized.

39 **FAMOUS PEOPLE.** In this section, some of the best-known citizens of the state are listed. When a person is noted in a state that is not the state of his of her birth, the birthplace is given.

40 **BIBLIOGRAPHY.** The bibliographic and web site listings at the end of each profile are provided as a guide for further reading.

Because many terms used in this encyclopedia will be new to students, each volume includes a glossary and a list of abbreviations and acronyms. A keyword index to all four volumes appears in Volume 4.

Acknowledgments

Junior Worldmark Encyclopedia of the States, Third Edition, draws on the fifth edition of the *Worldmark Encyclopedia of the States.* Readers are directed to that work for a complete list of contributors, too numerous to list here. Special acknowledgment goes to the government officials throughout the nation who gave their cooperation to this project.

Reviewers

The following individuals reviewed state articles for this or previous editions. In all cases the reviewers added important information and updated facts that might have gone unnoticed. The reviewers were also instrumental in suggesting changes and improvements.

Patricia L. Harris, Executive Director, Alabama Public Library Service

Patience Frederiksen, Head, Government Publications, Alaska State Library

Jacqueline L. Miller, Curator of Education, Arizona State Capitol Museum

John A. Murphey, Jr., State Librarian, Arkansas State Library

Eugene Hainer, School Library Media Consultant, Colorado State Library

Susan Cormier, Connecticut State Library

Dr. Annette Woolard, Director of Development, Historical Society of Delaware

Reference Staff, State Library of Florida

Cheryl Rogers, Consultant, Georgia Department of Education, Public Library Services

Lorna J. T. Peck, School Library Services, Specialist, State of Hawaii Department of Education

Marcia J. Beckwith, Director, Information Services/Library, Centennial High School, Boise, Idaho

Karen McIlrath-Muskopf, Youth Services Consultant, Illinois State Library

Cordell Svengalis, Social Science Consultant, Iowa Department of Education

Marc Galbraith, Director of Reference Services, Kansas State Library

James C. Klotter, State Historian, Kentucky Historical Society

Virginia R. Smith, Head, Louisiana Section, State Library of Louisiana

Ben Keating, Division Director, Maine State Library

Patricia V. Melville, Director of Reference Services, Maryland State Archives

Brian Donoghue, Reference Librarian, Massachusetts Board of Library Commissioners

Denise E. Carlson, Head of Reference, Minnesota Historical Society

Ronnie Smith, Reference Specialist, Mississippi Library Commission

Darlene Staffeldt, Director, Statewide Library Resources, Montana State Library

Rod Wagner, Director, Nebraska Library Commission

Reference Services and Archives Staff, Nevada State Library & Archives

Kendall F. Wiggin, State Librarian, New Hampshire State Library

John H. Livingstone, Acting Assistant Commissioner and State Librarian, New Jersey State Library

Robert J. Torrez, State Historian, New Mexico State Records and Archives

R. Allan Carter, Senior Librarian, New York State Library

Staff, Information Services and State Archives Research, State Library of North Carolina

Doris Daugherty, Assistant State Librarian, North Dakota State Library

Carol Brieck and Audrey Hall, Reference Librarians, State Library of Ohio

Audrey Wolfe-Clark, Edmond, Oklahoma

Paul Gregorio, Assistant Professor of Education, Portland State University, Portland, Oregon

Alice L. Lubrecht, Acting Bureau Director, State Library of Pennsylvania

Barbara Weaver, Director, Department of State Library Services, Rhode Island

Michele M. Reid, Director of Public Services, South Dakota State Library

Dr. Wayne C. Moore, Archivist, Tennessee State Library and Archives

Douglas E. Barnett, Managing Editor, New Handbook of Texas, Texas State Historical Association

Lou Reinwand, Director of Information Services, Utah State Library

Paul J. Donovan, Senior Reference Librarian, Vermont Department of Libraries

Catherine Mishler, Head, Reference, Library of Virginia

Gayle Palmer, Senior Library Information Specialist, Washington/Northwest Collections, Washington State Library

Karen Goff, Head of Reference, West Virginia Library Commission

Richard L. Roe, Research Analyst, Wisconsin Legislative Reference Bureau

Priscilla Golden, Principal Librarian, Wyoming State Library

Staff, Washingtoniana Division, Martin Luther King Memorial Library, Washington, D.C.

Jean Hanson, MLS, Consultant, web sites.

Advisors

The following persons were consulted on the content and structure of this encyclopedia. Their insights, opinions, and suggestions led to many enhancements and improvements in the presentation of the material.

Mary Alice Anderson, Media Specialist, Winona Middle School, Winona, Minnesota

Pat Baird, Library Media Specialist and Department Chair, Shaker Heights Middle School, Shaker Heights, Ohio

Pat Fagel, Library Media Specialist, Shaker Heights Middle School, Shaker Heights, Ohio

Nancy Guidry, Young Adult Librarian, Santa Monica Public Library, Santa Monica, California

Ann West LaPrise, Children's Librarian, Redford Branch, Detroit Public Library, Detroit, Michigan

Nancy C. Nieman, Teacher, U.S. History, Social Studies, Journalism, Delta Middle School, Muncie, Indiana

Madeleine Obrock, Library Media Specialist, Woodbury Elementary School, Shaker Heights, Ohio

Ernest L. O'Roark, Teacher, Social Studies, Martin Luther King Middle School, Germantown, Maryland

Ellen Stepanian, Director of Library Services, Shaker Heights Board of Education, Shaker Heights, Ohio

Mary Strouse, Library Media Specialist, Woodbury Elementary School, Shaker Heights, Ohio

Comments and Suggestions

We welcome your comments on the *Junior Worldmark Encyclopedia of the States, Third Edition,* as well as your suggestions for features to be included in future editions. Please write to: Editors, *Junior Worldmark Encyclopedia of the States,* U•X•L, 27500 Drake Road, Farmington Hills, Michigan 48331-3535; or call toll-free: 1-800-877-4253.

Guide to State Articles

All information contained within a state article is uniformly keyed by means of a boxed number to the left of the subject headings. A heading such as "Population," for example, carries the same key numeral (6) in every article. Therefore, to find information about the population of Alabama, consult the table of contents for the page number where the Alabama article begins and look for section 6.

Introductory matter for each state includes: Origin of state name
Nickname
Capital
Date and order of statehood
Song
Motto
Flag
Official seal
Symbols (animal, tree, flower, etc.)
Time zone.

Flag color symbols

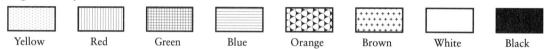

| Yellow | Red | Green | Blue | Orange | Brown | White | Black |

Sections listed numerically

1 Location and Size
2 Topography
3 Climate
4 Plants and Animals
5 Environmental Protection
6 Population
7 Ethnic Groups
8 Languages
9 Religions
10 Transportation
11 History
12 State Government
13 Political Parties
14 Local Government
15 Judicial System
16 Migration
17 Economy
18 Income
19 Industry
20 Labor
21 Agriculture

22 Domesticated Animals
23 Fishing
24 Forestry
25 Mining
26 Energy and Power
27 Commerce
28 Public Finance
29 Taxation
30 Health
31 Housing
32 Education
33 Arts
34 Libraries and Museums
35 Communications
36 Press
37 Tourism, Travel, and
   Recreation
38 Sports
39 Famous Persons
40 Bibliography

Alphabetical listing of sections

Explanation of symbols

A fiscal split year is indicated by a stroke (e.g. 1999/00).
Note that 1 billion = 1,000 million = 10^9.
The use of a small dash (e.g., 1998–99) normally signifies the
   full period of calendar years covered (including the end year indicated).

ALABAMA

State of Alabama

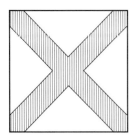

ORIGIN OF STATE NAME: Probably after the Alabama Indian tribe.
NICKNAME: The Heart of Dixie.
CAPITAL: Montgomery.
ENTERED UNION: 14 December 1819 (22d).
SONG: "Alabama."
MOTTO: *Audemus jura nostra defendere* (We dare defend our rights).
COAT OF ARMS: Two eagles, symbolizing courage, support a shield bearing the emblems of the five governments (France, England, Spain, Confederacy, US) that have held sovereignty over Alabama. Above the shield is a sailing vessel modeled upon the ships of the first French settlers of Alabama; beneath the shield is the state motto.
FLAG: Crimson cross of St. Andrew on a square white field.
OFFICIAL SEAL: Map of Alabama, including names of major rivers and neighboring states, surrounded by the words "Alabama Great Seal."
BIRD: Yellowhammer.
FISH: Tarpon.
FLOWER: Camellia.
TREE: Southern (longleaf) pine.
STONE: Marble.
MINERAL: Hematite.
TIME: 6 AM CST = noon GMT.

1 LOCATION AND SIZE

Located in the eastern south-central US, Alabama ranks 29th in size among the 50 states, with a total area of 51,705 square miles (133,915 square kilometers). Alabama extends roughly 200 miles (320 kilometers) east-west; the minimum north-south extension is 325 miles (520 kilometers). Its total boundary length is 1,044 miles (1,680 kilometers).

2 TOPOGRAPHY

Alabama is divided into four major regions: the Gulf Coastal Plain, Piedmont Plateau, Ridge and Valley section, and the Appalachian (or Cumberland) Plateau.

The largest lake wholly within Alabama is Guntersville Lake, covering about 108 square miles (280 square kilometers). The longest rivers are the Alabama, the Tennessee, and the Tombigbee. Archaeologists believe that Russell Cave, in northeastern Alabama, was the earliest site of human habitation in the southeastern US.

3 CLIMATE

Alabama's three climatic divisions are the lower coastal plain, the northern plateau, and the Black Belt and upper coastal plain, lying between the two extremes. Birmingham's temperature ranges from a normal January daily minimum of 34°F (1°C) to a normal July daily maximum of 90°F (32°C); for Mobile, the comparable minimum and maximum figures are 41°F (51°C) and 91°F (33°C). The record low temperature for the state is –27°F (–33°C), registered in 1966; the all-time high is 112°F (44°C), registered in 1925. Mobile, one of the rainiest cities in the US, recorded an average precipitation of 63.96 inches (162.5 centimeters) a year between 1961 and 1990.

4 PLANTS AND ANIMALS

Alabama was once covered by vast forests of pine, which still form the largest proportion of the state's forest growth. The state also has an abundance of poplar, cypress, hickory, oak, and various gum trees. Red cedar grows throughout the state; southern white cedar is found in the southwest; hemlock in the north.

Mammals include the white-tailed deer, bobcat, muskrat, and weasel. Alabama's birds include golden and bald eagles, osprey, and yellowhammer (the state bird). Game birds include quail, duck, and wild turkey. Freshwater fish such as bream, shad, and bass are common. Endangered or threatened animals include the Alabama cavefish, bald eagle, wood stork, Red Hills salamander, and Eastern indigo snake.

5 ENVIRONMENTAL PROTECTION

The Alabama Environmental Management Commission is charged with managing the state's land, air, and water resources. The most active environmental groups in the state are the Alabama Rivers Alliance,

Alabama Population Profile

Total population in 2000:	4,447,100
Population change, 1990–2000:	10.1%
Hispanic or Latino†:	0.9%
Population by race	
One race:	99.0%
White:	71.1%
Black or African American:	26.0%
American Indian/Alaska Native:	0.5%
Asian:	0.7%
Native Hawaiian/Pacific Islander:	—
Some other race:	0.7%
Two or more races:	1.0%

Population by Age Group

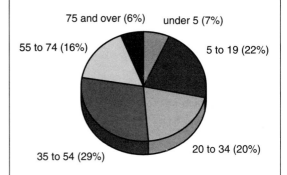

75 and over (6%) under 5 (7%)
55 to 74 (16%)
5 to 19 (22%)
20 to 34 (20%)
35 to 54 (29%)

Top Cities by Population

City	Population	% change 1990–2000
Birmingham	242,820	8.7
Mobile	201,568	7.7
Montgomery	198,915	1.3
Huntsville	158,216	–1.0
Tuscaloosa	77,906	0.2
Hoover	62,742	57.7
Dothan	57,737	7.7
Decatur	53,929	10.6
Auburn	42,987	27.1
Gadsden	38,978	–8.3

Notes: †A person of Hispanic or Latino origin may be of any race. NA indicates that data are not available.
Sources: U.S. Census Bureau. Public Information Office. *Demographic Profiles.* [Online] Available http://www.census.gov/Press-Release/www/2001/demoprofile.html. Accessed June 1, 2001. U.S. Census Bureau. *Census 2000: Redistricting Data.* Press release issued by the Redistricting Data Office. Washington, D.C., March, 2001.

ALABAMA

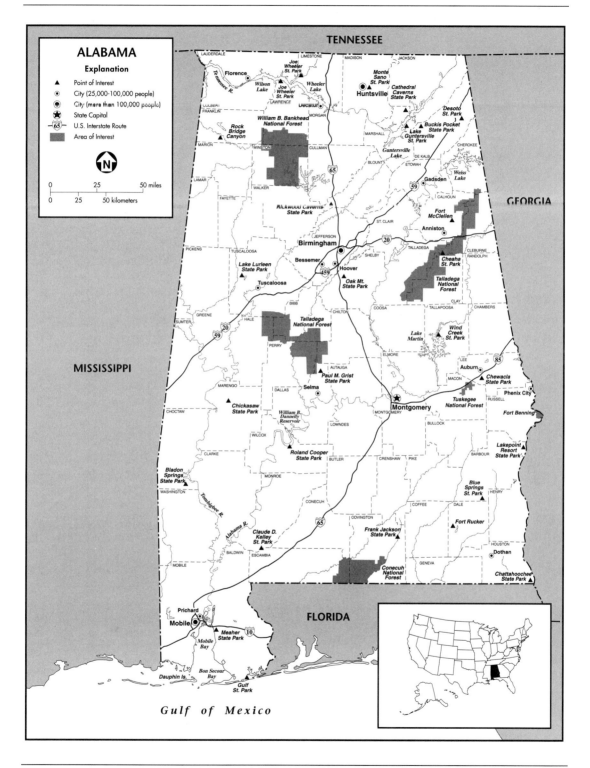

Photo credit: Dan Brothers, Alabama Bureau of Tourism.

Looking south, Spanish moss clings to bald cypress at Florala State Park along Lake Jackson. The 31st parallel, "Ellicott's Line," established in 1799 as the boundary between the United States and Spanish West Florida, passes through Lake Jackson.

Sierra Club, Alabama Audubon Council, and League of Women Voters.

Nuclear power has been a source of conflict in Alabama. In 1983, one Browns Ferry reactor was ordered to shut down temporarily for inspection. In 1998, there were 12 hazardous waste sites in Alabama. There are 108 municipal land fills and 8 curbside recycling programs in the state. Air quality is generally satisfactory, and Birmingham was the only metropolitan area not meeting federal ozone standards as of 1997.

6 POPULATION

Alabama ranked 23rd in population among the 50 states in 2000 with a census total of over 4.4 million. Alabama's population is projected at 4.6 million for 2005. The state has a population density of 87.6 persons per square mile (33.8 persons per square kilometer). About two out of every three Alabamians live in urban areas. First in size among Alabama's cities is Birmingham with an estimated 242,820 residents in 2000. Other major cities are Mobile, 201,568, and Montgomery, 198,915.

Alabama Population by Race

Census 2000 was the first national census in which the instructions to respondents said, "Mark one or more races." This table shows the number of people who are of one, two, or three or more races. For those claiming two races, the number of people belonging to the various categories is listed. The U.S. government conducts a census of the population every ten years.

	Number	Percent
Total population	4,447,100	100.0
One race	4,402,921	99.0
Two races	41,684	0.9
White *and* Black or African American	6,356	0.1
White *and* American Indian/Alaska Native	17,566	0.4
White *and* Asian	4,772	0.1
White *and* Native Hawaiian/Pacific Islander	415	—
White *and* some other race	5,930	0.1
Black or African American *and* American Indian/Alaska Native	2,326	0.1
Black or African American *and* Asian	1,119	—
Black or African American *and* Native Hawaiian/Pacific Islander	292	—
Black or African American *and* some other race	1,234	—
American Indian/Alaska Native *and* Asian	247	—
American Indian/Alaska Native *and* Native Hawaiian/Pacific Islander	23	—
American Indian/Alaska Native *and* some other race	392	—
Asian *and* Native Hawaiian/Pacific Islander	310	—
Asian *and* some other race	629	—
Native Hawaiian/Pacific Islander *and* some other race	73	—
Three or more races	2,495	0.1

Source: U.S. Census Bureau. *Census 2000: Redistricting Data.* Press release issued by the Redistricting Data Office. Washington, D.C., March, 2001. A dash (—) indicates that the percent is less than 0.1.

7 ETHNIC GROUPS

Alabama's population is largely divided between whites of English and Scots-Irish descent, and blacks descended from African slaves. The 1990 census counted about 17,000 Native Americans, mostly of Creek or Cherokee descent. The black population of Alabama in 1990 was about 1,021,000. As of 1990, Birmingham was 64% nonwhite, Mobile 40%, and Montgomery 43%. In 1997, the state's population was estimated at 73.1% white, 25.9% black (7th highest among the states), 0.6% Asian, and 0.4% American Indian. About 0.9% of the population was Hispanic in 1997.

In 1990, Alabama had 3,686 Asian Indians, 3,969 Koreans, and 3,529 Chinese. The population of Hispanic origin was about 25,000. Among persons reporting a single ancestry group, the leaders were Irish, 617,065, and English, 479,499.

Alabama's Cajuns, numbering perhaps 5,700, are thought to combine Anglo-Saxon, French, Spanish, Choctaw, Apache, and African ancestry. They are ethnically not related to the Cajuns of Louisiana.

Having made ports of call at Florence and Decatur, a day of steamboating aboard the Delta Queen draws to a close on the waters of Lake Guntersville. Steamboat transportation was extremely important to Alabama's cotton merchants in the mid-1800s.

8 LANGUAGES

Alabama English is mostly a Southern dialect. Alabama has experienced only minor foreign immigration, and 97.1% of all residents five years old or older speak only English at home. The three principal languages other than English spoken at home are Spanish (with 42,653 speakers), French (17,965), and German (14,603).

9 RELIGIONS

Alabama is predominantly Baptist. The first Baptist church in the state, the Flint River Church in Madison County, was organized in 1808. As of 1990, the major Protestant denominations are the Southern Baptist Convention, with 1,313,907 members; the United Methodist Church, with 332,029; and Churches of Christ, with 118,561. Roman Catholics in Alabama number 137,834, and there are an estimated 8,350 Jews.

10 TRANSPORTATION

The first rail line in the state was the Tuscumbia Railroad, chartered in 1830. It made its first run, of 44 miles (71 kilometers) around the Muscle Shoals from Tuscumbia to Decatur, on 15 December 1834. As of 1998, Alabama had 3,318 rail miles (5,339 kilometers) of track. As of 1998 there were 93,356 miles (150,210 kilometers) of public streets, roads, and highways. In the same year, the state had 1.9 million registered automobiles and 1.75 million trucks.

Thanks to the Tennessee Valley Authority, the Tennessee River has been transformed since the 1930s into a year-round navigable waterway. The 234-mile (377-kilometer), $2-billion Tennessee-Tombigbee project, which opened in 1985, provided a new barge route from the Midwest to the Gulf of Mexico. This was not only the largest civilian engineering project in the US during the early 1980s, but it was also by far the largest earth-moving project in US history.

Mobile, on the Gulf of Mexico, is Alabama's only international port, handling 49.2 million tons in 1998. Alabama's largest and busiest facility is Birmingham Municipal Airport, which boarded 1.3 million passengers during 1996.

11 HISTORY

Moundville (near Tuscaloosa) is one of the most important Native American Mound Builder sites in the southeastern US. This site includes 20 "platform mounds" for Native American buildings, dating from 1200 to 1500. When the first Europeans arrived, half the inhabitants of present-day Alabama were members of either the Creek tribe or smaller groups living under Creek control.

During the 16th century, five Spanish expeditions entered or explored the region now called Alabama. The most extensive was that of Hernando de Soto, whose army marched from the Tennessee Valley to the Mobile Delta in 1540. In 1702, two French naval officers established Ft. Louis de la Mobile, the first permanent European settlement in Alabama. Mobile remained in French hands until 1763, when it was turned over to the British under the terms of the Treaty of Paris.

A British garrison held Mobile during the American Revolution until it was captured in 1780 by the forces of Spain, an ally of the rebellious American colonists. Spanish control of Mobile lasted until the city was again seized during the War of 1812, this time by American troops. West Florida, including Mobile, was the only territory added to the US as a result of that war.

At the start of the 19th century, Native Americans still held most of present-day Alabama. War broke out in 1813 between American settlers and a Creek faction known as the Red Sticks, who were determined to resist the advancing whites. After General Andrew Jackson and his Tennessee militia crushed the Red Sticks in 1814 at the Battle of Horseshoe Bend in central Alabama, he forced the Creek to sign a treaty ceding some 40,000 square miles (103,600 square kilometers) of land to the US, thereby opening about three-fourths of the present state to white settlement.

Statehood

From 1814 onward, pioneers, caught up by what was called "Alabama fever," poured into the state. They came from the Carolinas, Virginia, Georgia, Tennessee, and Kentucky looking for opportunities in what Andrew Jackson called "the best unsettled country in America." In 1817,

Alabama Governors: 1819–2001

1819–1820	William Wyatt Bibb	Democrat	1900–1901	William James Samford	Democrat
1820–1821	Thomas Bibb	Democrat	1901–1904	William Dorsey Jelks	Democrat
1821–1825	Israel Pickens	Democrat	1904–1905	Russell McWhortor Cunningham	Democrat
1825–1829	John Murphy	Democrat	1905–1907	William Dorsey Jelks	Democrat
1829–1831	Gabriel Moore	Democrat	1907–1911	Braxton Bragg Comer	Democrat
1831	Samuel B. Moore	Democrat	1911–1915	Emmett O'Neal	Democrat
1831–1835	John Gayle	Democrat	1915–1919	Charles Henderson	Democrat
1835–1837	Clement Comer Clay	Democrat	1919–1923	Thomas Erby Kilby	Democrat
1837	Hugh McVay	Democrat	1923–1927	William Woodward Brandon	Democrat
1837–1841	Arthur Pendleton Bagby	Democrat	1924	Charles Samuel McDowell	Democrat
1841–1845	Benjamin Fitzpatrick	Democrat	1927–1931	David Bibb Graves	Democrat
1845–1847	Joshua Lanier Martin	Democrat	1931–1935	Benjamin Meek Miller	Democrat
1847–1849	Reuben Chapman	Democrat	1935–1939	David Bibb Graves	Democrat
1849–1853	Henry Watkins Collier	Democrat	1939–1943	Frank Murray Dixon	Democrat
1853–1857	John Anthony Winston	Democrat	1943–1947	George Chauncey Sparks	Democrat
1857–1861	Andrew Barry Moore	Whig	1947–1951	James Elisha Folsom	Democrat
1861–1863	John Gill Shorter	Democrat	1951–1955	Seth Gordon Persons	Democrat
1863–1865	Thomas Hill Watts	Whig	1955–1959	James Elisha Folsom	Democrat
1865	Lewis Eliphalet Parsons	Whig	1959–1963	John Malcolm Patterson	Democrat
1865–1868	Robert Miller Patton	Whig	1963–1967	George Corley Wallace	Democrat
1868–1870	William Hugh Smith	Democrat	1967–1968	Lurleen Burns Wallace	Democrat
1870–1872	Robert Burns Lindsay	Democrat	1968–1971	Albert Preston Brewer	Democrat
1872–1874	David Peter Lewis	Republican	1971–1972	George Corley Wallace	Democrat
1874–1878	George Smith Houston	Democrat	1972	Jere Locke Beasley	Democrat
1878–1882	Rufus Wills Cobb	Democrat	1972–1979	George Corley Wallace	Democrat
1882–1886	Edward Asbury O'Neal	Democrat	1979–1983	Forrest Hood (Fob) James, Jr.	Democrat
1886–1890	Thomas Seay	Democrat	1983–1987	George Corley Wallace	Democrat
1890–1894	Thomas Goode Jones	Democrat	1987–1993	Harold Guy Hunt	Republican
1894–1896	William Calvin Oates	Democrat	1993–1995	James Elisha Folsom, Jr.	Democrat
1896–1900	Joseph Forney Johnston	Democrat	1995–1999	Forrest Hood (Fob) James, Jr.	Republican
1900	William Dorsey Jelks	Democrat	1999–	Donald Siegelman	Democrat

Alabama became a territory; on 2 August 1819, a state constitution was adopted. On the following 14 December, Alabama was admitted to statehood.

Alabama seceded from the Union in January 1861 and shortly thereafter joined the Confederacy. Montgomery served as capital of the Confederacy until May, when the seat of government was moved to Richmond, Virginia. During the Confederacy's dying days in the spring of 1865, federal troops swept through Tuscaloosa, Selma, and Montgomery. Estimates of the number of Alabamians killed in the Civil War range from 25,000 upward.

During Reconstruction, Alabama was under military rule until readmitted to the Union in 1868.

Cotton remained the foundation of the Alabama economy in the late 19th and early 20th centuries. However, with the abolition of slavery it was now raised by sharecroppers. Alabama also attempted to create a "New South" in which agriculture would be balanced by industry. In the 1880s and 1890s, at least 20 Alabama towns were touted as ironworking centers. Birmingham, founded in 1871, became the New South's leading industrial center.

Photo credit: Dan Brothers, Alabama Bureau of Tourism.

Birmingham's most famous Civil Rights landmark, Sixteenth Street Baptist Church, is just across the street from the Civil Rights Institute. On 15 September 1963, a fatal bomb explosion at the church horrified the city and the nation and became a turning point in the Civil Rights Movement.

Civil Rights

During the 1950s and 1960s, national attention focused on civil rights demonstrations in Alabama, including the Montgomery bus boycott of 1955, the Birmingham and University of Alabama demonstrations of 1963, and the voting rights march from Selma to Montgomery in 1965. The leading opponents were Dr. Martin Luther King, Jr., head of the Southern Christian Leadership Conference, and Governor George C. Wallace, who was against racial integration. These black protests and the sometimes violent reactions to them—such as the 1963 bombing of a church in Birmingham in which four young black girls were killed—helped influence the US Congress to pass the Civil Rights Act of 1964 and the Voting Rights Act of 1965.

The civil rights era brought other momentous changes to Alabama. New racial attitudes among most whites have contributed to a vast improvement in the climate of race relations since 1960. Hundreds of thousands of black voters are now an important force in state politics. Blacks attend school, colleges, and universities of their choice and enjoy equal access to all public facilities. In 1984 there were 314 black elected officials, including 25 mayors, 19 lawmakers in the Alabama state legislature, and an associate justice of the state supreme court. In 1990, 704 blacks held elective office.

12 STATE GOVERNMENT

Alabama's legislature consists of a 35-seat senate and a 105-seat house of representatives, all of whose members are elected at the same time for four-year terms. Elected executive officials include the governor and lieutenant-governor (separately elected), secretary of state, attorney general, treasurer, and auditor. The governor is limited to a maximum of two consecutive terms.

A bill becomes a law when it is passed by a majority of both houses and is either signed by the governor or left unsigned for six days while the legislature is in session, or passed over the governor's veto by a majority of the elected members of each house. The governor may "pocket veto" a measure submitted fewer than five days before adjournment by not signing it within ten days after adjournment.

13 POLITICAL PARTIES

During the 20th century, the Democratic Party has commanded practically every statewide office, major and minor. However, in recent years Republicans have made gains in national and statewide races. In the 2000 presidential elections, 57% of the vote went to Republican

George W. Bush; 42% to Democrat Al Gore; and 1% to others.

Alabama's delegation of US Representatives in 2000 consisted of 2 Democrats and 5 Republicans. The state legislature in 2000 consisted of 24 Democrats and 11 Republicans in the State Senate, and 68 Democrats and 37 Republicans in the State House. Democrat Don Siegelman was first elected governor in 1998. Minority elected officials in 1995 included 758 blacks. There were 13 women serving in the state legislature in 2000.

Alabama Presidential Vote by Political Parties, 1948–2000

Year	Alabama Winner	Democrat	Republican
1948	Thurmond (SRD)	—	40,930
1952	Stevenson (D)	275,075	149,231
1956	Stevenson (D)	279,542	195,694
1960	*Kennedy (D)	318,303	236,110
1964	Goldwater (R)	—	479,085
1968	Wallace (AI)	195,918	146,591
1972	*Nixon (R)	256,923	728,701
1976	*Carter (D)	659,170	504,070
1980	*Reagan (R)	636,730	654,192
1984	*Reagan (R)	551,899	872,849
1988	*Bush (R)	549,506	815,576
1992	Bush (R)	690,080	804,283
1996	Dole (R)	662,165	769,044
2000	*Bush (R)	692,611	941,173

*Won US presidential election.

14 LOCAL GOVERNMENT

Alabama has 67 counties, 446 municipalities, and at least 490 special districts. Counties are governed by county commissions, usually consisting of three to seven commissioners, elected by district. Until the late 1970s, the most common form of municipal government was the commission, whose members are elected either at-large or by district. Partly in response to court orders requiring district elections in order to permit the election of more black officials, there has since been a trend toward the mayor-council form.

15 JUDICIAL SYSTEM

The high court of Alabama is the supreme court, consisting of a chief justice and eight associate justices, all elected for staggered six-year terms. It issues opinions on constitutional issues and hears cases appealed from the lower courts. The court of civil appeals has exclusive appeals jurisdiction in all suits involving sums up to $10,000. This court's three judges are elected for six-year terms, and the one who has served the longest is the presiding judge. The five judges of the court of criminal appeals are also elected for six-year terms; those judges choose the presiding judge by majority vote.

Circuit courts, which included 40 districts and 131 judgeships in 1999, have exclusive original jurisdiction over civil actions involving sums of more than $5,000, and over criminal prosecutions involving felony offenses. They also have original jurisdiction and appeals jurisdiction over most cases from district and municipal courts.

A new system of district courts replaced county and juvenile courts as of January 1977, staffed by judges who serve six-year terms. Municipal court judges are appointed by the municipality. Alabama had an FBI Crime Index rate in 1998 of 4,597 crimes per 100,000 population. As of June 1999, 24,283 prisoners were held in state and federal prisons in Alabama.

16 MIGRATION

Since the Civil War, migration to Alabama has been slight. Many blacks left Alabama from World War I through the 1960s, and the proportion of blacks fell from 35% in 1940 to 26% in 1998. Following the civil rights revolution, more blacks chose to remain in the state, and some who had gone elsewhere returned. Overall, Alabama lost as many as 944,000 residents through migration between 1940 and 1970, but enjoyed a net gain from migration of over 143,000 between 1970 and 1990, and about 126,000 during 1990–98. As of 1990, about 76% of Alabamians were born in the state.

17 ECONOMY

Cotton dominated Alabama's economy from the mid-19th century to the 1870s, when large-scale industrialization began. Although Alabama's prosperity has increased, particularly in recent decades, the state still lags in wage rates and per capita income. One factor that has hindered the growth of the state's economy is declining investment in resource industries owned by large corporations outside the state. Between 1974 and 1983, manufacturing grew at little more than half the rate of all state goods and services. In 1994 the goods-producing sector accounted for 30% of the state's total economic output, services accounted for 54%, and government for 16%.

18 INCOME

Alabama's per capita (per person) income in 1998 was $22,054, for a rank of 45th among the 50 states. In 1998, 14.7% of all

Alabamians were living below the federal poverty level. Median household income in 1998 was $33,394.

19 INDUSTRY

Alabama's industrial boom, which began in the 1870s, quickly transformed Birmingham into the leading industrial city in the South, producing pig iron more cheaply than its northern US and English competitors. By the late 1970s, the older smokestack industries were clearly in decline, but Birmingham received a boost in 1984 when US Steel announced it would spend $1.3 billion to make its Fairfield plant the newest fully integrated steel mill in the nation. In 1997 the Mercedes Benz facility in Vance began manufacturing sport utility vehicles.

The principal employers among industry groups are food and kindred products, textile mill, apparel, and other textile products, primary metal industries, industrial machinery, electronic equipment, and transportation equipment.

20 LABOR

Alabama's civilian labor force in 1998 averaged 2.15 million. Alabama's total employment was 2.07 million, yielding an unemployment rate of 3.7%. As of 1998, 11.8% of the state's workers were union members.

21 AGRICULTURE

Alabama ranked 24th among the 50 states in agricultural income in 1999, with $3.4 billion. There was considerable diversity in Alabama's earliest agriculture. By the mid-19th century, however, cotton had

Photo credit: Dan Brothers, Alabama Bureau of Tourism.

Sculpted in Italy and dedicated in 1919, the Boll Weevil Monument in Enterprise is thought to be the world's only statue commemorating an insect pest. The "boll weevil" was not added to the top of the cast lead statue until 1948.

taken over. Diversification began early in the 20th century, a trend accelerated by the destructive effects of the boll weevil on cotton growing. As of 1998 there were some 49,000 farms in Alabama, occupying approximately 9.5 million acres (3.8 million hectares), or roughly 30% of the state's land area.

In 1998, Alabama ranked third in the US in production of peanuts, with 411.6 million pounds (186.7 million kilograms), valued at $114 million. The 1998 cotton crop of

570,000 bales was worth $277.6 million. Other crops (and their values) included corn, 12.6 million bushels ($27.7 million); soybeans, 7.4 million bushels ($38.7 million); wheat, 3.5 million bushels ($9.2 million); and sweet potatoes, 629,000 hundredweight/28.5 million kilograms, ($11.3 million).

22 DOMESTICATED ANIMALS

The principal livestock-raising regions of Alabama are the far north, the southwest, and the Black Belt. During 1998, production of cattle and calves amounted to 531.9 million pounds (241.3 million kilograms), valued at $321 million. Hog production that year totaled 116.7 million pounds (52.9 million kilograms), valued at $56.8 million. There were 1,550,000 cattle and 200,190 hogs on Alabama farms and ranches. In addition, 31,000 milk cows yielded 418 million pounds (190 million kilograms) of milk in 1997.

Alabama is a leading producer of chickens, broilers, and eggs. In broiler production, the state ranked third in 1997 (after Arkansas and Georgia), with 4.3 billion pounds (2 billion kilograms), valued at $1.65 billion. That year, Alabama ranked third in chicken production, with 66.1 million pounds (30 million kilograms), worth $11.2 million. Egg production ranked tenth, with 2.5 billion pounds (1 billion kilograms), worth $220.7 million.

23 FISHING

Alabama's commercial fish catch was 30 million pounds (13.6 million kilograms) in 1998. The principal fishing port is Bayou La Batre, which brought in about 23.6 million pounds (10.6 million kilograms) worth $36.4 million in 1998, 11th-highest by value in the nation. Catfish farming is of growing importance. As of 1999, there were 246 catfish farms (down from 370 in 1999), covering 21,016 acres (9,534 hectares) of water surface. There were 84 processing and wholesaling plants with a combined total of about 12,300 employees in 1997. The US Fish and Wildlife Service spent over $2.9 million for the Sport Fish Restoration Program in 1996.

24 FORESTRY

Forestland in Alabama, predominantly pine, covers 21.9 million acres (8.8 million hectares). This is nearly 3% of the nation's total, and 67% of the state's land area. Nearly all of that was classified as commercial timberland, 95% of it privately owned. Four national forests covered a gross area of 1.2 million acres (516,400 hectares) in 1999.

25 MINING

In 1998, Alabama's nonfuel mineral industry mined and processed an estimated $947 million worth of mineral commodities. That year, over 4.4 million metric tons of cement and over 2.6 million metric tons of clay were produced. The combined value of crushed stone, lime, sand, and portland cement accounted for 90% of the total. The state ranked 16th nationally in total mineral production, remained first in the production of common clays, and third in kaolin, fire clays, and masonry cement.

26 ENERGY AND POWER

Electrical generating plants in Alabama produced a total of 113.4 billion kilowatt hours of electricity in 1998. About half came from private sources (the Alabama Power Company and Alabama Electric Cooperative), with most of the remainder from the Tennessee Valley Authority, which also owned three of the state's five nuclear reactors.

Significant petroleum finds in southern Alabama date from the early 1950s. The 1999 output was 11.1 million barrels; proved reserves as of 31 December 1998 totaled 39 million barrels. During 1998, 563.8 billion cubic feet of natural gas were extracted, from 4,171 wells, leaving reserves of 4.6 billion cubic feet. Coal production reached 23 million tons in 1998, of which all was bituminous. Coal reserves in 1998 totaled 373.7 million tons.

27 COMMERCE

Alabama had $43.3 billion in wholesale sales in 1997. That year, Alabama also had retail sales of $37.6 billion. In 1992, service establishments generated $14.9 billion in receipts and ranked 26th in the nation.

Alcoholic beverages, except for beer, are sold in ABC (Alcoholic Beverage Control) stores, run by the state. Prohibition of alcoholic beverages is by local option; 26 of the 67 counties were dry in 1994, but some dry counties had wet cities (cities that allowed alcoholic beverages).

Alabama exported $6.4 billion worth of goods in 1998.

28 PUBLIC FINANCE

The Division of the Budget within the Department of Finance prepares and administers the state budget, which the governor submits to the legislature for amendment and approval. The state's fiscal year runs from 1 October through 30 September. Total revenues amounted to over $14 billion in 1997, while expenditures amounted to $12.9 billion. As of 1997, the total debt of Alabama state government was $3.78 billion, or $875.32 per capita (per person).

29 TAXATION

Per capita (per person) tax revenues of all state and local governments in Alabama were $1,317 in 1997/98. This was less than the revenues of every other state except Arkansas and Mississippi. The state property tax receipts ($32.13 per capita) were still the lowest in the nation.

As of 2000, the personal income tax, which is designated for education, ranged from 2% to 5%, depending on income and marital status. The tax on corporate net income was 5% for most enterprises, but 6% for financial institutions. The state also imposed a sales tax of 4%; localities might charge up to an additional 3%. Alabama residents paid $12.1 billion in federal taxes in 1995. In that same year, the state received federal expenditures totaling $22.7 billion—a ratio of 53¢ in taxes for every $1 received.

30 HEALTH

Alabama's infant death rate for 1997, 9.2 per 1,000 live births, was second highest among the states. The state's overall death rate in 1998, 1,009.9 deaths per 100,000 population, included a death rate from heart disease of 304.1 per 100,000, compared to the national rate of 268.2.

Alabama had 110 hospitals in 1998; there were 16,998 beds. The average expense to hospitals in the state for care in 1998 was $1,171 per inpatient day. Alabama had about 194 physicians for every 100,000 state residents in 1997.

31 HOUSING

In October 1998, there were nearly 1.86 million housing units in Alabama. A total of 20,500 new privately owned units valued at $1.8 billion were authorized in 1998. During 1999, Alabama received $170.3 million in aid from the US Department of Housing and Urban Development (HUD), including $59 million in HUD community development block grants. In 1998, the median home value in Birmingham was $122,700.

32 EDUCATION

In 1995, 72% of Alabamians age 25 and older were high school graduates, the third-lowest rate in the nation. Approximately 10% of adult Alabamians had no education beyond the eighth grade.

The total enrollment in Alabama's public schools as of December during the 1997/98 school year was 749,187. Of these, 541,039 attended schools from kindergarten through grade eight, and 208,148 attended high school. Minority students made up approximately 38% of total enrollment in public elementary and secondary schools. In fall 1997, estimated

Photo credit: Dan Brothers, Alabama Bureau of Tourism.

The W.C. Handy Music Festival in Florence won a 1994 Regional Designation Award in the Arts by the Cultural Olympiad of Atlanta. The festival was so named to honor the musical genius of W.C. Handy, the "Father of the Blues."

enrollment in nonpublic schools was 72,486.

There are 64 institutions of higher education in Alabama, 48 public and 16 private. The largest state universities are Auburn University, with a fall 1993 enrollment of 21,363, and the three University of Alabama campuses. The latter's main campus in Tuscaloosa has an enrollment of 19,480; Birmingham, 15,913; and Huntsville, 8,232. Tuskegee University, founded as a normal and industrial school in 1881 under the leadership of Booker T.

Washington, became one of the nation's most famous black colleges. Its fall 1993 enrollment was 3,371. The fall 1994 total enrollment in institutions of higher education was 229,511.

33 ARTS

The Alabama Council on the Arts and Humanities, established by the legislature in 1967, provides aid to local nonprofit arts organizations.

The Alabama Shakespeare Festival State Theater performs in Montgomery and also tours. The festival has been attended by over one million people. The Birmingham Festival of Arts was founded in 1951, and the city's Alabama School of Fine Arts has been state-supported since 1971. Huntsville, Montgomery, and Tuscaloosa have symphony orchestras.

34 LIBRARIES AND MUSEUMS

As of 1998, Alabama had 20 county and multi-county regional library systems. Alabama public libraries had a combined total of nearly 7.6 million volumes in 1998, when the total circulation was 13.9 million. The Amelia Gayle Gorgas Library of the University of Alabama had 1.9 million volumes; the Birmingham Public and Jefferson County Free Library had 19 branches and 973,936 volumes. The Alabama Department of History and Archives Library, at Montgomery, has special collections on Alabama history and the Civil War.

Collections on aviation and space exploration in Alabama's libraries, particularly its military libraries, may be the most extensive in the US outside of Washington, D.C. Memorabilia of Werner von Braun are in the library at the Alabama Space and Rocket Center at Huntsville. Also, the Redstone Arsenal's Scientific Information Center holds some 227,000 volumes and 1.8 million technical reports.

Alabama had 81 museums in 2000. The most important art museum is the Birmingham Museum of Art. Russell Cave National Monument has an archaeological exhibit. In Florence is the W.C. Handy Home; at Tuscumbia is Helen Keller's birthplace, Ivy Green.

35 COMMUNICATIONS

In 1999, 91.5% of Alabama's occupied housing units had telephones. During 2000, Alabama had 333 operating radio stations (154 AM, 179 FM) and 48 television stations. In 2000, 69% of television households in Birmingham subscribed to cable television; a total of 44,371 Internet domain names had been registered.

36 PRESS

The oldest Alabama newspaper still in existence in the state is the *Mobile Register,* founded in 1813. As of 1998, Alabama had 19 morning dailies; 5 evening dailies; and 20 Sunday papers. The leading daily, the *Birmingham News,* had a 1998 daily circulation of 156,343.

37 TOURISM, TRAVEL, AND RECREATION

A top tourist attraction is the Alabama Space and Rocket Center at Huntsville, home of the US Space Camp. Among the

Photo credit: © A. Ramey/Woodfin Camp.

The U.S. Space and Rocket Center is located at Huntsville.

many antebellum houses and plantations to be seen in the state are Magnolia Grove (a state shrine) at Greensboro; Gaineswood and Bluff Hall at Demopolis; Arlington in Birmingham; Oakleigh at Mobile; Sturdivant Hall at Selma; and Shorter Mansion at Eufaula.

The celebration of Mardi Gras in Mobile, which began in 1704, predates that in New Orleans and now occupies several days before Ash Wednesday. The state fair is held at Birmingham every October.

During 1995, over 1 million tourists visited Alabama's four national park sites, which include Tuskegee Institute National Historic Site and Russell Cave National Monument, an almost continuous archaeological record of human habitation from at least 7000 BC to about AD 1650.

During 1995, an estimated 4 million tourists visited Alabama's 23 state parks which cover a total of 49,710 acres (20,118 hectares).

38 SPORTS

There are no major league professional sports teams in Alabama. There are minor league baseball clubs at Birmingham, Huntsville, and Mobile. Two major professional stock car races, the Winston 500 and DieHard 500, in May and July respectively, are held at Alabama International Motor Speedway in Talladega. Dog racing was legalized in Mobile in 1971; attendance was 929,000 in 1996. Four of the major hunting-dog competitions in the US are held annually in the state.

Football reigns supreme among collegiate sports, especially at the University of Alabama, which finished number one in 1961, 1965 (with Michigan State), 1978 (with USC), 1979, and 1992, and is a perennial top-ten entry. The Blue-Gray game, an all-star contest, is held at Montgomery on Christmas Day, and the Senior Bowl game is played in Mobile.

Boat races include the Lake Eufaula Summer Spectacular Boat Race in August, and the Dixie Cup Regatta in Guntersville in July. The Alabama Sports Hall of Fame is located at Birmingham; the International Motor Sports Hall of Fame is in Talladega.

mary on 15 May 1972, Wallace was shot and paralyzed from the waist down by a would-be assassin.

Civil rights leader Martin Luther King, Jr. (b.Georgia, 1929–68), winner of the Nobel Peace Prize in 1964, first came to national prominence as leader of the Montgomery bus boycott of 1955. He also led demonstrations at Birmingham in 1963 and at Selma in 1965. His widow, Coretta Scott King (b.1927) is a native Alabamian.

Famous musicians from Alabama include Nat "King" Cole (1917–65) and Hank Williams (1923–53). Alabama's prominent sports figures include Jesse Owens (James Cleveland Owens, 1913–80), winner of four gold medals in track and field at the 1936 Olympic Games in Berlin; Joe Louis (Joseph Louis Barrow, 1914–81), world heavyweight boxing champion from 1937 to 1949; and baseball stars Willie Mays (b.1931), and (Louis) Henry Aaron (b.1934), all-time US home-run leader.

40 BIBLIOGRAPHY

Marks, Henry S., and Marsha Marks. *Alabama Past Leaders*. Huntsville, Ala.: Strode, 1981.

McAuliffe, Emily. *Alabama Facts and Symbols*. Mankato, Minn.: Hilltop Books, 2000.

Shirley, David. *Alabama*. New York: Benchmark Books, 2000.

Web sites

Alabama Bureau of Tourism and Travel. *Alabama Unforgettable*. [Online] Available http://www.touralabama.org/ Accessed May 29, 2001.

AlaWeb. The Alabama Information Network. [Online] Available http://www.state.al.us/2k1 Accessed May 29, 2001.

Photo credit: EPD Photos/CSU Archives

Helen Keller (1880–1968), deaf and blind as the result of a childhood illness, was the first such multihandicapped person to earn a college degree; she later became a world-famous author and lecturer.

39 FAMOUS ALABAMIANS

Alabama's most widely known contempory political figure was George Corley Wallace (1919–98), who served as governor 1963–67 and 1971–79, and was elected to a fourth term in 1982. Wallace, an outspoken opponent of racial desegregation in the 1960s, was a candidate for the Democratic presidential nomination in 1964 and 1972. While campaigning in Maryland's Democratic presidential pri-

Alaska

State of Alaska

ORIGIN OF STATE NAME: From the Aleut world *"alyeska,"* meaning "great land."

NICKNAME: Land of the Midnight Sun.

UNOFFICIAL NICKNAME: The Last Frontier.

CAPITAL: Juneau.

ENTERED UNION: 3 January 1959 (49th).

SONG: "Alaska's Flag."

MOTTO: North to the Future.

FLAG: On a blue field, eight gold stars form the Big Dipper and the North Star.

OFFICIAL SEAL: In the inner circle symbols of mining, agriculture, and commerce are depicted against a background of mountains and the northern lights. In the outer circle are a fur seal, a salmon, and the words "The Seal of the State of Alaska."

BIRD: Willow ptarmigan.

FISH: King salmon.

FLOWER: Wild forget-me-not.

TREE: Sitka spruce.

GEM: Jade.

MINERAL: Gold.

SPORT: Dogteam racing (mushing).

TIME: 3 AM Alaska Standard Time, 2 AM Hawaii-Aleutian Standard Time = noon GMT.

1 LOCATION AND SIZE

Situated at the northwest corner of the North American continent, Alaska is separated by Canadian territory from the conterminous 48 states. Alaska is the largest of the 50 states, with a total area of 591,004 square miles (1,530,699 square kilometers). Land takes up 570,833 square miles (1,478,456 square kilometers) and inland water 20,171 square miles (52,243 square kilometers). Alaska is more than twice the size of Texas, the next-largest state, and occupies 16% of the total US land area; the east-west extension is 2,261 miles (3,639 kilometers); the maximum north-south extension is 1,420 miles (2,285 kilometers).

Alaska is bounded on the north by the Arctic Ocean and Beaufort Sea; on the east by Canada's Yukon Territory and province of British Columbia; on the south by the Gulf of Alaska, Pacific Ocean, and Bering Sea; and on the west by the Bering Sea, Bering Strait, Chukchi Sea, and Arctic Ocean.

Alaska's many offshore islands include St. Lawrence, St. Matthew, Nunivak, and the Pribilof group in the Bering Sea; Kodiak Island in the Gulf of Alaska; and the Aleutian Islands in the Pacific.

The total boundary length of Alaska is 8,187 miles (13,176 kilometers), including a general coastline of 6,640 miles (10,686 kilometers); the tidal shoreline extends 33,904 miles (54,563 kilometers). Alaska's geographic center is about 60 miles (97 kilometers) northwest of Mt. McKinley. The northernmost point in the US—Point Barrow, at 71°23′30″N, 156°28′30″W—lies within the state of Alaska, as does the westernmost point—Cape Wrangell on Attu Island in the Aleutians, at 52°55′30″N, 172°28′E. Little Diomede Island, belonging to Alaska, is less than 2 miles (3 kilometers) from Big Diomede Island, belonging to Russia.

2 TOPOGRAPHY

Topography varies sharply among the six distinct regions of Alaska. In the southeast is a narrow coastal panhandle cut off from the main Alaskan land mass by the St. Elias Range. This region, featuring numerous mountain peaks of 10,000 feet (3,000 meters) in elevation, is paralleled by the Alexander Archipelago. South-central Alaska, which covers a 700-mile (1,100-kilometer) area along the Gulf of Alaska, includes the Kenai Peninsula and Cook Inlet, a great arm of the Pacific penetrating some 200 miles (320 kilometers) to Anchorage. The southwestern region includes the Alaska Peninsula, filled with lightly wooded, rugged peaks, and the 1,700-miles (2,700-kilometers) sweep of the Aleutian islands, barren masses of volcanic origin. Western Alaska extends from

Alaska Population Profile

Total population in 2000:	626,932
Population change, 1990–2000:	14.0%
Hispanic or Latino†:	4.1%
Population by race	
One race:	94.6%
White:	69.3%
Black or African American:	3.5%
American Indian/Alaska Native:	15.6%
Asian:	4.0%
Native Hawaiian/Pacific Islander:	0.5%
Some other race:	1.6%
Two or more races:	5.4%

Population by Age Group

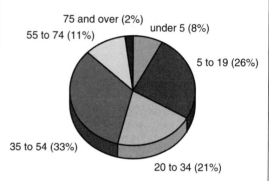

75 and over (2%)
55 to 74 (11%)
under 5 (8%)
5 to 19 (26%)
35 to 54 (33%)
20 to 34 (21%)

Top Cities by Population

City	Population	% change 1990–2000
Anchorage	260,283	15.0
Juneau	30,711	14.8
Fairbanks	30,224	–2.0
Sitka	8,835	2.9
Ketchikan	7,922	–4.1
Kenai	6,942	9.7
Kodiak	6,334	–0.5
Bethel	5,471	17.1
Wasilla	5,469	35.8
Barrow	4,581	32.1

Notes: †A person of Hispanic or Latino origin may be of any race. NA indicates that data are not available.
Sources: U.S. Census Bureau. Public Information Office. *Demographic Profiles.* [Online] Available http://www.census.gov/Press-Release/www/2001/demoprofile.html. Accessed June 1, 2001. U.S. Census Bureau. *Census 2000: Redistricting Data.* Press release issued by the Redistricting Data Office. Washington, D.C., March, 2001.

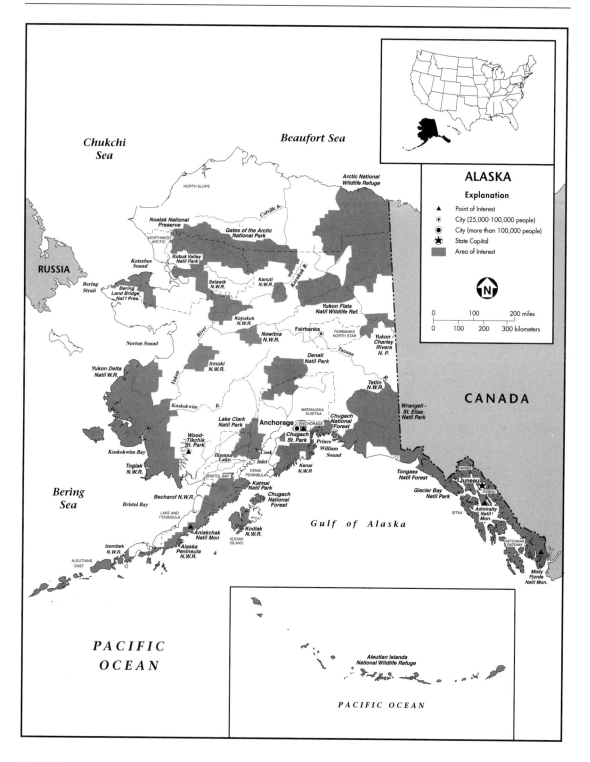

Chukchi Sea

Beaufort Sea

Arctic National Wildlife Refuge

NORTH SLOPE

Noatak National Preserve

Colville R.

Gates of the Arctic National Park

NORTHWEST ARCTIC

Kobuk Valley Natil Park

Kotzebue Sound

Selawik N.W.R.

Kanuti N.W.R.

Koyukuk R.

RUSSIA

Bering Strait

Bering Land Bridge Nat'l Pres.

Koyukuk N.W.R.

Yukon Flats Natil Wildlife Ref.

River

Yukon-Charley Rivers N. P.

Nowitna N.W.R.

Fairbanks

FAIRBANKS NORTH STAR

Norton Sound

Yukon

Innoki N.W.R.

Denali Natil Park

Tanana

Tetlin N.W.R.

R.

Yukon Delta Natil W.R.

Kuskokwim

R.

Lake Clark Natil Park

MATANUSKA SUSITNA

Wrangell - St. Elias Natil Park

CANADA

Wood-Tikchik St. Park

Anchorage

ANCHORAGE

Chugach National Forest

Kuskokwim Bay

Iliamna Lake

Chugach St. Park

Prince

Cook

Togiak N.W.R.

Inlet

William Sound

Kenai N.W.R

Kenai PENINSULA

BRISTOL BAY

Tongass Natil Forest

HAINES

Bering Sea

Bristol Bay

Becharof N.W.R.

LAKE AND PENINSULA

Katmai Natil Park

Chugach National Forest

Gulf of Alaska

Glacier Bay Natil Park

Juneau

JUNEAU

Izembek N.W.R.

Aniakchak Natil Mon

Kodiak N.W.R.

KODIAK ISLAND

Admiralty Natil Mon.

SITKA

ALEUTIANS EAST

Alaska Peninsula N.W.R.

KETCHIKAN GATEWAY

PACIFIC OCEAN

Misty Fjords Natil Mon.

ALASKA

Explanation

▲ Point of Interest
◉ City (25,000-100,000 people)
● City (more than 100,000 people)
★ State Capital
Area of Interest

N

| 0 | | 100 | | 200 miles |
| 0 | 100 | 200 | | 300 kilometers |

Aleutian Islands National Wildlife Refuge

PACIFIC OCEAN

Photo credit: Susan D. Rock.

An active glacier in Glacier Bay.

Bristol Bay to the Seward Peninsula, an immense tundra dotted with lakes and containing the deltas of the Yukon and Kuskokwim rivers, the longest in the state at 1,875 miles (3,017 kilometers) and 680 miles (1,094 kilometers), respectively. Interior Alaska extends north of the Alaska Range and south of the Brooks Range, including most of the drainage of the Yukon and its major tributaries, the Tanana and Porcupine rivers. The Arctic region extends from Kotzebue, north of the Seward Peninsula, east to Canada.

The 11 highest mountains in the US—including the highest in North America, Mt. McKinley (20,320 feet—6,194 meters), located in the Alaska Range—are in the state, which also contains half the world's glaciers; the largest, Malaspina, covers more area than the entire state of Rhode Island. Ice fields cover 5% of the state. Alaska has more than 3 million lakes larger than 20 acres (8 hectares), and more than one-fourth of all the inland water wholly within the US lies inside the state's borders. The largest lake is Iliamna, occupying about 1,100 square miles (2,850 square kilometers).

3 CLIMATE

Americans who called Alaska "Seward's icebox" when it was first purchased from the Russians were unaware of the variety of climatic conditions within its six topographic regions. Although minimum daily winter temperatures in the Arctic region of the state and in the Brooks Range average –20°F (–29°C) and the ground at Point Barrow is frozen permanently to 1,330 feet (405 meters), summer maximum daily temperatures in the Alaskan lowlands average above 60°F (16°C) and have been known to exceed 90°F (32°C). The southeastern region is moderate, ranging from a daily average of 30°F (–1°C) in January to 56°F (13°C) in July; the south-central zone has a similar summer range, but winters are somewhat harsher. The Aleutian Islands have chilly, damp winters and rainy, foggy weather for most of the year; western Alaska is also rainy and cool. The all-time high for the state was 100°F (38°C), recorded at Ft. Yukon on 27 June 1915; the reading of –79.8°F (–62°C) registered at Prospect Creek Camp, in the northwestern part of the state, on 23 January 1971, is the lowest temperature ever officially recorded in the US.

Juneau receives an average of 54.3 inches (138 centimeters) of precipitation each year. The average annual snowfall there is 104 inches (264 centimeters).

4 PLANTS AND ANIMALS

Life zones in Alaska range from grasslands, mountains, and tundra to thick forests, in which Sitka spruce (the state tree), western hemlock, tamarack, white birch, and western red cedar predominate.

Mammals abound in the wilderness. Reindeer and elk inhabit coastal islands. Moose are found mainly in the southcentral and interior parts of the state. There

are at least 13 large caribou herds that migrate across the state. Kodiak, polar, black, and grizzly bears, Dall sheep, and an abundance of small mammals are also found. The sea otter and musk ox have been successfully reintroduced. Round Island, along the north shore of Bristol Bay, has the world's largest walrus rookery. North America's largest population of bald eagles nests in Alaska, and whales migrate annually to the icy bays. Pristine lakes and streams are famous for trout and salmon fishing. In all, 386 species of birds, 430 fishes, 105 mammals, 7 amphibians, and 3 reptiles have been found in the state. Endangered species include the Eskimo curlew and American peregrine falcons. Threatened species are the Aleutian Canada goose and speckled eider; numerous species considered endangered in the conterminous US remain common in Alaska.

5 ENVIRONMENTAL PROTECTION

Alaska's number one environmental health problem is the unsafe water and sanitation facilities in over 135 of Alaska's communities—mostly Alaska Native villages. The people of these communities must carry their water from streams or watering points to their homes; people must use "honey buckets" or privies for disposal of human waste; and solid waste lagoons are usually a collection of human waste, trash, and junk, infested with flies and other carriers of disease. Alaska is using state and federal funds to build new water, sewer, and solid waste facilities to end the need for privies by 2005.

The 1989 oil spill by the tanker *Exxon Valdez* highlighted the need for better prevention and response abilities. Since then these capabilities have been increased through stronger laws and more clearly defined roles among all the various governments and communities.

Mining throughout the state, timber harvesting, and oil development continue to be areas of concern for environmental protection, as do winter violations of air quality standards for carbon monoxide in Anchorage and Fairbanks.

6 POPULATION

Alaska, with a land area one-fifth the size of the conterminous US, surpassed Vermont in population in 2000 and ranked 48th out of the 50 states. Its population totaled 626,932 that year. Regions of settlement and development constitute less than 0.001% of Alaska's total land area. The population density was 1.1 persons per square mile (0.42 persons per square kilometer) in 2000, much less than the national average of 79.6 per square mile (30.7 per square kilometer). The population increased by 14% from 1990 to 2000. The Census Bureau projects a population of 700,000 in 2005.

The Alaska gold rush of the 1890s resulted in a population boom from 32,052 in 1890 to 63,592 a decade later; by the 1920s, however, when mining had declined, Alaska's population had decreased to 55,036. The region's importance to US national defense during the 1940s led to a rise in population from 72,524 to 128,643 during that decade. Oil development, especially the construction of the Alaska pipeline, brought a 78% population increase between 1960 and 1980. Almost all of this gain was from migration; as of 1990, over 60% of all state residents had been born in another state. The state's population is about three years younger than that of the nation as a whole (the median age was only 32.4 in 2000 compared with the national of 35.3), and only 2% of all Alaskans were 75 years of age or older in 2000. Alaska is also one of the few states where men (nearly 52%) outnumber women.

Alaska's population is 67.5% urban. Over one-third of all state residents live in the city of Anchorage, which had an estimated population of 260,283 in 2000. Other leading cities are Juneau, 30,711, and Fairbanks, 30,224.

7 ETHNIC GROUPS

Indians—primarily Athapaskan, Tlingit, Haida, and Tsimshian living along the southern coast—number around 34,000. Eskimos (42,024) and Aleuts (10,244), the other native people, live mostly in scattered villages to the north and northwest. Taken together, Alaskan natives, Eskimos, Aleuts, and Native Americans numbered about 97,100 or 15.9% of the population in 1997, the highest rate among the states.

The number of blacks was estimated around 23,800, or 3.9% of the population in 1997. Among those of Asian and Pacific Islands origin are 8,584 Filipinos, 3,009 Japanese, and 4,349 Koreans. Out of Alaska's total population, about 23,300 individuals are of Hispanic origin, with 6,888 of those claiming Mexican ancestry.

Alaska Population by Race

Census 2000 was the first national census in which the instructions to respondents said, "Mark one or more races." This table shows the number of people who are of one, two, or three or more races. For those claiming two races, the number of people belonging to the various categories is listed. The U.S. government conducts a census of the population every ten years.

	Number	Percent
Total population	626,932	100.0
One race	592,786	94.6
Two races	31,743	5.1
White *and* Black or African American	2,460	0.4
White *and* American Indian/Alaska Native	16,920	2.7
White *and* Asian	4,103	0.7
White *and* Native Hawaiian/Pacific Islander	647	0.1
White *and* some other race	3,113	0.5
Black or African American *and* American Indian/Alaska Native	1,064	0.2
Black or African American *and* Asian	310	—
Black or African American *and* Native Hawaiian/Pacific Islander	92	—
Black or African American *and* some other race	393	0.1
American Indian/Alaska Native *and* Asian	811	0.1
American Indian/Alaska Native *and* Native Hawaiian/Pacific Islander	208	—
American Indian/Alaska Native *and* some other race	503	0.1
Asian *and* Native Hawaiian/Pacific Islander	582	0.1
Asian *and* some other race	450	0.1
Native Hawaiian/Pacific Islander *and* some other race	87	—
Three or more races	2,403	0.4

Source: U.S. Census Bureau. *Census 2000: Redistricting Data.* Press release issued by the Redistricting Data Office. Washington, D.C., March, 2001. A dash (—) indicates that the percent is less than 0.1.

Foreign-born persons numbered approximately 25,000, or 4.4% of the population.

8 LANGUAGES

From the Tlingit, Haida, and Tsimshian groups of lower Alaska almost no language influence has been felt, save for *hooch* (from Tlingit *hoochino)*; but some native words have escaped into general usage, notably Inuit *mukluk* and Aleut *parka*. Native place-names abound: Skagway and Ketchikan (Tlingit), Kodiak and Katmai (Inuit), and Alaska and Akutan (Aleut).

Almost 88% of the population five years old and older speaks only English in the home. Other major languages spoken in the home, and the number of people speaking them, include various Native American, Alaskan, and Aleut languages, 26,780; Spanish, 10,020; and Tagalog, 5,124.

9 RELIGIONS

The largest religious organization in the state is the Roman Catholic Church, which has over 45,203 members. Southern Baptists constitute the largest Protestant denomination, with 28,718 members in 1990. Other major groups are the Church of Jesus Christ of Latter-day Saints (Mormons), 15,751; Assembly of God, 8,779;

ters) and is not directly connected to any other North American line (although rail-barge service provides access to the rest of the US rail network); it was federally operated until 1985, when it was bought by the state government for $22.3 million. The line handled over 5.9 million tons of freight in 1995, mostly nonmetallic minerals (43%), coal (28%), and petroleum (24%).

The Alaska Highway, which extends 1,523 miles (2,451 kilometers) from Dawson Creek, British Columbia, to Fairbanks, is the only road link with the rest of the US. Only 12,775 miles (20,555 kilometers) of roads were in use as of 1997. During the same year, the state had 542,398 registered vehicles and 446,247 licensed drivers. The state's major ports, Nikishka and Anchorage, handled 5 and 3.4 million tons of cargo, respectively, in 1996. Valdez, the terminus of the Trans-Alaska Pipeline, handled 77.1 million tons, almost entirely crude oil. It was the seventh-busiest US port.

Air travel is the primary means of intrastate transportation, with several bush carriers serving the remote communities. There are approximately 8,800 active pilots and 5,400 active aircraft registered in the state, with about 643,000 hours flown—2.4% of the nation's total. Anchorage International Airport, the state's largest, carried over 1.6 million passengers and 268,000 tons of freight in 1996. Alaska has a total of 248 air facilities operated by the state, and 854 smaller privately owned airports.

Photo credit: © George Herben/Woodfin Camp.

An oil tanker is on its way to Alaska.

Presbyterians, 6,307; and Episcopalians, 7,540. There was also a very small population of Jews as of 1997.

Many Aleuts were converted to the Russian Orthodox religion during the 18th century, and small Russian Orthodox congregations are still active on the Aleutian Islands, in Kodiak and southeastern Alaska, and along the Yukon River.

10 TRANSPORTATION

Alaska had no regular rail service until 1923, when the Alaska Railroad linked Seward, Anchorage, and Fairbanks. This railroad of 482 route miles (776 kilome-

A shopping and business district in Juneau.

11 HISTORY

At some time between 10,000 and 40,000 years ago, the ancestors of all of America's aboriginal peoples trekked over a land bridge that connected northeastern Siberia with northwestern America. These early hunter-gatherers dispersed, eventually becoming three distinct groups: Aleut, Eskimo, and Indian.

Ages passed before overseas voyagers rediscovered Alaska. Separate Russian parties led by Aleksei Chirikov and Vitas Bering (who had sailed in 1728 through the strait that now bears his name) landed in Alaska in 1741. In 1784, the first permanent Russian settlement was established on Kodiak Island: 15 years later, the Russian American Company was granted a monopoly over the region. Its manager, Aleksandr Baranov, established Sitka as the company's headquarters. In 1802, the Tlingit Indians captured Sitka but two years later lost the town and the war with the Russian colonizers. Increasingly, the imperial Russian government viewed the colonies as a drain on the treasury. In 1867, as a result of the persistence of Secretary of State William H. Seward, a devoted American expansionist, Russia agreed to sell its American territories to the US for $7,200,000. From 1867 until the first Organic Act of 1884, which provided for a federally appointed governor, Alaska was administered first by the US Army, then by the US Customs Service.

The Gold Rush

The pace of economic development quickened after the discovery of gold in 1880 at Juneau. But it was the major strike in Canada's Klondike region in 1898 that sparked a mass stampede to the Yukon Valley and other regions of Alaska, including the Arctic.

Subsequent development of the fishing and timber industries increased Alaska's prosperity and prospects, although the region suffered from a lack of transportation facilities. A significant achievement came in 1914 when construction started on the Alaska Railroad connecting Seward, a new town with an ice-free port, with Anchorage and Fairbanks. Congress granted territorial status to the region in 1912, and the first statehood bill was introduced in Congress four years later.

Mineral production declined sharply after 1914. Population declined too, and conditions remained depressed through the 1920s, although gold mining was helped by a rise in gold prices in 1934. World War II provided the next great economic impetus for Alaska; the Aleutian campaign following the Japanese invasion of the islands, though not as pivotal as the combat in other areas of the Pacific, did show American policymakers that Alaska's geography was in itself an important resource.

Statehood

The US government built the Alaska Highway and many other facilities, including docks, airfields, and an extension of the Alaska Railroad. Population soared as thousands of civilian workers and military personnel moved to the territory. The Alaska Statehood Act was adopted by Congress in June 1958 and ratified by Alaska voters that August. On 3 January 1959, President Dwight Eisenhower signed the proclamation that made Alaska the 49th state.

In 1971, the Native Claims Settlement Act provided an extensive grant to the state's natives but also precipitated a long federal-state controversy over land allocations. A major oil field was discovered in 1968, and in 1974, over the opposition of many environmentalists, construction began on the 789-mile (1,270-kilometer) Trans-Alaska Pipeline from Prudhoe Bay to Valdez.

The state's dependence on oil—82% of its revenue came from oil industry taxes and royalties—became a disadvantage when overproduction in the Middle East drove the price of oil down from $36 a barrel at the peak of Alaska's oil boom in 1980–81 to $13.50 a barrel in 1988. In 1986, the state's revenues had declined by two-thirds. Alaska lost 20,000 jobs between 1985 and 1989.

On 24 March 1989, the *Exxon Valdez*, a 987-foot oil tanker, hit a reef and ran aground. The tanker spilled 11 million gallons of crude oil. The oil eventually contaminated 1,285 miles of shoreline, fouling Prince William Sound and its wildlife sanctuary, the Gulf of Alaska, and the Alaska Peninsula. In the settlement of the largest environmental suit in US history brought by the state and federal governments, Exxon was fined $1.025 billion in civil and criminal penalties.

12 STATE GOVERNMENT

Under Alaska's first and only constitution—adopted in 1956, effective since the time of statehood, and amended 19 times by the end of 1983—the house of representatives consists of 40 members elected for two-year terms; the senate has 20 members elected for staggered four-year terms. The minimum age is 21 for a representative, 25 for a senator; legislators must have resided in the state for at least three years before election and in the district at least one year.

Alaska's executive branch, modeled after New Jersey's, features a strong governor who appoints all cabinet officers (except the commissioner of education) and judges subject to legislative confirmation. The lieutenant governor is the only other elected executive. The governor must be at least 30 years of age and must have been a US citizen for seven years and an Alaska resident for seven years. The term of office is four years, and the governor is limited to two consecutive terms. The qualifications for the lieutenant governor are the same as for the governor.

After a bill has been passed by the legislature, it becomes law if it is: signed by the governor; left unsigned for 15 days (Sundays excluded) while the legislature is in session or for 20 days after it has adjourned; or passed by a two-thirds vote of the combined houses over a gubernatorial veto (to override a veto of an appropriations bill requires a three-fourths vote). Constitutional amendments require a two-thirds vote of the legislature and ratification by the electorate.

Alaska Governors: 1959–2001

1959–1966	William Allen Egan	Democrat
1966–1969	Walter Joseph Hickel	Democrat
1969–1970	Keith Harvey Miller	Republican
1970–1974	William Allen Egan	Democrat
1974–1982	Jay Sterner Hammond	Republican
1982–1986	William Jennings Sheffield	Democrat
1986–1990	Steve Camberling Cowper	Democrat
1990–1994	Walker Joseph Hickel	Independent
1994–	Tony Knowles	Democrat

13 POLITICAL PARTIES

As of 2000, of 473,648 registered voters, approximately 18% were Democrats, while 25% were Republican, and 42% were unaffiliated. In presidential elections since 1968, Alaskans have voted Republican nine consecutive times. Alaskans gave Al Gore 28% of the vote in 2000, while George W. Bush received 59% and others received 13%.

Alaska Presidential Vote by Major Political Parties, 1960–2000

YEAR	ALASKA WINNER	DEMOCRAT	REPUBLICAN
1960	Nixon (R)	29,809	30,953
1964	*Johnson (D)	44,329	22,930
1968	*Nixon (R)	35,411	37,600
1972	*Nixon (R)	32,967	55,349
1976	Ford (R)	44,058	71,555
1980	*Reagan (R)	41,842	186,112
1984	*Reagan (R)	62,007	138,377
1988	*Bush (R)	72,584	119,251
1992**	Bush (R)	78,294	102,000
1996**	Dole (R)	80,380	122,746
2000	*Bush (R)	79,004	167,398

* Won US presidential election.
** Independent candidate Ross Perot received 73,481 votes in 1992 and 26,333 votes in 1996.

Both US Senators and its sole US Representative are Republicans. Alaska's state legislature consisted of 6 Democrats and 14 Republicans in the state senate, and 13 Democrats and 27 Republicans in the state house. Democrat Tony Knowles won reelection to a second term as governor in 1998.

14 LOCAL GOVERNMENT

Alaska is divided into 25 districts, 14 of which are counties. As of 1997 there were 149 cities, most of them governed by elected mayors and village councils. 44 million acres of federal land have been returned to native Alaskan tribes, operated under The Bureau of Indian Affairs. Juneau, Sitka, and Anchorage, Alaska's three unified municipalities, have consolidated city and borough functions.

15 JUDICIAL SYSTEM

The supreme court, consisting of a chief justice and four associate justices, hears appeals for civil matters from the 15 superior courts, whose 30 judges are organized among the four state judicial districts, and for criminal matters from the three-member court of appeals. The superior court has original jurisdiction in all civil and criminal matters, and it hears appeals from the district court. The lowest court is the district court, of which there are 56 in four districts.

All judges are appointed by the governor from nominations made by the Judicial Council, but are thereafter subject to voter approval; supreme court justices serve terms of 10 years; court of appeals and superior court judges, 6 years; and

district judges, 4 years. In 1998, the crime rate was 4,777 crimes per 100,000 population. Alaska has no capital punishment statute. There were 4,211 inmates in state and federal prisons as of June 1999. Alaska had 2,196 practicing attorneys in 1996.

16 MIGRATION

The earliest immigrants to North America, more than 10,000 years ago, likely came to Alaska via a land bridge across what is now the Bering Strait. The Russian fur traders who arrived during the 1700s found Aleuts, Eskimos, and Indians already established there. Despite more than a century of Russian sovereignty over the area, however, few Russians came, and those that did returned to the mother country with the purchase of Alaska by the US in 1867.

Virtually all other migration to Alaska has been from the continental US—first during the gold rush of the late 19th century, and most recently during the oil boom of the 1970s. Between 1970 and 1983, Alaska's net gain from migration was 78,000, but from 1985 to 1990, Alaska suffered a net loss from migration of over 37,500. There was a net loss of 21,000 during 1990–98 from domestic migration, but a net gain of 1,008 from abroad.

Urbanization increased with migration during the 1980s; the urban population increased from 64.5% in 1980 to 67.5% of the total population in 1990. In the 1980s, migration added 36,000 people to the state, or 34% of the total population increase. Only 34% of the 1990 popula-

Photo credit: Alaska Division of Tourism.

Mt. McKinley (20,320 feet—6,194 meters) is the tallest mountain in North America.

tion was born within the state, a lower percentage than any other state except Florida and Nevada.

17 ECONOMY

When Alaska gained statehood in 1959, its economy was almost totally dependent on the US government. Fisheries, limited mining (mostly gold and gravel), and some lumber production made up the balance. That all changed with development of the petroleum industry during the 1970s. Construction of the Trans–Alaska Pipeline brought a massive infusion of money and people into the state.

The collapse of oil prices in the mid-1980s hit Alaska hard. But by 1990, a recovery was underway. Alaska depends on oil for 85% of its total revenue.

Commercial fishing is one of the foundations of the Alaska economy. Alaska's fishery accounts for 50% of the total annual US catch.

The value of Alaska's forest products grew from $248 million in 1986 to $641 million in 1990. Log exports began to decline in 1990 and are expected to drop 50% by 2000 as the supply of timber shrinks.

In 1994, private goods-producing industries accounted for 30% of Alaska's economic output, private services-producing industries for 49%, and government for 21%. Tourism is the second largest primary employer in the state.

18 INCOME

Alaska boasts the 17th highest per capita (per person) income in the US: $27,835 in 1998. The median household income in 1998 was $51,421.

Living costs are high: in 1995, Anchorage, Fairbanks, and Juneau all had a cost of living some 25–35% above the US urban average, and costs in some other Alaskan cities were much higher. A total of 8.5% of all Alaskans were living below the federal poverty level in 1996–97.

19 INDUSTRY

Alaska's small but growing manufacturing sector is centered on petroleum refining and the processing of lumber and food products, especially seafood.

Five of Alaska's ten top employers are engaged in the petroleum industry: ARCO Alaska, VECO, BP Exploration, Alyeska Pipeline Service, and Alaska Petroleum Contractors.

20 LABOR

Following completion of the Trans-Alaska Pipeline in 1977, the state entered a period of high unemployment that lasted through the end of the decade and into the 1980s and 1990s. Of the 317,800 in the civilian labor force in 1998, 19,800 were unemployed, for a rate of 6.2%. Alaska's economy features significant seasonal fluctuations.

In 1998, 20.4% of Alaskan workers were union members. Wage rates averaged $464 per week for production workers in December 1996.

21 AGRICULTURE

Hampered by a short but intense growing season, frequent frosts, and difficulties getting agricultural products to market, Alaska has limited commercial agriculture. Farm income in 1999 was only $54 million. Greenhouse and nursery items, hay, and potatoes are the main commodities produced. In 1998 there were about 560 farms and 910,000 acres (368,000 hectares) in farms; the leading farming region is the Matanuska Valley, northeast of Anchorage.

22 DOMESTICATED ANIMALS

Dairy and livestock products account for about 65% of Alaska's agricultural income. Alaska had 9,900 cattle and 1,700 sheep at the beginning of 1995. In 1997, an estimated 14 million pounds (5.1 million kilograms) of milk, valued at $3.1 million, were produced by 900 milk cows. Meat and poultry production is negligible by national standards.

23 FISHING

Alaska is the leading fishing state in terms of earnings and in the total weight of catch. The salmon catch, the staple of the industry, amounted to 626.1 million pounds (284 million kilograms) of fish and over $242.7 million in 1998. Pink,

Photo credit: © George Herben/Woodfin Camp.

The central Alaskan pipeline is located near the Tazlina River.

sockeye, and chum salmon accounted for 93% of the salmon catch. The cod catch in 1995 was a record 589.7 million pounds (267.5 million kilograms), worth $109 million. Crab, a major export item, has recently declined in availability. In all, Alaska's commercial catch in 1998 totaled 4.8 billion pounds (2.2 billion kilograms), some 53% of the total US commercial catch, valued at $951.5 million. In 1998, Dutch Harbor–Unalaska ranked first and Kodiak ranked second among US fishing ports in both quantity and value. Alaska had 414 processing and wholesale plants with an average of about 7,988 employees during 1997, as well as a commercial fishing fleet of 16,442 boats and vessels in 1996.

There were over 399,680 licensed sport anglers in Alaska in 1998.

24 FORESTRY

Alaska's timber resources are vast, but full-scale development of the industry awaits fundamental land-use decisions at the federal and state levels. Alaska's forested area covers 127.3 million acres (51.5 million hectares), far more than any other state. However, the area of harvestable timberland is only 12.4 million acres (5.0 million acres). Alaska contains the nation's largest natural forests, Tongass in the southeast (17.4 million acres—7 million hectares) and Chugach along the Gulf Coast (6.6 million acres—2.7 million hectares).

Lumbering and related industries employed about 10,500 workers in 1995. The value added by the manufacture of the lumber and wood products industries was $219.5 million in 1997.

Photo credit: Susan D. Rock.

A pair of Huskies hitched to a sled team wait for the signal to start the Iditarod Trail Sled Dog Race—a long, strenuous race across Alaska.

25 MINING

The US Geological Survey estimated the 1998 value for Alaska nonfuel mineral production at $911 million, down 7% from 1997. Metallic minerals accounted for 91% of the total value, especially gold, zinc, lead, and silver.

State estimates show that about 3,400 people were employed in all aspects of the mineral industry in 1995.

26 ENERGY AND POWER

As of 1998, Alaskan production of crude oil was 18% of the nation's total, and second only to that of Texas. Of the 383.2 million barrels produced, 97% came from the vast North Shore fields and 3% from the Cook Inlet area. The Trans-Alaska Pipeline, which runs 789 miles (1,270 kilometers) from the North Slope oil fields to the port of Valdez on the southern coast, carried 1.45 million barrels of crude oil a day in 1996. Proven reserves in Alaska total 5.05 billion barrels, or about one-quarter of national reserves in 1998.

Natural gas production in 1998 was 466.6 billion cubic feet (13.2 billion cubic meters), seventh among states. Proved reserves are 9.9 trillion cubic feet (.3 trillion cubic meters). Electric power production totaled over 5.1 billion kilowatt hours; installed capacity was nearly 1.9 million kilowatts, and almost all generating facilities were government-owned. Alaska also had proved coal reserves totaling 6.5 billion tons in 1996. Production of coal in 1998 was 1.34 million tons, from a single mine at Healy. Alaska's total consumption of energy per capita was 1,151.8 million Btu (289.1 million kilocalories) in 1996, over three times greater than the national average.

27 COMMERCE

Sales from wholesale trade in 1992 amounted to $3.6 billion, 49th among states, and retail sales totaled $5 billion that year. More than 71% of all retail sales were in the Anchorage metropolitan area.

Food stores accounted for 23.2% of all retail sales, followed by automotive dealers, 15.7%; department stores, 14.1%; eating and drinking places, 13.1%; and others, 33.9%. Service establishments had receipts of $2.8 billion in 1992, 45th among the states.

Exports of goods made in Alaska came to nearly $2 billion in 1998. One-third of Alaska's manufactured goods are exported to other countries, the highest ratio of all the states, with paper and food products the leading items. Alaska is the leading fish-exporting state and the largest exporter of salmon. By federal law, Alaskan petroleum cannot be exported to foreign countries.

28 PUBLIC FINANCE

Alaska's annual budget is prepared by the Division of Budget and Management, within the Office of the Governor, and submitted by the governor to the legislature for amendment and approval. The fiscal year runs from 1 July through 30 June.

In 1997, Alaska led the nation in state government revenues and expenditures per person, at $15,498.28 and $9,396.48, respectively. Total revenues that year were nearly $9.44 billion, while expenditures were about $5.72 billion—for every $1 spent the state government took in $1.65. As of 1997, the outstanding debt of Alaska was over $3.29 billion. At about $5,403 per capita (per person), Alaska's ratio of state government debt per person was the highest of any state that year.

29 TAXATION

The huge sums generated by the sale of oil leases and by oil and gas royalties make Alaska's tax structure highly unusual. Government derived 78% of its revenue from oil in 1996. There are no state sales or personal income taxes, and the business tax was ended in 1979. Some localities impose a sales tax, as well as a property tax. The corporate tax rate in 2000 ranged from 1% on the first $10,000 of taxable income to 9.4% on amounts over $90,000. Other taxes include ones on alcoholic beverages, motor fuels and vehicles, estates, cigarettes, insurance companies, and fisheries. Nevertheless, Alaska had the lowest of all states in per capita (per person) state tax burden, with $2,657, in 1996. Each Alaskan resident also receives a dividend from the state's oil earnings—in 1999 the dividend was $1,770.

30 HEALTH

Alaska's birthrate of 15.9 per 1,000 population in 1997 was fourth highest among the states. The infant mortality rate of 5.9 per 1,000 live births for 1997 was below the national average. The abortion ratio was 15 per 1,000 births in 1996.

Alaska's overall death rate of 418.7 per 100,000 population in 1998 was less than half the US rate, but the death rate from accidents (40.9 per 100,000) was one of the highest in the US, and the suicide rate of 22.1 was nearly twice the national average. The commercial fishing industry has one of the highest occupational fatality rates in Alaska; in the early 1990s the fishing industry annually had about one occupational fatality for every 200 workers. per 1000,000. The 1998 death rate of 24.9 per 100,000 for cerebrovascular diseases was significantly lower than the national rate of 58.6, due to the relative youth of the state's population.

Alaska's 17 community hospitals in 1998 had 1,240 beds and 41,294 admissions. The state had 993 physicians in 1996, lower than the national average. The average daily expense to Alaskan hospitals per inpatient amounted to $970 in 1998. Over 17% of the state's residents did not have health insurance in 1998.

31 HOUSING

Despite the severe winters, housing designs in Alaska do not differ notably from those in other states. Builders do usually provide thicker insulation in walls and ceilings, but the high costs of construction have not encouraged more energy-efficient adaptation to the environment. In 1980, the state legislature passed several measures to encourage energy conservation in housing and in public buildings. In native villages, traditional dwellings like the half-buried huts of the Aleuts have long since given way to conventional, low-standard housing.

In 1998, there were an estimated 248,000 housing units, 66% of which were owner occupied. From 1970 to 1978, 43,009 building permits were issued, as construction boomed during the years of pipeline building. As of 1990, only 87.5% of Alaska's housing units had complete plumbing facilities, the lowest

proportion of all states. In 1996, the state authorized 2,640 new privately-owned housing units, valued at $316.4 million. The median house value was $94,400 in 1990, down 22.1% from 1980 after adjusting for inflation. The median monthly cost for an owner-occupied unit with a mortgage was $1,059 in 1990 (fourth highest in the US); the median rent was $559 per month.

32 EDUCATION

As of 1998, 91% of the population over 25 years of age had completed high school. Some 24% had obtained a bachelor's degree. Minority students make up almost 37% of total enrollment in public schools. The University of Alaska is the state's leading higher educational institution. The main campus at Fairbanks, established in 1917, had 5,072 students in 1993, while the Anchorage campus had 13,519. Private institutions included two colleges with four-year programs, a theological seminary, and Alaska Pacific University. The University of Alaska's Rural Education Division has a network of education centers and offers 90 correspondence courses in 22 fields of study.

33 ARTS

The Council on the Arts sponsors tours by performing artists, supports artists' residences in the schools, aids local arts projects, and purchases the works of living Alaskans for display in state buildings.

By 1996, there were 250 arts-related associations in Alaska and 32 local art groups. Fairbanks, Juneau, and Anchorage have symphony orchestras, and Anchorage has a civic opera.

34 LIBRARIES AND MUSEUMS

Alaska public libraries had an estimated combined book stock of 2 million and a circulation of 3.7 million in 1998; facilities are located in seven boroughs and in most larger towns. Anchorage had the largest public library system, with four branches and 554,686 volumes in 1998. Also notable are the State Library in Juneau and the library of the University of Alaska at Fairbanks.

Alaska had 44 museums in 2000. The Alaska State Museum in Juneau offers an impressive collection of native crafts and Alaskan artifacts. Sitka National Historical Park features Indian and Russian items, and the nearby Museum of Sheldon Jackson College holds important native collections. Noteworthy historical and archaeological sites include the Totem Heritage Center in Ketchikan. Anchorage has the Alaska Zoo.

35 COMMUNICATIONS

Considering the vast distances traveled and the number of small, scattered communities, the US mail is a bargain for Alaskans. In 1999, 6 percent of the state's households had telephones. There were 106 radio stations (41 AM, 65 FM) in 1999, along with 19 television stations (5 noncommercial educational). A total of 13,558 Internet domain names had been registered by the year 2000.

36 PRESS

One of Alaska's seven daily newspapers and two Sunday newspapers are in Anchorage. The *Anchorage Daily News* (mornings) in 1997 had a daily circulation of 71,239 and a Sunday circulation of 91,863. The *Tundra Times,* also published in Anchorage, is a statewide weekly devoted to native concerns. The University of Alaska Press is the state's main academic publisher.

37 TOURISM, TRAVEL, AND RECREATION

With thousands of miles of unspoiled scenery and hundreds of mountains and lakes, Alaska has vast tourist potential. An estimated 1.8 million travelers visited Alaska in 1996. Alaska's tourism industry revenue was about $1 billion in 1998.

One of the most popular tourist destinations is Glacier Bay National Monument. Alaska's state and national parks, preserves, historical parks, and monuments total 52.9 million acres (21.7 million hectares). Licenses were held by 216,977 hunters who were state residents in 1995.

38 SPORTS

There are no major league professional sports teams in Alaska; Anchorage, however, has a minor league hockey franchise. Sports in Alaska generally revolve around the outdoors, including skiing, fishing, hiking, mountain biking, and camping. Perhaps the biggest sporting event in the state is the Iditarod Trail Sled Dog Race, covering 1,159 miles from Anchorage to

Photo credit: EPD Photos/National Archives

Secretary of State William H. Seward (b.New York, 1801–72), was instrumental in the 1867 purchase of Alaska, and ranks as the state's "founding father," although he never visited the region.

Nome. The race is held in March, and men and women compete against each other. With a $50,000 purse, it is the richest sled dog race in the world.

39 FAMOUS ALASKANS

Alaskan's best-known officeholder was Ernest Gruening (b.New York, 1887–1974), a territorial governor from 1939 to 1953 and US senator from 1959 to 1969. Outstanding historical figures include Vitus Bering (b.Denmark, 1680–1741), a seaman in Russian service who commanded the discovery expedition in 1741, and Aleksandr Baranov (b.Russia, 1746–1819), the first governor of Russian America.

40 BIBLIOGRAPHY

Alaska, State of. Department of Education. Division of Libraries, Archives, and Museums. *Alaska Blue Book 1993–94.* Juneau, 1994.

Dubois, Muriel. *Alaska Facts and Symbols.* Mankato, Minn.: Hilltop Books, 2000.

McNamara, Katharine. *Narrow Road to the Deep North: A Journey into the Interior of Alaska.* San Francisco, Calif.: Mercury House, 2001.

Naske, Claus M. *A History of Alaska Statehood.* Lanham, Md.: University Press of America, 1985.

Strudwick, Leslie. *Alaska.* Mankato, Minn.: Weigl, 2001.

Web sites

Official Tourism Marketing Organization for the State of Alaska. *Welcome to Alaska.* [Online] Available http://www.travelalaska.com/homepage.html Accessed May 29, 2001.

State of Alaska. *Alaska Kids.* [Online] Available http://www.state.ak.us/kids/ Accessed May 29, 2001.

ARIZONA

State of Arizona

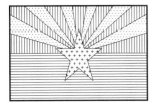

ORIGIN OF STATE NAME: Probably from the Pima or Tohono O'Odham word *arizonac,* meaning "place of small springs."

NICKNAME: The Grand Canyon State.

CAPITAL: Phoenix.

ENTERED UNION: 14 February 1912 (48th).

SONG: "Arizona" and "Arizona March Song."

MOTTO: *Ditat Deus* (God enriches).

FLAG: A copper-colored five-pointed star symbolic of the state's copper resources rises from a blue field; six yellow and seven red segments radiating from the star cover the upper half.

OFFICIAL SEAL: Depicted on a shield are symbols of the state's economy and natural resources, including mountains, a rising sun, and a dam and reservoir in the background, irrigated farms and orchards in the middle distance, a quartz mill, a miner, and cattle in the foreground, as well as the state motto. The words "Great Seal of the State of Arizona 1912" surround the shield.

BIRD: Cactus wren.

FLOWER: Blossom of the saguaro cactus.

TREE: Palo Verde.

OFFICIAL NECKWEAR: Bola tie.

TIME: 5 AM MST = noon GMT. Arizona does not observe daylight savings time.

1 LOCATION AND SIZE

Located in the Rocky Mountains region of the southwestern US, Arizona ranks sixth in size among the 50 states. The total area of Arizona is 114,000 square miles (295,260 square kilometers). Arizona extends about 340 miles (547 kilometers) east-west; the state's maximum north-south extension is 395 miles (636 kilometers). Arizona's total boundary length is 1,478 miles (2,379 kilometers).

2 TOPOGRAPHY

Arizona is a state of extraordinary topographic diversity and beauty. The Colorado Plateau, which covers two-fifths of the state in the north, is a dry highland region characterized by deep canyons. The most notable is the Grand Canyon, a vast gorge more than 200 miles (320 kilometers) long, up to 18 miles (29 kilometers) wide, and more than 1 mile (1.6 kilometers) deep. Also within this region are the Painted Desert and Petrified Forest.

The Mogollon Rim separates the northern plateau from a central region of alternating basins and ranges. The Sonora Desert, in the southwest, contains the lowest point in the state, 70 feet (21 meters) above sea level. The Colorado is the state's major river. Arizona has few natural lakes, but there are several large artificial lakes formed by dams.

3 CLIMATE

Arizona has a dry climate. Average daily temperatures at Yuma, in the southwestern desert, range from 43°F to 67°F (6°C to 19°C) in January and from 81°F to 106°F (27°C to 41°C) in July. The maximum recorded temperature was 128°F (53°C), registered at Lake Havasu City on 29 June 1994; the minimum, –40°F (–40°C), was set at Hawley Lake on 7 January 1971.

Annual precipitation ranges from 3 inches (8 centimeters) in the extreme southwest to between 25 and 30 inches (63 to 76 centimeters) at the highest elevations of the state. Snow, sometimes as much as 100 inches (254 centimeters) of it, falls on the highest peaks each winter.

4 PLANTS AND ANIMALS

The desert is known for many varieties of cacti, from the saguaro, whose blossom is the state flower, to the cholla and widely utilized yucca. Desert flowers include the night-blooming cereus. Among medicinal desert plants is the jojoba, also harvested for its oil-bearing seeds. Trees include spruce, fir, juniper, ponderosa pine, oak, and piñon.

Arizona's native animals range from desert species of lizards and snakes to the deer, elk, and antelope of the northern highlands. Prairie dog "towns" dot the northern regions. Rattlesnakes are abundant, and the desert is rife with reptiles such as the collared lizard. Native birds

Arizona Population Profile

Total population in 2000:	5,130,632
Population change, 1990–2000:	40.0%
Hispanic or Latino†:	25.3%
Population by race	
One race:	97.1%
White:	75.5%
Black or African American:	3.1%
American Indian/Alaska Native:	5.0%
Asian:	1.8%
Native Hawaiian/Pacific Islander:	0.1%
Some other race:	11.6%
Two or more races:	2.9%

Population by Age Group

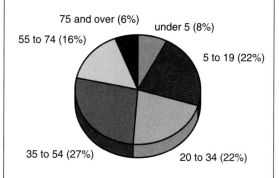

75 and over (6%)
under 5 (8%)
55 to 74 (16%)
5 to 19 (22%)
35 to 54 (27%)
20 to 34 (22%)

Top Cities by Population

City	Population	% change 1990–2000
Phoenix	1,321,045	34.3
Tucson	486,699	20.1
Mesa	396,375	37.6
Glendale	218,812	47.7
Scottsdale	202,705	55.8
Chandler	176,581	95.0
Tempe	158,625	11.8
Gilbert	109,697	275.8
Peoria	108,364	114.1
Yuma	77,515	41.1

Notes: †A person of Hispanic or Latino origin may be of any race. NA indicates that data are not available.
Sources: U.S. Census Bureau. Public Information Office. *Demographic Profiles.* [Online] Available http://www.census.gov/Press-Release/www/2001/demoprofile.html. Accessed June 1, 2001. U.S. Census Bureau. *Census 2000: Redistricting Data.* Press release issued by the Redistricting Data Office. Washington, D.C., March, 2001.

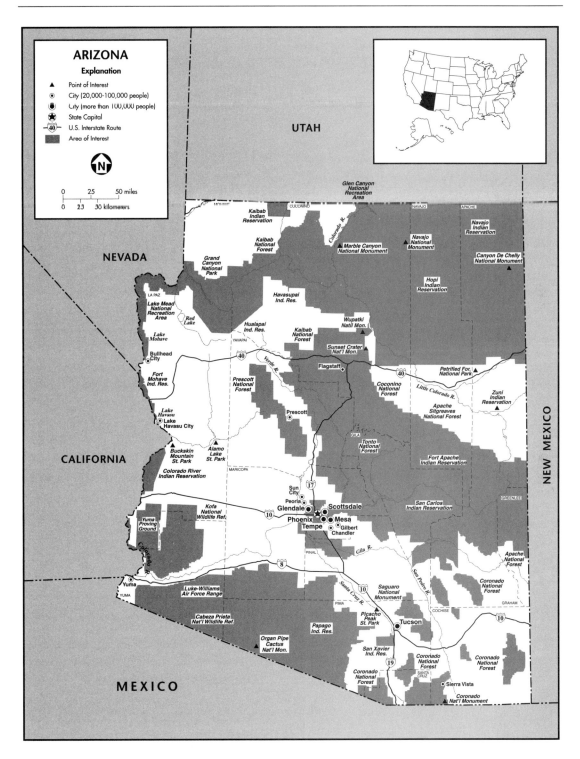

include the thick-billed parrot, white pelican, and cactus wren (the state bird). Arizona counts the osprey, desert tortoise, spotted bat, and Gila monster among its threatened wildlife.

5 ENVIRONMENTAL PROTECTION

Aside from Phoenix, whose air quality is poorer than that of most other US cities, Arizona has long been noted for its clear air, open lands, and beautiful forests. Legislation enacted in 1980 attempts to allocate water use among cities, mining, and agriculture. As of 1998, Arizona had 10 hazardous waste sites, and some 13 communities had curbside recycling programs.

6 POPULATION

Arizona ranked 20th in the US, with a 2000 census population of over 5.1 million. This number was a 40% increase from 1990, placing the state second (behind Nevada) in percentage change of population (Arizona's population growth rate has been one of the nation's highest for two decades). A projection of 5.2 million is estimated for 2005.

Approximately 6% of Arizonans are 75 years of age or older with the median age at 36 years of age, slightly older than the national average of 35.3. Despite its rapid population growth, Arizona still had a population density of only 45.2 persons per square mile (17.5 persons per square kilometer) in 2000. Three out of four Arizonans live in metropolitan areas. The largest cities are Phoenix, with a 2000 population of 1,321,045; Tucson, 486,699; Mesa, 396,375; and Glendale,

218,812. Phoenix was the nation's sixth-largest city in 2000.

7 ETHNIC GROUPS

Arizona has by far the nation's greatest expanse of Native American lands. The largest single American Indian nation, the Navajo, had an estimated 1995 registered reservation population exceeding 125,000 in Arizona. This group is located primarily in the northeastern part of the state. After the Navajo, the leading tribes are the Tohono O'Odham (formerly known as Papago) in the south, Apache in the east, and Hopi in the northeast. Altogether, an estimated 262,000 Arizonans had primarily Native American ancestry in 2000.

The southern part of Arizona has most of the state's largest ethnic majority, which consists of a Hispanic population estimated in 1997 at 1 million (21.9% of the population, fourth among the states). The bulk of Hispanics are of Mexican origin. There were an estimated 409,000 black Americans in Arizona in 2000. Filipinos, Chinese, Japanese, and other Asian and Pacific Island peoples make up 2.1% of the population.

8 LANGUAGES

The linguistic influence of Arizona's Tohono O'Odham, Pima, Apache, Navajo, and Hopi tribes is almost totally limited to some place-names, including Arizona itself. Most borrowed Indian words are derived from the Nahuatl speech of the Mexican Aztecs—for example, *coyote, chili, mesquite,* and *tamale.*

Arizona Population by Race

Census 2000 was the first national census in which the instructions to respondents said, "Mark one or more races." This table shows the number of people who are of one, two, or three or more races. For those claiming two races, the number of people belonging to the various categories is listed. The U.S. government conducts a census of the population every ten years.

	Number	Percent
Total population	5,130,632	100.0
One race	4,984,106	97.1
Two races	138,655	2.7
White *and* Black or African American	13,732	0.3
White *and* American Indian/Alaska Native	23,009	0.4
White *and* Asian	15,624	0.3
White *and* Native Hawaiian/Pacific Islander	2,044	—
White *and* some other race	62,927	1.2
Black or African American *and* American Indian/Alaska Native	2,889	0.1
Black or African American *and* Asian	1,346	—
Black or African American *and* Native Hawaiian/Pacific Islander	200	—
Black or African American *and* some other race	4,537	0.1
American Indian/Alaska Native *and* Asian	809	—
American Indian/Alaska Native *and* Native Hawaiian/Pacific Islander	249	—
American Indian/Alaska Native *and* some other race	5,430	0.1
Asian *and* Native Hawaiian/Pacific Islander	1,556	—
Asian *and* some other race	3,537	0.1
Native Hawaiian/Pacific Islander *and* some other race	766	—
Three or more races	7,871	0.2

Source: U.S. Census Bureau. *Census 2000: Redistricting Data.* Press release issued by the Redistricting Data Office. Washington, D.C., March, 2001. A dash (—) indicates that the percent is less than 0.1.

English in the state is a blend of North Midland and South Midland dialects without clear regional differences. Over 2,674,000 Arizonans—79.2% of all residents five years old and older—speak only English at home. Other languages spoken at home, and the number of people speaking them, include Spanish, 478,234; various Native American languages, 110,559; and German, 21,344.

9 RELIGIONS

The state has over 655,000 Catholics. The Church of Jesus Christ of Latter-day Saints (Mormons) has about 200,000 known members in Arizona. The Southern Baptist Convention has 163,000 members and the United Methodist Church has 60,000 members in Arizona. Arizona's estimated Jewish population approaches 70,800, nearly all of whom live in the Phoenix or Tucson metropolitan areas.

10 TRANSPORTATION

There was a total of 1,845 rail miles (2,969 kilometers) of railroad track in 1998, with 10 railroads operating in the state. Amtrak provides limited passenger service. In 1997, the state had 55,712 miles (89,641 kilometers) of public streets and roads. Interstate highways in Arizona totaled 1,228 miles (1,976 kilometers). Of

Photo credit: Arizona Office of Tourism.

Montezuma Castle National Monument.

tures—the Anasazi, the Mogollon, and the Hohokam. For reasons unknown—a devastating drought is the most likely explanation—these cultures were in decay and the population much reduced by the 14th century. Two centuries later, when the first Europeans arrived, most of the natives were living in simple shelters in fertile river valleys, dependent on hunting, gathering, and small-scale farming for subsistence. The Hopi were the oldest group, their roots reaching back to the Anasazi.

The Spanish presence in Arizona involved exploration, missionary work, and settlement. Between 1539 and 1605, four expeditions crossed the land, followed by Franciscan and Jesuit missionaries. The Spanish military outpost, or *presidio*, established at Tubac on the Santa Cruz River in 1752 was the first major European settlement in Arizona. The end of the 18th century and the beginning of the 19th were periods of relative peace on the frontier.

When Mexico revolted against Spain in 1810, the Arizona settlements were not affected. However, with the outbreak of the Mexican War in 1846, two US armies marched across the region. The California gold rush of 1849 saw thousands of Americans pass along the Gila River. In 1850, most of present-day Arizona became part of the new US Territory of New Mexico; the southern strip was added by the Gadsden Purchase in 1853.

The outbreak of the Civil War in 1861 saw the declaration of southern Arizona as Confederate territory. A small Confederate force entered Arizona in 1862 but was

the 3.14 million motor vehicles registered in that year, nearly 1.85 million were passenger automobiles. Arizona had 302 airports and 89 heliports in 1996. The leading air terminal in 1996 was Phoenix Sky Harbor International Airport, which handled 14.8 million arriving and departing passengers (sixth highest in the nation).

11 HISTORY

It is believed that by AD 500, early inhabitants of present-day Arizona had acquired a basic agriculture from what is now Mexico. They were divided into several cul-

driven out by a volunteer Union army from California. On 24 February 1863, President Abraham Lincoln signed into law the Organic Act of Arizona, a measure creating the new Territory of Arizona.

Statehood

The development of rich gold mines along the lower Colorado River and in the interior mountains attracted both people and money to Arizona, as did the discovery of silver in Tombstone and other districts in the late 1870s. Phoenix, established in 1868, grew steadily as an agricultural center, eventually becoming the state capital in 1889. On 14 February 1912, Arizona entered the Union as the 48th State.

World War I spurred the expansion of the copper industry, intensive agriculture, and livestock production, but the 1920s brought depression: banks closed, mines shut down, and agricultural production declined. To revive the economy, local citizens pushed highway construction, tourism, and the resort business. Arizona also shared in the general distress caused by the Great Depression of the 1930s and received large amounts of federal aid for relief and recovery.

Prosperity returned during World War II as camps for military training, prisoners of war, and displaced Japanese-Americans were built throughout the state. Arizona emerged from World War II a modern state. Wartime industries spawned an expanding peacetime manufacturing boom that soon provided the principal source of income, followed by tourism, agriculture, and mining.

Arizona Governors: 1913–2001

1913–1916	George Wylie Paul Hunt	Democrat
1917	Thomas Edward Campbell	Republican
1918	George Wylie Paul Hunt	Democrat
1919–1922	Thomas Edward Campbell	Republican
1923–1928	George Wylie Paul Hunt	Democrat
1929–1930	John C. Phillips	Republican
1931–1932	George Wylie Paul Hunt	Democrat
1933–1936	Benjamin Baker Moeur	Democrat
1937–1938	Rawghlie Clement Stanford	Democrat
1939–1940	Robert Taylor Jones	Democrat
1941–1948	Sidney Preston Osborn	Democrat
1948–1950	Dan E. Garvey	Democrat
1951 1954	John Howard Pyle	Republican
1955–1958	Ernest William McFarland	Democrat
1959–1964	Paul Jones Fannin	Republican
1965–1966	Samuel Pearson Goddard, Jr.	Democrat
1967–1975	John Richard Williams	Republican
1975–1977	Raul Hector Castro	Democrat
1977–1978	Wesley H. Bolin	Democrat
1978–1987	Bruce Edward Babbitt	Democrat
1987–1988	Evan Mecham	Republican
1988–1991	Rose Mofford	Democrat
1991–1998	Fife Symington (resigned)	Republican
1998–	Jane D. Hull	Republican

During the 1950s, the political scene changed. Arizona Republicans captured the governorship, gained votes in the legislature, won congressional seats, and brought a viable two-party system to the state. The rise of Barry Goldwater of Phoenix to national prominence further encouraged Republican influence. Meanwhile, air conditioning changed lifestyles, prompting a significant migration to the state.

Arizona politics in recent years have been rocked by the discovery of corruption in high places. In 1988, Governor Evan Mecham was impeached on two charges of official misconduct. In 1989, two senators, John McCain and Dennis DeConcini, were indicted for influencing federal bank regulators on behalf of Lincoln Savings and Loan Association. Lincoln's president,

Charles Keating Jr., had contributed large sums to the senators' re-election campaigns. In 1990, Peter MacDonald, the leader of the Navajo Nation, was convicted in the Navajo Tribal Court of soliciting $400,000 in bribes and kickbacks.

12 STATE GOVERNMENT

Legislative authority is vested in a 30-member senate and a 60-member house of representatives. All senators and representatives serve two-year terms and are chosen at the general election in November of each even-numbered year. Chief executive officials elected statewide include the governor, secretary of state, treasurer, attorney general, state mine inspector, and superintendent of public instruction, all of whom serve four-year terms.

Bills may originate in either house of the legislature and must be passed by both houses and approved by the governor in order to become law. A two-thirds vote in each house is necessary to override the governor's veto. Under the initiative procedure, legislation and proposed constitutional amendments can be placed on the ballot by petition.

13 POLITICAL PARTIES

Conservative Republican Senator Barry Goldwater, who was first elected in 1952 and won the Republican presidential nomination in 1964, led the Republican party to dominance in Arizona politics in the post-World War II period. Arizonans gave the most votes to Republican presidential candidates in every election from 1952 through 1992. Several Arizona Republicans were appointed to high office during the Nixon years. Democrat and former governor Bruce Babbitt was named Secretary of the Interior for the Clinton administration in 1992.

Although Democrat Bill Clinton carried the state in the 1996 Presidential election, Republicans continue to dominate Arizona politics. In 1998 Republican Jane

Arizona Presidential Vote by Political Party, 1948–2000

Year	Electoral Vote	Arizona Winner	Democrat	Republican	Progressive
1948	4	*Truman (D)	95,251	77,597	3,310
1952	4	*Eisenhower (R)	108,528	152,042	—
1956	4	*Eisenhower (R)	112,880	176,990	—
1960	4	Nixon (R)	176,781	221,241	—
1964	5	Goldwater (R)	237,753	242,535	—
					American Ind.
1968	5	*Nixon (R)	170,514	266,721	46,573
					American
1972	6	*Nixon (R)	198,540	402,812	21,208
1976	6	Ford (R)	295,602	418,642	7,647
1980	6	*Reagan (R)	246,843	529,688	18,784
1984	7	*Reagan (R)	333,854	681,416	10,585
1988	7	*Bush (R)	454,029	702,541	13,351
					Ind. (Perot)
1992	8	Bush (R)	543,086	572,086	353,741
1996	8	*Clinton (D)	653,288	622,073	112,072
2000	8	*Bush (R)	685,341	781,652	45,645

*Won US presidential election.

Hull was elected governor and John McCain was reelected US Senator. Arizona's other Senator, Jon Kyle, is also a Republican, and the state's US House delgation consists of five Republicans and one Democrat. In addition, Republican George W. Bush was the Arizona winner in the 2000 presidential elections. The state House has 36 Republicans and 24 Democrats, while the state Senate consists of 15 Republicans and 15 Democrats.

14 LOCAL GOVERNMENT

Arizona is divided into 15 counties. Local governmental units include towns, cities, and charter cities. Towns generally follow the council-mayor form of government. In all, there were 600 local government units in 1997, of which 88 were municipal governments. Each of the 22 Indian reservations in Arizona has a tribal council or board with members elected by the people.

15 JUDICIAL SYSTEM

The supreme court is the highest court in Arizona and has administrative responsibility over all other courts in the state. The court of appeals is organized in two geographical divisions which together have 22 judges. The superior court is the general trial court of the state; there must be at least one superior court judge in every Arizona county.

Counties are divided into precincts, each of which has a justice court. Every incorporated city and town has a police court. According to the FBI Crime Index of 1998, Arizona had a crime rate of 6,575 per 100,000 population. In 1999, federal and state institutions held 26,092 prisoners at year-end.

16 MIGRATION

In the 1980s, half of Arizona's total population increase was from migration; about 530,000 persons moved there during that time. By 1990, only 34.2% of state residents had been born in Arizona; only three other states had a lower proportion. Arizona showed a net gain of 296,449 immigrants from 1985 to 1990. During 1990–98, movements between the states added 518,800 more residents, and movements from abroad added 95,800. Mexico is the main source of foreign immigrants. The federal government estimated that in 1996 there were 115,000 illegal immigrants living in Arizona.

17 ECONOMY

Mining and cattle-raising were the main economic activities during the territorial period. With the introduction of irrigation in the early 1900s, farming became more important. Leading industries today include electronic components from the manufacturing sector, copper from the mining sector, and cattle and cotton from the farming sector. Tourism is also an important contributor to revenues.

18 INCOME

In 1998, Arizona ranked 36th among the 50 states with a per capita (per person) income of $24,206. The median household income was estimated at $34,402 in 1998. In the same year, it is estimated that about 18.1% of the population was below the federal poverty level.

Photo credit: EPD Photos/CSU Archives

César Chávez (1927–93) was a well-known activist for migrant workers and president of the United Farm Workers of America.

19 INDUSTRY

Manufacturing, which has grown rapidly since World War II, became the state's leading economic activity in the 1970s. The major manufacturing centers are the Phoenix and Tucson areas. Principal industries include machinery, electrical and electronic equipment (computers, semiconductors, communication equipment), aircraft equipment, food products, and printing and publishing. Military equipment accounts for much of the output.

20 LABOR

In mid-1998, the civilian labor force totaled 2.27 million, with an unemployment rate of 4.1%. Arizona's nonfarm employment distribution in 1997 consisted of 0.1% in mining; 6.6% in construction; 10.4% in manufacturing; 4.9% in transportation, communications, and utilities; 24.7% in trade; 6.2% in finance, insurance, and real estate; 30.5% in services; and government, 16.6%. In 1998, only 6.5% of all workers belonged to labor unions, despite labor's long history in this state.

21 AGRICULTURE

In 1998 there were about 7,900 farms covering 28.3 million acres (11.4 million hectares), or about 39% of the state's total area. Only 1.96 million acres (389,000 hectares), or 1.3% of the state's total area, were actually farmed for crops that year. About 95% of all farmland is dependent on irrigation provided by dams and water projects. Cotton is the leading cash crop in Arizona. In 1995 the state was the second highest among all states in cotton yield per acre, producing a total of 865,200 bales of cotton lint, valued at $355.4 million. Vegetables, especially head lettuce, had a value of $353.9 million that year. Arizona's lemon production accounts for 25% of national production value for that crop. Other crops are wheat, sorghum, barley, grapes, broccoli, cauliflower, cantaloupes, oranges, tangerines, and grapefruit.

Photo credit: Arizona Office of Tourism.

Sheep herding in Monument Valley.

22 DOMESTICATED ANIMALS

The total inventory of cattle and calves was 810,000 in 1999. In 1997, the state had 111,000 sheep and lambs. In 1998 there were 115,000 hogs and pigs. Cattle production has accounted for about 25% of the states's agricultural receipts.

23 FISHING

Arizona has no commercial fishing. The state's lakes and mountain streams lure the state's 468,500 licensed sport fishermen and are an increasingly important tourist attraction.

24 FORESTRY

Arizona's forests are more valuable for soil conservation and recreation than for lumber. There are 19.9 million acres (8 million hectares) of forestland in Arizona, 27% of the state's area. National forests covered 11.8 million acres (4.8 million hectares).

25 MINING

Arizona ranks third in the nation in nonfuel mineral production value, thanks to the state's copper industry. In 1998 the value of the state's nonfuel mineral production exceeded $2.82 billion, with copper accounting for 75%. Production figures for principal minerals are as follows: copper, 1.2 million metric tons; sand and gravel, 46.9 million metric tons; gold, 2,100 kilograms (1998); and crushed stone, 7.4 million short tons. Arizona led the nation in US copper production and was also the leading producer of molybdenum and second gemstones.

26 ENERGY AND POWER

In 1998, Arizona produced 81.3 billion kilowatt hours of electric power. Hydroelectric plants accounted for 17% of power output. Surplus electricity production is sold to other states, primarily California. In 1997, the state marketed 457 billion cu ft (12.8 billion cubic meters) of natural gas. Coal production in 1998 was 11.3 million metric tons, all of it from two surface mines.

27 COMMERCE

In 1992, wholesale sales in Arizona totaled $28 billion. Most wholesale establishments are located in Maricopa and Pima counties. Retail sales in 1992 totaled $29.3 billion. Goods produced in Arizona worth $9.9 billion were exported in 1996.

28 PUBLIC FINANCE

Government revenues for 1997 were $13.69 billion, while expenditures for the same period were $12.42 billion. As of 1997, Arizona's total outstanding debt was $2.7 billion, or about $602 per person.

29 TAXATION

State taxes in 1997 came to over $6.83 billion, or $1,500 per person. Arizona has a state sales tax, with the retail sales tax rate

at 5%. An estate tax, luxury tax, insurance premium tax, and transport fuel tax are also levied. The state also receives tax revenue from collections of the general property tax and the motor-vehicle license tax, and it has a lottery.

30 HEALTH

The percentage of deaths from accidents and suicide in 1998 was above the national average, while the death rate for heart disease and cardiovascular diseases was lower. Serious public-health problems include tuberculosis and San Joaquin Valley fever (coccidioidomycosis), especially among Native Americans. In 1998 there were 64 state-licensed hospitals, with 10,857 beds. At least 24.4% of the adult population has no health insurance.

31 HOUSING

In October 1999, Arizona had an estimated 2 million units of year-round housing. The median value of a home in Arizona was $80,100 in 1990. An owner-occupied unit with a mortgage had a median monthly cost of $769 in 1990; the median cost for a rental unit was $438. In 1996, 53,715 new units were authorized.

32 EDUCATION

In 1997, enrollment at public schools was 814,113, minorities making up 44% of total enrollment. Expenditures for public elementary and secondary schools amounted to $4,012 per student in 1965/96 (49th among the states). Private schools enrolled 43,765 students in 1997. The leading public higher educational institutions are the University of Arizona

Navajo children, Monument Valley.

at Tucson and Arizona State University at Tempe. As of 1997, the state had 12 colleges and universities and 17 community colleges, with a total enrollment of 292,730.

33 ARTS

Arizona has traditionally been a center for Native American folk arts and crafts, which are displayed at museums throughout the state. Modern Arizona artists are featured at the Tucson Museum of Art and the Yuma Art Center. Phoenix and Tucson have symphony orchestras, and the Arizona Opera Company performs in both cities.

34 LIBRARIES AND MUSEUMS

In 1998, Arizona's public libraries had a combined book stock of 8.2 million volumes, and total circulation was 28 million. Spending on libraries per capita (per person) was $10 in 1994. Arizona has more than 120 museums and historic sites. Attractions in Tucson include the Arizona State Museum, the Flandreau Planetarium, and the Gene C. Reid Zoological Park. Phoenix's facilities include the Heard Museum (anthropology and primitive art),

Photo credit: EPD Photos.

Tourists about to enter an abandoned mine in Bisbee, Arizona.

Arizona Mineral Resources Museum, and Desert Botanical Garden. Archaeological and historical sites include the cliff dwellings at the Canyon De Chelly. The town of Tombstone was the site of the famous gunfight at the O. K. Corral in the early 1880s.

35 COMMUNICATIONS

Over 93% of the households in Arizona had telephones in 1999. There were 188 radio stations broadcasting in Arizona in 2000 (72 AM and 116 FM). The state also had 37 television stations in the same year, with 7 large cable television systems providing service. A total of 131,164 Internet domain names had been registered in 2000.

36 PRESS

As of 1998 there were 6 morning dailies, and 10 evening dailies. Leading dailies (with 1998 daily circulation figures) include the *Arizona Republic* (435,330); the *Arizona Daily Star* (91,798); and *The Citizen* (41,115). Among the most notable magazines and periodicals published in Arizona are *Arizona Highways*, *Phoenix Magazine*, *Phoenix Living*, and *Arizona Living*, devoted to the local and regional lifestyle.

37 TOURISM, TRAVEL, AND RECREATION

Tourism and travel is a leading industry in Arizona. There are 22 national parks and monuments located entirely within Arizona. By far the most popular is Grand Canyon National Park, which had over 5 million visitors in 1995. Petrified Forest National Park and Saguaro National Monument are also popular national parks. Popular for sightseeing and shopping are the state's Indian reservations, particularly those of the Navajo and Hopi.

38 SPORTS

There are five major league professional teams in Arizona, all in Phoenix: the Cardinals of the National Football League, the Suns of the National Basketball Association and the Mercury of the Women's National Basketball Association, the Arizona Diamondbacks of Major League Baseball, and the Coyotes of the National Hockey League. Several major league baseball teams hold spring training in Arizona. Phoenix and Tucson have entries in the Pacific Coast League, the Firebirds and the Toros, respectively. There is also horse racing, dog racing, and auto racing; rodeos are held throughout the state.

The Thunderbird Hot Air Balloon Races are held annually in Glendale. Both Arizona State and the University of Arizona joined the Pacific 10 Conference in 1978. College football's Fiesta Bowl is held annually at Sun Devil Stadium in Tempe.

39 FAMOUS ARIZONANS

Although Arizona entered the Union relatively late, many of its citizens have achieved national prominence, especially since World War II. William H. Rehnquist (b. Wisconsin, 1924) was appointed associ-

Photo credit: EPD Photos/National Archives

Important to the state's history and development were Chiricahua Apache leaders Cochise (1812?–74) and Geronimo (1829–1909), pictured above, who fought against the U.S. Army and avoided capture in the Southwest for over two decades.

ate justice of the US Supreme Court in 1971 and chief justice in 1986. In 1981 Sandra Day O'Connor (b. Texas, 1930) became the first woman to serve on the Supreme Court. Barry Goldwater (1909–98), son of a pioneer family, was elected to the US Senate in 1952, won the Republican presidential nomination in 1964, and returned to the Senate in 1968.

Wyatt Earp (b. Illinois, 1848–1929) was a legendary lawman of Tombstone during the early 1880s. César Chávez (1927–93) was a well-known activist for migrant workers and president of the United Farm Workers of America.

A writer whose name has been associated with Arizona is Zane Grey (b.Ohio, 1875–1939), who wrote many of his western adventure stories in his summer home near Payson.

40 BIBLIOGRAPHY

Alampi, Gary, ed. *Gale State Rankings Reporter*. Detroit: Gale Research Inc., 1994.

Arizona: Its People and Resources. 2d ed., rev. Tucson: University of Arizona Press, 1972.

Aylesworth, Thomas G. *The West: Arizona, Nevada, Utah*. New York: Chelsea House Publishers, 1992.

Blashfield, Jean F. *Arizona*. New York: Children's Press, 2000.

McAuliffe, Emily. *Arizona Facts and Symbols*. New York: Hilltop Books, 1999.

McDaniel, Melissa. *Arizona*. Tarrytown, N.Y.: Benchmark Books, 2000.

Web sites

State of Arizona. *Welcome to the State of Arizona Website*. [Online] Available http://www.state.az.us/ Accessed May 29, 2001.

ARKANSAS

State of Arkansas

ORIGIN OF STATE NAME: French derivation of *Akansas* or *Arkansas,* a name given to the Quapaw Indians by other tribes.

NICKNAME: The Natural State.

CAPITAL: Little Rock.

ENTERED THE UNION: 15 June 1836 (25th).

SONG: "Arkansas", "Arkansas (You Run Deep in Me)," "Oh, Arkansas," and "The Arkansas Traveler."

MOTTO: *Regnat populus* (The people rule).

COAT OF ARMS: In front of an American eagle is a shield displaying a steamboat, plow, beehive, and sheaf of wheat, symbols of Arkansas's industrial and agricultural wealth. The angel of mercy, the goddess of liberty encircled by 13 stars, and the sword of justice surround the eagle, which holds in its talons an olive branch and three arrows, and in its beak a banner bearing the state motto.

FLAG: On a red field, 25 stars on a blue band border a white diamond containing the word "Arkansas" and four blue stars.

OFFICIAL SEAL: Coat of arms surrounded by the words "Great Seal of the State of Arkansas."

BIRD: Mockingbird.

FLOWER: Apple blossom.

TREE: Pine.

GEM: Diamond.

INSECT: Honeybee.

TIME: 6 AM CST = noon GMT.

1 LOCATION AND SIZE

Located in the western south-central US, Arkansas ranks 27th in size among the 50 states. The total area of Arkansas is 53,187 square miles (137,754 square kilometers). Arkansas extends about 275 miles (443 kilometers) east-west and 240 miles (386 kilometers) north-south. The total boundary length of Arkansas is 1,168 miles (1,880 kilometers).

2 TOPOGRAPHY

The Boston Mountains in the northwest and the Ouachita Mountains in the west-central region constitute Arkansas's major uplands. Aside from the Arkansas River valley, the state's lowlands belong to the Mississippi Alluvial Plain and the Gulf Coastal Plain. The highest elevation in Arkansas, at 2,753 feet (839 meters), is Magazine Mountain. The state's lowest point, at 55 feet (17 meters), is on the Ouachita River in south-central Arkansas.

Arkansas's largest lake is the artificial Lake Ouachita, covering 63 square miles (163 square kilometers); Lake Chicot, in southeastern Arkansas, is the state's largest natural lake, with a length of 18 miles (29 kilometers). Principal rivers include the Mississippi, the Arkansas, and the Red, White, Ouachita, and St. Francis rivers, all of which drain south and southeast into the Mississippi. Numerous springs are found in Arkansas, including Mammoth Springs, one of the largest in the world, with a flow rate averaging nine million gallons an hour. Crowley's Ridge, a unique strip of hills formed by sedimentary deposits and windblown sand, lies west of the St. Francis River.

3 CLIMATE

Arkansas has a temperate climate, warmer and more humid in the southern lowlands than in the mountainous regions. At Little Rock, the normal daily temperature ranges from 40°F (4°C) in January to 81°F (27°C) in July. A record low temperature of –29°F (–34°C) was set on 13 February 1905 at the Pond weather station, and a record high of 120°F (49°C) on 10 August 1936 at the Ozark station.

Average yearly precipitation is approximately 45 inches (114 centimeters) in the mountainous areas and greater in the lowlands. Little Rock receives an annual average of 49 inches (124 centimeters). Snowfall in the capital averages 5.4 inches (13.7 centimeters) a year.

Arkansas Population Profile

Total population in 2000:	2,673,400
Population change, 1990–2000:	13.7%
Hispanic or Latino†:	3.2%
Population by race	
One race:	98.7%
White:	80.0%
Black or African American:	15.7%
American Indian/Alaska Native:	0.7%
Asian:	0.8%
Native Hawaiian/Pacific Islander:	0.1%
Some other race:	1.5%
Two or more races:	1.3%

Population by Age Group

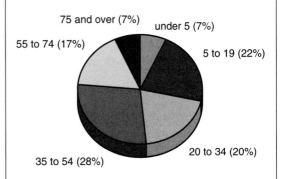

75 and over (7%)
under 5 (7%)
55 to 74 (17%)
5 to 19 (22%)
20 to 34 (20%)
35 to 54 (28%)

Top Cities by Population

City	Population	% change 1990–2000
Little Rock	183,133	4.2
Fort Smith	80,268	10.3
North Little Rock	60,433	–2.1
Fayetteville	58,047	37.9
Jonesboro	55,515	19.3
Pine Bluff	55,085	–3.6
Springdale	45,798	53.0
Conway	43,167	63.0
Rogers	38,829	57.3
Hot Springs	35,750	10.1

Notes: †A person of Hispanic or Latino origin may be of any race. NA indicates that data are not available.
Sources: U.S. Census Bureau. Public Information Office. *Demographic Profiles*. [Online] Available http://www.census.gov/Press-Release/www/2001/demoprofile.html. Accessed June 1, 2001. U.S. Census Bureau. *Census 2000: Redistricting Data*. Press release issued by the Redistricting Data Office. Washington, D.C., March, 2001.

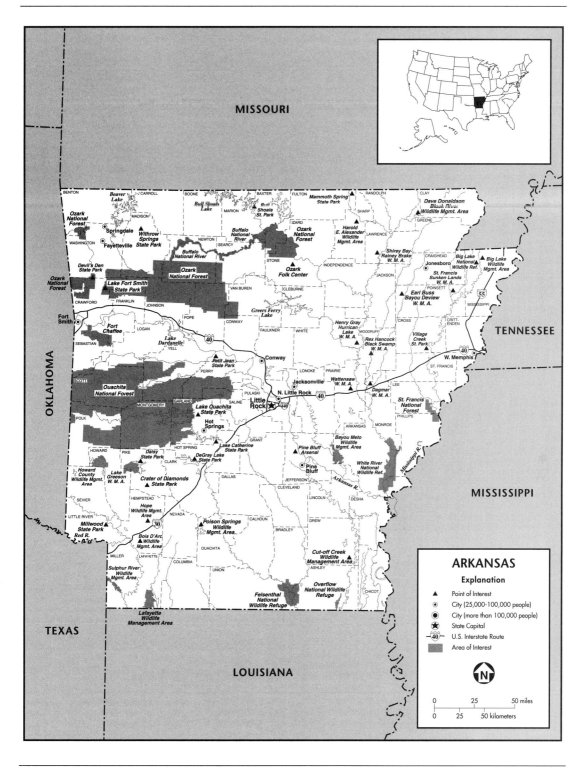

ARKANSAS

Explanation

▲ Point of Interest

◉ City (25,000-100,000 people)

◉ City (more than 100,000 people)

★ State Capital

〰40〰 U.S. Interstate Route

▨ Area of Interest

4 PLANTS AND ANIMALS

Arkansas has at least 2,600 native plants, and there are many adopted exotic species. Cypresses, water oak, hickory, and ash grow in the Mississippi Valley, while Crowley's Ridge is thick with tulip trees and beeches. A forest belt of oak, hickory, and pine stretches across south-central and southwestern Arkansas. The state has at least 26 native varieties of orchid, and the passion flower is abundant.

Arkansas's native animals include mink, armadillo, white-tailed deer, and eastern chipmunk. Black bears roam the swamp and mountain regions. Among 300 native birds are such game birds as the eastern wild turkey, mourning dove, and bobwhite quail. Among local fish are catfish, gar, and the unusual paddle fish. The Arkansas Game and Fish Commission lists the leopard darter and fat pocketbook pearly mussel as threatened species. The peregrine falcon, Indiana and gray bats, and the eastern prairie fringed orchid are among those listed as endangered.

5 ENVIRONMENTAL PROTECTION

In 1987, the state adopted what is believed to be the first "eco-region" water quality standards in the nation; they are based on individual characteristics within each of six district eco-regions of the state, as opposed to having blanket standards that apply statewide. There are 64 municipal landfills in the state and only two curbside recycling programs. Arkansas had 11 hazardous waste sites, as of 1998.

6 POPULATION

At the time of the 2000 census, Arkansas had a population of over 2.6 million (retaining its rank of 33rd in the US). The average population density was 51.3 persons per square mile (19.8 per square kilometer). The Census Bureau estimates that the population will be over 2.7 million in 2005.

Over 40% of all state residents live in metropolitan areas. The largest city in Arkansas is Little Rock, which had a 2000 population of 183,133. Other major cities in 2000 included Fort Smith, 80,268; North Little Rock, 60,433; Fayetteville, 58,047; and Jonesboro, 55,515.

7 ETHNIC GROUPS

Arkansas's population is predominantly white, composed mainly of descendants of immigrants from the British Isles. The largest minority group consists of black Americans, estimated at 409,000 in 2000, or 15.9% of the population, followed by Asians and Pacific Islanders, 17,800 (0.7%). An estimated 45,100 Arkansans were of Hispanic origin. The 1990 census listed 1,788 Vietnamese, 1,575 Chinese, 2,166 Filipinos, 1,202 Asian Indians, and 754 Japanese.

8 LANGUAGES

Arkansas English is essentially a blend of Southern and South Midland speech, with South Midland dominating the mountainous northwest and Southern the southeastern agricultural areas. A few place-names—such as Arkansas itself, Choctaw, Caddo, and Ouachita—attest to the one-time presence of Native Americans, mostly

Arkansas Population by Race

Census 2000 was the first national census in which the instructions to respondents said, "Mark one or more races." This table shows the number of people who are of one, two, or three or more races. For those claiming two races, the number of people belonging to the various categories is listed. The U.S. government conducts a census of the population every ten years.

	Number	Percent
Total population	2,673,400	100.0
One race	2,637,656	98.7
Two races	33,818	1.3
White *and* Black or African American	4,773	0.2
White *and* American Indian/Alaska Native	16,439	0.6
White *and* Asian	3,061	0.1
White *and* Native Hawaiian/Pacific Islander	351	—
White *and* some other race	5,608	0.2
Black or African American *and* American Indian/Alaska Native	1,088	—
Black or African American *and* Asian	406	—
Black or African American *and* Native Hawaiian/Pacific Islander	89	—
Black or African American *and* some other race	600	—
American Indian/Alaska Native *and* Asian	146	—
American Indian/Alaska Native *and* Native Hawaiian/Pacific Islander	59	—
American Indian/Alaska Native *and* some other race	262	—
Asian *and* Native Hawaiian/Pacific Islander	275	—
Asian *and* some other race	484	—
Native Hawaiian/Pacific Islander *and* some other race	177	—
Three or more races	1,926	0.1

Source: U.S. Census Bureau. *Census 2000: Redistricting Data*. Press release issued by the Redistricting Data Office. Washington, D.C., March, 2001. A dash (—) indicates that the percent is less than 0.1.

members of the Caddoan tribes, in the Territory of Arkansas.

About 2,125,900 Arkansans—97.2% of the residents five years old or older—speak only English at home. The most common other languages spoken at home are Spanish (27,351 people), German (7,059), and French (8,210).

9 RELIGIONS

The largest denomination in Arkansas is the Southern Baptist Convention, which has over 617,000 members in 1990. Other leading Protestant groups are the United Methodist Church, with 197,402 members and the Baptist Missionary Associa-

tion of America, with 78,121. The Roman Catholic population of Arkansas numbers 73,000 and the estimated Jewish population is 2,400.

10 TRANSPORTATION

As of 1998, Arkansas was served by three major railroads and had 2,726 rail miles (4,280 kilometers) of track. In 1995/96, the number of Arkansas Amtrak riders amounted to 16,005. By 1997, Arkansas had 94,366 miles (151,835 kilometers) of public roads, streets, and highways. During the same year, 857,314 automobiles and 770,702 trucks were registered in Arkansas. In 1996, private and commer-

Photo credit: Little Rock Convention & Visitors Bureau.

The Old State House in Little Rock.

cial automobiles in the state came only to 34 per every 100 residents, fewer than in any other state.

Development of the Arkansas River, completed during the early 1970s, made the waterway commercially navigable all the way to Tulsa, Oklahoma. In 1996, Arkansas had 180 airports. The principal airport in the state, Adams Field at Little Rock, boarded 1.25 million passengers in that year.

11 HISTORY

Foremost among the Native American tribes in Arkansas were the Quapaw, an agricultural people who had migrated to southern Arkansas in the early 16th cen-

tury; the Caddo, fighters from Texas; the warlike Osage; and the Choctaw and Chickasaw of the northeast. Another prominent tribe, the Cherokee, arrived in the early 19th century, after federal and state authorities had driven them westward. Nearly all these tribes had been expelled to what is now Oklahoma by the time Arkansas became a state.

The first Europeans to set foot in Arkansas were Spaniards, led by Hernando de Soto in 1541. More than 100 years later, in 1673, a small band of Frenchmen led by Jacques Marquette, a Jesuit missionary, and Louis Jolliet, a fur trader and explorer, ended their voyage down the Mississippi at the mouth of the

Arkansas Governors: 1836–2001

1836–1840	James Sevier Conway	Democrat		1909	Jesse M. Martin	Democrat
1840–1844	Archibald Yell	Democrat		1909–1913	George W. Donaghey	Democrat
1844	Samuel Adams	Democrat		1913	Joseph Taylor Robinson	Democrat
1844–1849	Thomas Stevenson Drew	Democrat		1913	William Kavanaugh Oldham	Democrat
1849	John Williamson	Democrat		1913	Junius Marion Futrell	Democrat
1849	Richard C. Byrd	Democrat		1913–1917	George Washington Hays	Democrat
1849–1851	John Selden Roane	Democrat		1917–1921	Charles Hillman Brough	Democrat
1851	John R. Hampton	Democrat		1921–1925	Thomas Chipman McRae	Democrat
1852–1860	Elias Nelson Conway	Democrat		1925–1927	Tom Jefferson Terral	Democrat
1860–1862	Henry Massey Rector	Indep-Dem		1927–1928	John Ellis Martineau	Democrat
1862	Thomas Fletcher	Democrat		1928–1933	Harvey Parnell	Democrat
1862–1864	Harris Flanagin	Democrat		1933–1937	Junius Marion Futrell	Democrat
1864–1868	Isaac Murphy	Unionist		1937–1941	Carl Edward Bailey	Democrat
1868–1871	Powell Clayton	Republican		1941–1945	Homer Martin Adkins	Democrat
1871–1873	Ozra A. Hadley	Republican		1945–1949	Benjamin Travis Laney	Democrat
1873–1874	Elisha Baxter	Republican		1949–1953	Sidney Sanders McMath	Democrat
1874–1877	Augustus Hill Garland	Democrat		1953–1955	Francis Adams Cherry	Democrat
1877–1881	William Read Miller	Democrat		1955–1967	Orval Eugene Faubus	Democrat
1881–1883	Thomas James Churchill	Democrat		1967–1971	Winthrop Rockefeller	Republican
1883–1885	James Henderson Berry	Democrat		1971–1975	Dale Leon Bumpers	Democrat
1885	Ben T. Embry	Democrat		1975	Robert Cowley Riley	Democrat
1885–1889	Simon P. Hughes	Democrat		1975–1979	David Hampton Pryor	Democrat
1889–1893	James Philip Eagle	Democrat		1979	Joe Purcell	Democrat
1893–1895	William Meade Fishback	Democrat		1979–1981	William Jefferson Clinton	Democrat
1895–1897	James Paul Clarke	Democrat		1981–1983	Frank D. White	Republican
1897–1901	Daniel Webster Jones	Democrat		1983–1992	William Jefferson Clinton	Democrat
1901–1907	Jeff Davis	Democrat		1992–1999	James Guy Tucker	Democrat
1907	John Sebastian Little	Democrat		1999–	Mike Huckabee	Republican
1907	John I. Moore	Democrat				
1907–1909	Xenophon Overton Pindall	Democrat			Independent Democrat – Indep-Dem	

Arkansas River. Nine years later, the French explorer Robert Cavelier, Sieur de la Salle, claimed all the Mississippi Valley for his king, Louis XIV.

Statehood

In 1762 France ceded the territory to Spain. Restored to France in 1800, the territory was sold to the US in the Louisiana Purchase of 1803. After first becoming part of the Missouri Territory, Arkansas gained territorial status in its own right in 1819. The territorial capital was moved from Arkansas Post to Little Rock in 1821. By 1835, Arkansas Territory had a population of 52,240, including 9,838

slaves. It was admitted to the Union in 1836 as a slave state, paired with the free state of Michigan in accordance with the Missouri Compromise.

Increasing numbers of slaves were brought into the largely agricultural state as the cultivation of cotton spread. Arkansas, like the rest of the South, was headed for secession, although it waited to commit itself until the Civil War had begun. There was considerable Union sentiment in the state, but pro-Union sympathies crumbled after Confederate guns fired on Fort Sumter, South Carolina. On 6 May 1861, at a convention held in Little Rock, Arkansans voted 69–1 to secede.

By September 1863, the Union Army had taken Little Rock, and the Capital was moved to Washington, in Hempstead County, until the conclusion of hostilities in 1865. Like virtually all white southerners, Arkansas's white majority hated the postwar Reconstruction government. In 1874 the white Democratic majority adopted a new state constitution, throwing out the carpetbagger constitution of 1868.

Modernization

Industrialization, urbanization, and modernization did not come to Arkansas until after the depression of the 1930s. Following World War II, the state became the first in the South to racially integrate its public colleges and universities. Little Rock's school board decided in 1954 to comply with the US Supreme Court's racial desegregation decision. Nevertheless, in September 1957, Governor Orval E. Faubus called out the National Guard to block the integration of Central High School at Little Rock. US President Dwight D. Eisenhower enforced a federal court order to integrate the school by sending in federal troops. Faubus, then in his second term, was elected to a third term and then to three more.

The contrast between Faubus and his successor could not have been greater. Winthrop Rockefeller, millionaire heir of a famous family, moved to Arkansas from New York in the early 1950s, establishing himself as a gentleman rancher and building a Republican Party organization in one of the most strongly Democratic states in

Arkansas Presidential Vote by Political Parties, 1948–2000

YEAR	ARKANSAS WINNER	DEMOCRAT	REPUBLICAN	STATES' RIGHTS DEMOCRAT
1948	*Truman (D)	149,659	50,959	40,068
1952	Stevenson (D)	226,300	177,155	—
				CONSTITUTION
1956	Stevenson (D)	213,277	186,287	7,008
				NAT'L STATES' RIGHTS
1960	*Kennedy (D)	215,049	184,508	28,952
1964	*Johnson (D)	314,197	243,264	2,965
				AMERICAN IND.
1968	Wallace (AI)	188,228	190,759	240,982
				AMERICAN
1972	*Nixon (R)	199,892	448,541	2,887
1976	*Carter (D)	498,604	267,903	—
				LIBERTARIAN
1980	*Reagan (R)	398,041	403,164	8,970
1984	*Reagan (R)	388,646	534,774	2,221
1988	*Bush (R)	349,237	466,578	3,297
				IND. (Perot)
1992	*Clinton (D)	505,823	337,324	99,132
1996	*Clinton (D)	475,171	325,416	69,884
				PROGRESSIVE (Nader)
2000	*Bush (R)	422,768	472,940	28,747

* Won US presidential election.

The state capitol building in Little Rock.

the Union. In 1966, Rockefeller became the first Republican governor of Arkansas since Reconstruction. He helped bring a new image and spirit to the state.

Rockefeller's successors have continued his progressive approach. Governor Bill Clinton, who became United States President in 1992, introduced investment tax credits to help corporations modernize their facilities and thereby to create jobs. Clinton also signed a "bare bones" health insurance law which dropped state requirements for some of the more costly coverages and thus made health insurance affordable for small businesses.

He increased spending for education and passed legislation requiring compe-tency tests for teachers. But Clinton remained hampered in his efforts to increase government spending because the state constitution requires that any increase in the state income tax obtain approval of two-thirds of the Legislature. Arkansas continues to rank among the poorest states in the nation, with a per capita (per person) income in 1994 of only $16,817 (49th among the states).

12 STATE GOVERNMENT

Arkansas's legislature, the general assembly, consists of a 35-member senate and a 100-member house of representatives. Senators serve four-year terms; representatives serve for two years. A bill passed by both houses of the legislature becomes law

Photo credit: The White House.

Former President of the United States, Bill Clinton. Clinton was born in Hope, Arkansas, and was elected governor of Arkansas in 1978. He won reelection in 1982, 1984, 1986, and 1990.

if: it is signed by the governor; the governor's veto is overridden by a majority of all elected members of each house; or the bill is neither signed nor returned by the governor within five days when the legislature is in session.

13 POLITICAL PARTIES

Republicans ruled during Reconstruction, which ended in Arkansas after the election of 1872. During the 1890s, as in the rest of the South, Democrats succeeded in passing laws imposing segregation and disenfranchising blacks as well as poor whites.

Although elected to the governorship as a progressive in 1954, Democrat Orval Faubus took a segregationist stand on racial matters in 1957. Faubus's successor, progressive Republican Winthrop Rockefeller, was followed by three more progressives, all Democrats: Dale Bumpers, David Pryor, and Bill Clinton. In a major upset, Clinton was defeated in 1980 by Republican Frank White, but Clinton recaptured the statehouse in 1982 and won reelection in 1984, 1986, and 1990. Clinton ran for and won the US presidency in 1992 and was reelected to a second term in 1996. On 8 November 1994, Democratic governor Jim Guy Tucker was one of the few of his party nationwide to resist a Republican landslide. Tucker was subsequently forced to resign due to scandal and was succeeded by his Lieutenant-Governor, Republican Mike Huckabee who was elected to a full term in 1998. In the 2000 presidential election, Arkansas made Republican George W. Bush its winner with 51% of the votes.

Democrat Blanche Lambert Lincoln became the state's second woman elected to the US Senate. Arkansas's other Senator is Republican Tim Hutchinson. The state's US Representatives in 2000 included two Republicans and two Democrats. In 2000 the state legislature had 27 Democrats and 8 Republicans in the state senate, and 72 Democrats and 28 Republicans in the state house.

14 LOCAL GOVERNMENT

There are 75 counties in Arkansas, ten of them with two county seats. Each county is governed by a quorum court, consisting of 9–15 justices of the peace, elected for two-year terms. Elected county executives, who serve two-year terms, include the sheriff, assessor, coroner, treasurer, and county judge. Arkansas had 490 municipalities in 1997.

15 JUDICIAL SYSTEM

Arkansas's highest court is the supreme court, consisting of a chief justice and six associate justices, elected for staggered eight-year terms. An appeals court of six judges, also elected for eight-year terms, was established in 1978. Other courts include the circuit courts (law) and the chancery courts (equity).

Arkansas had an FBI Crime Index rate of 4,283.4 per 100,000 population in 1998. In 1999 there were 10,926 prisoners in state and federal correctional institutions.

16 MIGRATION

During the depression years of the 1930s and afterwards, Arkansas lost much of its farm population to migration, and many blacks left the state for the industrial cities of the Midwest and the east and west coasts. The net loss from migration totaled 919,000 between 1940 and 1970.

Between 1970 and 1980, however, the state gained 180,000 residents through migration, as the Ozarks became one of the fastest-growing rural areas in the US. Net migration from 1985 to 1990 amounted to a gain of nearly 36,600. As of 1990, just over two-thirds of all Arkansans had been born in the state. During 1990–98, movements between states resulted in a net gain of 105,600 more residents.

17 ECONOMY

Not until the 1950s did Arkansas enjoy significant success in attracting industry, thanks in large part to the efforts of Winthrop Rockefeller. By the mid-1990s, Arkansas's principal industries had become manufacturing, dominated by lumber and wood products companies; agriculture; and forestry. Five Fortune 500 firms are headquartered in Arkansas: Walmart Stores, Tyson Foods, Dillard Department Stores, Beverly Enterprises, and Alltel. Private goods-producing industries account for 34% of the state's total economic output, while services-producing industries account for 54% and government for 12%.

18 INCOME

Total personal income for Arkansas was $54 billion in 1998. In the same year, Arkansas ranked 48th among the 50 states in per capita (per person) income, with $21,167. An estimated 17.2% of the population was living below the federal poverty level in 1998.

19 INDUSTRY

Manufacturing in Arkansas is diverse, ranging from blue jeans to bicycles, though resource industries such as rice processing and woodworking still play a major role. The total value of shipments of manufactured goods in 1995 was nearly $43 billion, with food products accounting for 25%.

20 LABOR

Arkansas's civilian labor force totaled 1.24 in mid-1998. About 58,000 Arkansans were unemployed, for an unemployment rate of 4.7% in mid-1998. In 1998, 9.3% of workers were union members.

21 AGRICULTURE

Farm marketings in Arkansas were over $5 billion in 1998 (11th in the US). The state is the nation's leading producer of rice and is among the leaders in cotton, soybeans, and sorghum. Confined mainly to slaveholding plantations before the Civil War, cotton farming became more widespread in the postwar period. As elsewhere in the South, sharecropping by tenant farmers predominated well into the 20th century, until modernization gradually brought an end to the system.

During 1998, Arkansas produced 112 million bushels of soybeans; 45.9 million bushels of wheat; 2.2 million tons of hay; and 6.8 million bushels of sorghum for grain. The rice harvest in 1998 was nearly 8.8 billion pounds (4 billion kilograms); the cotton crop in 1998 was 1.2 million bales.

22 DOMESTICATED ANIMALS

Poultry farms are found throughout Arkansas, but especially in the northern and western regions. Arkansas was the second highest broiler-producing state in the US in 1997, with 5.6 billion broilers valued at $2.1 billion. In 1999 Arkansas had 1.82 million cattle and calves valued at $855.4 million. In 1998 the state had 750,000 hogs and pigs valued at $41.3 million.

23 FISHING

Fish farming is an important part of the state's economy. As of 1999, the state ranked first in the US in minnow farming and second only to Mississippi in catfish farming. As of 1999, there were 152 catfish operations covering 28,900 acres (13,144 hectares) of water surface.

24 FORESTRY

Forestland comprised 18.8 million acres (7.6 million hectares), or 56% of the state's total land area, in 1997. The southwest and central plains, the state's timber belt, constitute one of the most concentrated sources of yellow pine in the US. Three national forests in Arkansas covered a total of 3.5 million acres (1,428,975 hectares) in 1999.

25 MINING

The US Geological Survey estimate of the value of mineral production in Arkansas in 1998 was $598 million. In 1998, 38.6 million metric tons of crushed stone were produced, valued at $248 million; the state is also the leading producer of bromine in the U.S.

26 ENERGY AND POWER

As of 1999, Arkansas's power production totaled 9.87 million kilowatt hours. During 1999, 7.14 million barrels of crude petroleum were produced, leaving proven reserves of 47 million barrels. Production of natural gas was 188.4 billion cubic feet (5.3 billion cubic meters), with 1.33 trillion cubic feet (0.4 billion cubic meters) of reserves remaining. About 24,000 tons of bituminous coal were mined in 1998.

27 COMMERCE

Arkansas had wholesale sales totaling $29 billion in 1997. Retail sales that year totaled $22 billion and ranked 18th in the US. In 1997, exports of goods produced within Arkansas amounted to $2.3 billion.

28 PUBLIC FINANCE

Under the 1874 constitution, state expenditures may not exceed revenues. For the fiscal year ending 30 June 1997, revenues for the General Fund were $8.84 billion and expenditures were $7.68 billion. State government debt totaled $2.25 billion, or about $891 per person.

29 TAXATION

As of 2000, Arkansas's state tax revenue per capita (per person) was $1,598, among the lowest in the US. In 2000, the state sales tax was 4.625%, and state income tax ranges from 0% to 6%. City and county property taxes in Arkansas are among the lowest in the nation.

30 HEALTH

The infant death rate for 1997 was 8.4 per 1,000 live births. In 1996 Arkansas's incidence of cerebrovascular disease— 91.4 per 100,000 population—led the US. Death rates from heart disease, cancer, accidents, motor vehicle accidents, homicide, and suicide also exceeded the national average. Arkansas's 82 community hospitals had 9,876 beds in 1998. Hospital expenses—$814 per day—were lower than the US average. The state had 5,000 nonfederal physicians (about 185 physicians for every 100,000 population), and 9,751 registered nurses in 1997.

31 HOUSING

In October 1999, there were nearly 1.1 million housing units in Arkansas. In 1990, the median value of a home in Arkansas was $46,300, lower than in 47 other states, and down 6.3% from 1980 after adjusting for inflation. The median monthly cost for an owner-occupied unit (including a mortgage) was $514; a rental unit had a median monthly cost of $328 in 1990.

32 EDUCATION

In 1998, 76.8% of all Arkansans 25 years of age and older were high school graduates. In 1983, in an effort to raise the quality of education in Arkansas, the state legislature approved a comprehensive program that included smaller classes, more high school level courses, and competency tests for teachers. Public school enrollment in 1997 totaled 456,497. Expenditures for public elementary and secondary schools amounted to $4,058 per student in 1995/96 (48th among the states). In 1996, Arkansas had 20 public and private four-year colleges and universities, of which the largest was the University of Arkansas at Fayetteville. Arkansas also has 12 two-year colleges, 6 vocational-technical schools, 5 technical institutes, and 13 technical colleges.

33 ARTS

Little Rock is the home of the Arkansas Symphony and the Arkansas Arts Center. The best-known center for traditional arts and crafts is the Ozark Folk Center at Mountain View. The Arkansas Folk Festival is held there during two weekends in

Photo credit: Wleck Photo DataBase.

Canoeing on the Buffalo River in the Buffalo National River Park.

April. In 1996, there were 55 arts-related associations in Arkansas and 25 local groups.

34 LIBRARIES AND MUSEUMS

During 1994, Arkansas had 72 county or regional library systems and 15 municipal libraries. That year, public libraries held a total of 4.9 million volumes and circulation amounted to over 9 million. There were 71 museums in 1994 and a number of historic sites. Principal museums include the Arkansas Arts Center and the Museum of Science and History, both at Little Rock.

35 COMMUNICATIONS

In 1999, 88.9% of the state's households had telephones, one of the lowest rates in the nation. There were 258 radio stations (87 AM, 171 FM) and 27 television stations. A total of 23,195 Internet domain names were registered in 2000.

36 PRESS

The first newspaper in Arkansas, the *Arkansas Gazette* (established in 1819), was the state's most widely read and influential journal In 1998 there were 14 morning dailies, 16 evening papers, and 16 Sunday papers. The leading dailies (with 1998 circulations) are the *Southwest Times Record* (41,224) and the *Arkansas Democrat Gazette* (173,316).

37 TOURISM, TRAVEL, AND RECREATION

In 1995, the five national parks had 2.5 million visitors. Leading attractions are the mineral waters and recreational facilities at Hot Springs, Eureka Springs, Mammoth Spring, and Heber Springs. The Crater of Diamonds, near Murfreesboro, is the only known public source of natural diamonds in North America. For a fee, visitors may hunt for diamonds and keep any they find. More than 100,000 diamonds have been found in the area since 1906.

38 SPORTS

Arkansas has no major league professional sports teams. The Razorback football team of the University of Arkansas won the Orange Bowl in 1978 and the Blue-

Photo credit: EPD Photos/National Archives

General Douglas MacArthur (1880–1964), born in Arkansas, was supreme commander of Allied forces in the Pacific during World War II and in Korea. In this famous WWII picture, MacArthur wades ashore at Leyte in the Philippine Islands after American troops had secured the area from the Japanese.

bonnet Bowl in 1982. The men's basketball team won or shared the Southwest Conference championship in 1977, 1978, 1979, 1981, 1982, 1994, and 2000.

39 FAMOUS ARKANSANS

Arkansas has produced one president of the United States, William Jefferson Clinton (b. 1946). Clinton, a Democrat, defeated incumbent George Bush in the 1992 presidential election and was reelected in 1996. Clinton was elected governor of Arkansas in 1978, becoming the nation's youngest governor.

Hattie W. Caraway (b.Tennessee, 1878–1950), was the first woman elected to the US Senate, serving from 1931 to 1945. Senator J. William Fulbright (b.Missouri, 1905–95) was chairman of the Senate Foreign Relations Committee.

John H. Johnson (b.1918), publisher of the nation's leading black-oriented magazines—*Ebony, Jet,* and others—is an Arkansan. John Gould Fletcher (1886–1950) was a Pulitzer Prize-winning poet.

Notable Arkansas sports personalities include football coach Paul "Bear" Bryant (1913–83); Brooks Robinson (b.1937), considered by some the best-fielding third baseman in baseball history; Lou Brock (b.1939), who holds the record for the most stolen bases; and star pass-catcher Lance Alworth (b.Mississippi, 1940).

40 BIBLIOGRAPHY

Altman, Linda Jacobs. *Arkansas.* New York: Benchmark Books, 2000.

Angelou, Maya. *I Know Why the Caged Bird Sings.* New York: Bantam, 1971.

Ashmore, Harry S. *Arkansas: A Bicentennial History.* New York: Norton, 1978.

McNair, Sylvia. *Arkansas.* New York: Children's Press, 2001.

Web sites

Arkansas Department of Parks and Tourism. Arkansas Vacation in the Natural State. [Online] Available http://www.arkansas.com Accessed May 31, 2001.

State of Arkansas. Welcome to the State of Arkansas. [Online] Available http://www.state.ar.us/ Accessed May 31, 2001.

CALIFORNIA

State of California

CALIFORNIA REPUBLIC

ORIGIN OF STATE NAME: Probably from the mythical island California in a 16th-century romance by Garci Ordóñez de Montalvo.

NICKNAME: The Golden State.

CAPITAL: Sacramento.

ENTERED UNION: 9 September 1850 (31st).

SONG: "I Love You, California."

MOTTO: Eureka (I have found it).

FLAG: The flag consists of a white field with a red star at upper left and a red stripe and the words "California Republic" across the bottom; in the center, a brown grizzly bear walks on a patch of green grass.

OFFICIAL SEAL: In the foreground is the goddess Minerva; a grizzly bear stands in front of her shield. The scene also shows the Sierra Nevada, San Francisco Bay, a miner, a sheaf of wheat, and a cluster of grapes, all representing California's resources. The state motto and 31 stars are displayed at the top. The words "The Great Seal of the State of California" surround the whole.

COLORS: Yale blue and golden yellow.

ANIMAL: California grizzly bear (extinct).

BIRD: California valley quail.

FISH: California golden trout.

FLOWER: Golden poppy.

TREE: California redwood.

ROCK: Serpentine.

MINERAL: Native gold.

GEMSTONE: Benitoite.

REPTILE: California desert tortoise.

INSECT: California dog-face butterfly (flying pansy).

MARINE MAMMAL: California gray whale.

FOSSIL: California saber-toothed cat.

TIME: 4 AM PST = noon GMT.

1 LOCATION AND SIZE

Situated on the Pacific coast of the southwestern US, California is the nation's third-largest state (after Alaska and Texas). The total area of California is 158,706 square miles (411,048 square kilometers). California extends about 350 miles (560 kilometers) east-west; its maximum north-south extension is 780 miles (1,260 kilometers).

The eight Santa Barbara islands lie from 20 to 60 miles (32–97 kilometers) off California's southwestern coast. The small islands and islets of the Farallon group are about 30 miles (48 kilometers) west of San Francisco Bay. The total boundary length of the state is 2,050 miles (3,299 kilometers).

2 TOPOGRAPHY

California is the only state in the US with an extensive seacoast, high mountains, and deserts. The state's extreme physical diversity is best illustrated by the fact that Mt. Whitney (14,495 feet—4,418 meters), the highest point in the continental US, is situated no more than 80 miles (129 kilometers) from the lowest point in the entire country, Death Valley (282 feet, or 86 meters, below sea level). California has 41 mountains exceeding 10,000 feet (3,050 meters). The mean elevation of the state is about 2,900 feet (900 meters).

California's principal geographic regions are the Sierra Nevada in the east, the Coast Ranges in the west, the Central Valley between them, and the Mojave and Colorado deserts in the southeast. The mountain-walled Central Valley is drained by the state's two principal rivers, the Sacramento River in the north and the San Joaquin River in the south. The Coast Ranges mountain system, extending more than 1,200 miles (1,900 kilometers) alongside the Pacific, is drained by the Klamath, Eel, Russian, Salinas, and other rivers.

The Salton Sea, in the Imperial Valley of the southeast, is the state's largest lake, occupying 374 square miles (969 square kilometers). The California coast is indented by two magnificent natural harbors, San Francisco Bay and San Diego Bay, and two smaller bays, Monterey and Humboldt. Two groups of islands lie off

California Population Profile

Total population in 2000:	33,871,648
Population change, 1990–2000:	13.8%
Hispanic or Latino†:	32.4%
Population by race	
One race:	95.3%
White:	59.5%
Black or African American:	6.7%
American Indian/Alaska Native:	1.0%
Asian:	10.9%
Native Hawaiian/Pacific Islander:	0.3%
Some other race:	16.8%
Two or more races:	4.7%

Population by Age Group

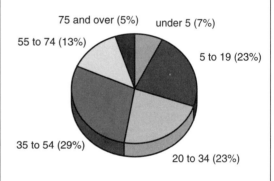

75 and over (5%)   under 5 (7%)
55 to 74 (13%)
5 to 19 (23%)
35 to 54 (29%)
20 to 34 (23%)

Top Cities by Population

City	Population	% change 1990–2000
Los Angeles	3,694,820	6.0
San Diego	1,223,400	10.2
San Jose	894,943	14.4
San Francisco	776,733	7.3
Long Beach	461,522	7.5
Fresno	427,652	20.7
Sacramento	407,018	10.2
Oakland	399,484	7.3
Santa Ana	337,977	15.1
Anaheim	328,014	23.1

Notes: †A person of Hispanic or Latino origin may be of any race. NA indicates that data are not available.
Sources: U.S. Census Bureau. Public Information Office. *Demographic Profiles.* [Online] Available http://www.census.gov/Press-Release/www/2001/demoprofile.html. Accessed June 1, 2001. U.S. Census Bureau. *Census 2000: Redistricting Data.* Press release issued by the Redistricting Data Office. Washington, D.C., March, 2001.

CALIFORNIA

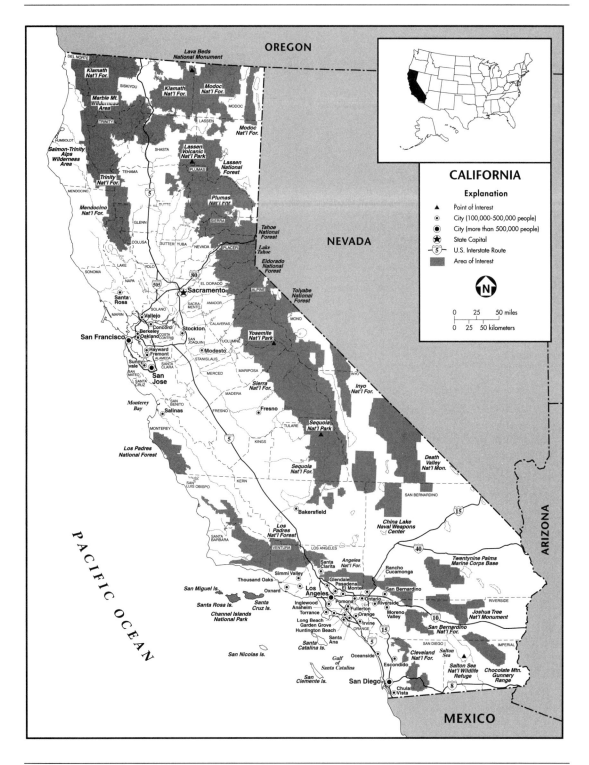

OREGON

Lava Beds
National Monument

DEL NORTE

Klamath
Nat'l For.

SISKIYOU

Klamath
Nat'l For.

Modoc
Nat'l For.

Marble Mt.
Wilderness
Area

MODOC

TRINITY

Modoc
Nat'l For.

HUMBOLDT

LASSEN

Salmon-Trinity
Alps
Wilderness
Area

SHASTA

Lassen
Volcanic
Nat'l Park

Trinity
Nat'l For.

TEHAMA

PLUMAS

Lassen
National
Forest

Mendocino

Mendocino
Nat'l For.

GLENN

BUTTE

Plumas
Nat'l For.

SIERRA

Tahoe
National
Forest

NEVADA

COLUSA

SUTTER YUBA

NEVADA

PLACER

Lake
Tahoe

LAKE

YOLO

Eldorado
National
Forest

SONOMA

NAPA

Santa
Rosa

MARIN

SOLANO

Vallejo

SACRA-
MENTO

EL DORADO

★ Sacramento

ALPINE

Tolyabe
National
Forest

AMADOR

Berkeley
Concord
Oakland

Stockton

CALAVERAS

MONO

San Francisco

COSTA
CONTRA

SAN
JOAQUIN

TUOLUMNE

Yosemite
Nat'l Park

Hayward
Fremont

ALAMEDA

Modesto

Sunny-
vale

SAN
MATEO

SANTA
CLARA

STANISLAUS

San Jose

SANTA
CRUZ

MERCED

MARIPOSA

Monterey
Bay

SAN
BENITO

MADERA

Sierra
Nat'l For.

Inyo
Nat'l For.

Salinas

FRESNO

Fresno

MONTEREY

TULARE

Sequoia
Nat'l Park

KINGS

Los Padres
National Forest

Sequoia
Nat'l For.

Death
Valley
Nat'l Mon.

SAN
LUIS OBISPO

KERN

SAN BERNARDINO

Bakersfield

China Lake
Naval Weapons
Center

15

Los
Padres
Nat'l Forest

Twentynine Palms
Marine Corps Base

SANTA
BARBARA

VENTURA

LOS ANGELES

40

Angeles
Nat'l For.

Santa
Clarita

Rancho
Cucamonga

RIVERSIDE

Simi Valley

Glendale
Pasadena
El Monte

San Bernardino

Thousand Oaks

Ontario

Joshua Tree
Nat'l Monument

San Miguel Is.

Oxnard

Los
Angeles

Inglewood
Anaheim
Torrance

Pomona

Riverside

Moreno
Valley

10

San Bernardino
Nat'l For.

Santa Rosa Is.

Santa
Cruz Is.

Fullerton

Orange

Long Beach
Garden Grove
Huntington Beach

Irvine

Channel Islands
National Park

ORANGE

15

Santa
Ana

SAN DIEGO

IMPERIAL

San Nicolas Is.

Santa
Catalina Is.

5

Oceanside

Cleveland
Nat'l For.

Salton
Sea

Gulf
of
Santa Catalina

Escondido

Salton Sea
Nat'l Wildlife
Refuge

Chocolate Mtn.
Gunnery
Range

San
Clemente Is.

San Diego

Chula
Vista

8

MEXICO

PACIFIC OCEAN

ARIZONA

CALIFORNIA

Explanation

▲ Point of Interest
⊙ City (100,000-500,000 people)
◉ City (more than 500,000 people)
★ State Capital
〈5〉 U.S. Interstate Route
▨ Area of Interest

Ⓝ

0   25   50 miles

0   25   50 kilometers

the California shore: the Santa Barbara Islands and the rocky Farallon Islands. Because water is scarce in the southern part of the state, more than 1,000 dams and reservoirs have been built in California. By 1993, there were 1,336 reservoirs in the state.

The San Andreas Fault extends from north of San Francisco Bay for more than 600 miles (970 kilometers) southeast to the Mojave Desert. This is a major active earthquake zone and was responsible for the great San Francisco earthquake of 1906.

3 CLIMATE

California has four main climatic regions. Mild summers and winters prevail in central coastal areas, where temperatures are steadier than practically anywhere else in the US. In the area between San Francisco and Monterey, for example, the difference between average summer and winter temperatures is seldom more than 10°F (6°C). Mountainous regions are characterized by milder summers and colder winters, with markedly low temperatures at high elevations. The Central Valley has hot summers and cool winters, while the Imperial Valley is marked by very hot, dry summers, with temperatures frequently exceeding 100°F (38°C).

Average annual temperatures for the state range from 47°F (8°C) in the Sierra Nevada to 73°F (23°C) in the Imperial Valley. The highest temperature ever recorded in the US was 134° (57°C), registered in Death Valley on 10 July 1913. The state's lowest temperature was –45°F (–43°C),

recorded on 20 January 1937 at Boca, near the Nevada border.

Los Angeles has an average January minimum temperature of 47°F (8°C) and an average July maximum of 83°F (28°C). Sacramento's January minimums average 37°F (3°C), with July maximums of 93°F (34°C). Annual precipitation varies from only 2 inches (5 centimeters) in the Imperial Valley to 68 inches (173 centimeters) at Blue Canyon, near Lake Tahoe.

4 PLANTS AND ANIMALS

The state's six life zones are the lower Sonoran (desert); upper Sonoran (foothill regions and some coastal lands); transition (coastal areas and moist northeastern counties); and the Canadian, Hudsonian, and Arctic zones, comprising California's highest elevations.

Plant life in the arid climate of the lower Sonoran zone features native cactus, mesquite, and paloverde. The Joshua tree *(Yucca brevifolia)* is found in the Mojave Desert. Flowering plants include the dwarf desert poppy and a variety of asters. Fremont cottonwood and valley oak grow in the Central Valley. The upper Sonoran zone includes the unique chaparral belt, with forests of small shrubs, stunted trees, and herbaceous plants. The golden poppy *(Eschscholtzia californica)*—the state flower—also flourishes in this zone.

The transition zone includes most of the state's forests, with such magnificent specimens as the redwood *(Sequoia sempervirens)* and "big tree" or giant sequoia *(Sequoia gigantea),* among the oldest living things on earth (some are believed to

Photo credit: Corel Corporation.

The General Sherman tree in the Sequoia National Forest.

be at least 4,000 years old). Characteristic wildflowers include varieties of mariposa, tulip, and tiger and leopard lilies.

The high elevations of the Canadian zone contain abundant Jeffrey pine, red fir, and lodgepole pine. Just below the timberline, in the Hudsonian zone, grow the whitebark, foxtail, and silver pines. At approximately 10,500 feet (3,200 meters) begins the Arctic zone, a treeless region whose plantlife includes a number of wildflowers, including Sierra primrose, yellow columbine, alpine buttercup, and alpine shooting star. Among the numerous plant species found in California that are federally classified as endangered are the Contra Costa wallflower, Antioch Dunes evening primrose, and San Clemente Island larkspur.

Mammals found in the deserts of the lower Sonoran zone include the jackrabbit, kangaroo rat, squirrel, and opossum. The Texas night owl, roadrunner, and various species of hawk are common birds, and reptiles include the sidewinder and horned toad. The upper Sonoran zone is home to such mammals as the antelope, brown-footed woodrat, and ring-tailed cat. Birds of this zone include the California thrasher and California condor.

Animal life is abundant amid the forests of the transition zone. Colombian black-tailed deer, black bear, gray fox, cougar, and bobcat are found. Garter snakes and rattlesnakes are common, and birds include the kingfisher, chickadee, towhee, and hummingbird.

Mammals of the Canadian zone include the mountain weasel, snowshoe hare, and several species of chipmunk. Birds include the blue-fronted jay and Sierra hermit thrush. Birds become scarcer as one ascends to the Hudsonian zone. Principal mammals of this region are also visitors from other zones, though the Sierra coney and white-tailed jackrabbit make their homes here.

Aquatic life in California is abundant. Many trout species are found, among them rainbow, golden, and Tahoe. Migratory species of salmon are also common. Deep-sea life-forms include sea bass, yellowfin tuna, barracuda, and several types of whale. Native to the cliffs of northern California are seals, sea lions, and many types of shorebirds.

Joint efforts by state and federal wildlife agencies have established an ambitious—if somewhat controversial—recovery program to revitalize the dwindling population of the majestic condor, the largest bird native to the US. As of 1997, some 81 California animals were on the federal endangered species list. These include the Jan Joaquin kit fox, salt marsh harvest mouse, California least tern, California condor, San Francisco garter snake, and Owens River pupfish. Ten butterflies listed as endangered on the federal list are California species. Among threatened aquatic animals are the Paiute cutthroat trout, and Southern sea otter. California

has a total of 290,821 acres (117,6791 hectares) of National Wildlife Refuges.

5 ENVIRONMENTAL PROTECTION

In 1892, naturalist John Muir and other wilderness lovers founded the Sierra Club. This group, with other private groups of conservationists, has been influential in saving the Muir Woods and other stands of redwoods from the lumbermen's axes. State land-reclamation programs have been important in providing new agricultural land and controlling flood damage.

California's primary resource problem is water: the southern two-thirds of the state accounts for about 75% of annual water consumption but only 30% of the supply. Water has been diverted from the Sierra Nevada snow runoff and from the Colorado River to the cities and dry areas largely by means of aqueducts. Some 700 miles (1,100 kilometers) of aqueducts have been constructed in federal and state undertakings.

Air pollution has been a serious problem since July 1943, when heavy smog enveloped Los Angeles for the first time. In 1960, the state legislature passed the first automobile antismog law in the nation, requiring that all cars be equipped with antismog exhaust devices within three years. The city's smog problem has since been reduced to a manageable level, but pollution problems still persist there and in other California cities. In 1996, southern California had the best air quality ever measured since 1945.

In the 1980s, the state legislature enacted stringent controls on toxic waste disposal. California has also been a leader in recycling waste products—for example, using acid waste from metal-processing plants as a soil additive in citrus orchards.

6 POPULATION

Nearly 13% of all Americans live in California, which retains its rank of first in population among the 50 states. Los Angeles is the second most populous city in the US (behind New York City) and Los Angeles County ranks first in population among all US counties.

At the 2000 census, the population of 33,871,648 was 49.8% male and 50.2% female. The population density in 2000 was 217.2 persons per square mile (83.8 persons per square kilometer), much higher than the national average of 79.6 persons per square mile (30.7 per square kilometer). Californians are younger than the nation as a whole—in 2000, nearly one-quarter of the state's population was 19 years of age or younger, and 5% of the population was 75 or older.

In 2000, Los Angeles had a population of nearly 3.7 million; San Diego, 1.2 million; San Jose, 894,943; San Francisco, 776,733; Long Beach, 461,522; and Fresno, 427,652.

7 ETHNIC GROUPS

At least 32% of all foreign-born persons in the US live in California. The state has the nation's largest populations of those born in: Mexico, the Philippines, Canada, Germany, the United Kingdom, Korea, Vietnam, China, El Salvador, India, Japan, Taiwan, Guatemala, Iran, Laos, Hong Kong, Peru, France, Cambodia, Honduras, and Thailand. California also has the most Native Americans and Asian Indians, more blacks than any state except New York, more Eskimos and Aleuts than any state except Alaska, and more native Hawaiians than any state except Hawaii.

The westward movement of American settlers in the third quarter of the 19th century, followed by Germans, Irish, North Italians, and Italian Swiss immigrants, overshadowed but did not obliterate California's Spanish heritage. In 1997, an estimated 9.9 million of the state's residents were of Hispanic origin, more than any other state and 33.9% of the US total. Hispanics represented 30.8% of the population, the second highest percentage among the states. The majority of these Hispanics were Mexican-Americans. About 10.6% of the state's population consisted of native-born Mexicans in 1996. As of 1990, there were also 113,548 Puerto Ricans, 143,017 Guatemalans, and 300,102 Salvadorans.

California had an estimated 3.8 million Asians and Pacific Islanders in 1997, 37.6% of the US total. In 1990, the state's Chinese population was 641,250, more than double that of New York State and by far the highest in the US. The nation's oldest and largest Chinatown is in San Francisco. In 1990 there were 353,251 Japanese-Americans in California. After their removal from their homes and internment during World War II, most Japanese, deprived of their landholdings,

California Population by Race

Census 2000 was the first national census in which the instructions to respondents said, "Mark one or more races." This table shows the number of people who are of one, two, or three or more races. For those claiming two races, the number of people belonging to the various categories is listed. The U.S. government conducts a census of the population every ten years.

	Number	Percent
Total population	33,871,648	100.0
One race	32,264,002	95.3
Two races	1,513,166	4.5
White *and* Black or African American	101,705	0.3
White *and* American Indian/Alaska Native	175,273	0.5
White *and* Asian	247,396	0.7
White *and* Native Hawaiian/Pacific Islander	26,920	0.1
White *and* some other race	684,475	2.0
Black or African American *and* American Indian/Alaska Native	25,204	0.1
Black or African American *and* Asian	25,203	0.1
Black or African American *and* Native Hawaiian/Pacific Islander	4,257	—
Black or African American *and* some other race	47,923	0.1
American Indian/Alaska Native *and* Asian	14,560	—
American Indian/Alaska Native *and* Native Hawaiian/Pacific Islander	1,837	—
American Indian/Alaska Native *and* some other race	29,004	0.1
Asian *and* Native Hawaiian/Pacific Islander	36,050	0.1
Asian *and* some other race	82,728	0.2
Native Hawaiian/Pacific Islander *and* some other race	10,631	—
Three or more races	94,480	0.3

Source: U.S. Census Bureau. *Census 2000: Redistricting Data*. Press release issued by the Redistricting Data Office. Washington, D.C., March, 2001. A dash (—) indicates that the percent is less than 0.1.

entered urban occupations. Many dispersed to other regions of the country.

While the Chinese and Japanese communities in California are the oldest in the state, they were not the most populous in 1990. This distinction was held by the Filipino community, which numbered 709,599 that year. There were also 260,822 Koreans, 242,946 Vietnamese, 112,560 Asian Indians, 43,418 native Hawaiians, 26,444 Samoans, and 19,820 Guamanians.

Native Americans were estimated at 307,000 in 1997. In 1990, there were 1,854 Eskimos and 1,091 Aleuts. Los Angeles has more Native Americans than any other US city. Black Americans constitute a smaller proportion of California's population than of the nation's as a whole: an estimated 7.4% in 1997.

8 LANGUAGES

As in much of the West, California English is a combination of the eastern dialects and subdialects brought by the continuing westward migration from the eastern states. The interior valley is Midland-oriented, but generally, in both northern and southern California, Northern speech is dominant.

Boonville, a village about 100 miles (160 kilometers) north of San Francisco, is notorious for "Boontling," a local dialect contrived in the mid-19th century by Scotch-Irish settlers who wanted privacy and freedom from obscenities in their conversation. Now declining in use, Boontling has about 1,000 vocabulary replacements of usual English words, together with some unusual pronunciations.

In 1990, 18,764,213 Californians—or 68.5% of the population five years old or over—reported speaking only English at home. Other languages spoken at home included the following:

Spanish	5,478,712
Chinese	575,447
Tagalog	464,644
Vietnamese	233,074
Other various Indo-European	231,654
Korean	215,845
Japanese	174,451
German	165,962
French	132,657
Indic	119,318
Italian	111,133
Portuguese	78,232
Arabic	73,738
Mon-Khmer	59,622
Russian	44,978
Other various West-Germanic	34,433
Greek	32,889

California's large foreign-language populations have posed major educational problems. In 1974, a landmark San Francisco case, *Lau v. Nichols,* brought a decision from the US Supreme Court that children who do not know English should not thereby be handicapped in school, but should receive instruction in their native tongue while learning English. In 1997, a federal judge in Orange County ruled against blocking English immersion classes, ending the bilingual education program.

9 RELIGIONS

In the early 20th century, many dissident sects sprang up, including such organizations as Firebrands for Jesus, the Psychosomatic Institute, the Mystical Order of Melchizedek, the Infinite Science Church, and Nothing Impossible, among many others. Canadian-born Aimee Semple McPherson, who preached her Foursquare Gospel during the 1920s at the Angelus Temple in Los Angeles, was typical of the many charismatic preachers of new doctrines who gave—and still give—California its exotic religious flavor. Since World War II, religions such as Zen Buddhism and Scientology have won enthusiastic followings, along with various cults devoted to self-discovery and self-improvement.

Nevertheless, the large majority of religious Californians continue to follow traditional faiths. In 1990, there were 7,142,067 Roman Catholics and 4,524,337 known Protestants. The largest non-Catholic Christian denominations were the Church of Jesus Christ of Latter-day Saints (Mormon) with 533,741 members; Southern Baptist, 504,516; United Methodist, 266,306; Presbyterian, 258,854; American Baptist, 184,723; Assembly of God, 263,059; Episcopal, 178,263; and the Lutheran Church-Missouri Synod, 143,987. In 1994, the Jewish population was estimated at 922,000, nearly two-thirds of whom lived in the Los Angeles metropolitan area.

10 TRANSPORTATION

California has—and for decades has had—more motor vehicles than any other state, and ranks second only to Texas in interstate highway mileage. A complex

Photo credit: Robert Holmes.

The Golden Gate Bridge, San Francisco.

included Santa Fe, Burlington Northern, and Union Pacific. Amtrak passenger trains connect the state's major population centers. In 1995/96, the number of riders throughout the state totaled 7.3 million.

Urban transit began in San Francisco in 1861 with horse-drawn streetcars. Cable-car service was introduced in 1873; a few cable cars are still in use, mainly for the tourist trade. The 71-mile (114-kilometer) Bay Area Rapid Transit System, or BART, connects San Francisco with Oakland.

In Los Angeles, competition from buses—which provided greater mobility, but aggravated the city's smog and congestion problems—forced the trolleys to end service in 1961.

The Pasadena Freeway, the first modern expressway in California, opened in 1941. During the 1960s and 1970s, the state built a complex toll-free highway network tying in with the federal highway system, and costing more than $10 billion. Local, state, and federal authorities combined spent almost $97, with $2 billion of that amount for maintenance.

Los Angeles County claims more automobiles, more miles of streets, and more intersections than any other US city. The 8-mile (13-kilometer) San Francisco–Oakland Bay Bridge was completed in 1936. The next year saw the opening of the magnificent Golden Gate Bridge, which at 4,200 feet (1,280 meters) was the world's longest suspension bridge until 1964.

In 1997, California had 170,598 miles (274,492 kilometers) of public roads and registered 24,944,976 motor vehicles.

8,300-mile (13,400-kilometer) network of urban freeways is one of the engineering wonders of the modern world—but the traffic congestion in the state's major cities during rush hours may well be the worst in the country.

The Central Pacific–Union Pacific transcontinental railroad was finished in 1869. The railroads dominated transportation in the state until motor vehicles came into widespread use in the 1920s.

As of 1998, California had 6,415 rail miles (10,322 kilometers) of track. Class I railroads operating within the state in 1998

The state's death rate per 100,000 vehicle miles—1.52—was slightly less than the US average of 1.73 in 1995.

In 1998, the port at Long Beach handled 57.7 million tons of cargo. The port at Los Angeles handled just 44 million tons. Other main ports are Richmond, Oakland, and San Francisco. California has 550 airports and 380 heliports. California's most active air terminal—and one of the nation's most active—is Los Angeles International Airport, which handles nearly 200,000 departing passenger aircraft and boards over 20 million passengers each year.

11 HISTORY

The region now known as California has been populated for at least 10,000 years, and possibly far longer. On the eve of European discovery, at least 300,000 Native Americans lived there. This large population was divided into no fewer than 105 separate tribes or nations speaking at least 100 different languages and dialects. In general, the California tribes depended for their survival on hunting, fishing, and gathering the abundant natural food resources. The basic unit of political organization was the village community, consisting of several small villages, or the family unit.

European contact with California began in 1533 when Hernán Cortés, Spanish conqueror of the Aztecs, sent a naval expedition northward along the western coast of Mexico in search of new wealth. The expedition led to the discovery of Baja California (now part of Mexico). On 28 September, Juan Rodriquez Cabrillo landed at the bay now known as San Diego, thus becoming the first European discoverer of Alta (or Upper) California.

European interest in the Californias declined in the succeeding decades, and California remained for generations on the fringe of European activity in the New World. Spanish interest in California revived during the late 18th century. Because rival colonial powers were becoming increasingly aggressive, Spain decided to establish permanent settlements in the north. Over the next half-century, the 21 missions established by Catholic Franciscans along the Pacific coast from San Diego to San Francisco formed the core of Hispanic California.

The principal concern of the missionaries was to convert the Native Americans to Christianity. They were also taught to perform a wide variety of new tasks: making bricks, tiles, pottery, shoes, saddles, wine, candles, and soap; herding horses, cattle, sheep, and goats; and planting, irrigating, and harvesting. In addition to transforming the way of life of these native Californians, the missions also reduced their number by introducing new diseases.

Spanish control of California ended with the successful conclusion of the Mexican Revolution in 1821. For the next quarter-century, California was a province of the independent nation of Mexico. During the Mexican period, California attracted a considerable minority of immigrants from within the US. The first organized group to cross the continent for the purpose of settlement in California was the Bidwell-Bartleson party of 1841. Sub-

Photo credit: Jeff Hyman.

Gateway to Chinatown Plaza, Los Angeles.

sequent groups of overland pioneers included the ill-fated Donner party of 1846, whose members, stranded by a snowstorm near the Sierra Nevada summit, resorted to cannibalism so that 47 of the 87 travelers could survive.

Gold Rush

Following the 1846–48 Mexican War, resulting from a dispute over the Texas border, Mexico ceded California and other territories to the US. Mexico received $15 million and the settlement by the US of some $3 million in claims by Mexican citizens. Just nine days before the treaty ending the war was signed, James Wilson Marshall discovered gold along the American River in California. The news of the gold discovery, on 24 January 1848, soon spread around the globe, and a massive rush of people poured into the region. By the end of 1848, about 6,000 miners had obtained $10 million worth of gold. In 1852, the peak year of production, about $80 million in gold was mined in the state.

California's census population quadrupled during the 1850s, reaching nearly 380,000 by 1860, and continued to grow at a rate twice that of the nation as a whole in the 1860s and 1870s. One of the most serious problems facing California in the early years of the gold rush was the absence of government. The US Congress, deadlocked over the slavery controversy, failed to provide any form of legal government for California from the end of the Mexican War until its admission as a state in the fall of 1850. Taking matters into their own hands, 48 delegates gathered at a constitutional convention in Monterey in September 1849 to draft a fundamental law for California. To the surprise of many, the convention decided by unanimous vote to exclude slavery from the region. California soon petitioned Congress for admission as a state, having bypassed the preliminary territorial stage. On 9 September 1850, President Millard Fillmore signed the admission bill, and California became the 31st state to enter the union.

Statehood

The early years of statehood were marked by racial discrimination and considerable ethnic conflict. The Native American population declined from an estimated 150,000 in 1845 to less than 30,000 by 1870. In 1850, the state legislature enacted a foreign miners' license tax, aimed at eliminating competition from Mexican and other Latin American miners. The 25,000 Chinese who replaced the Mexicans as the state's largest foreign minority—making up about a tenth of the state's population by 1852—soon became the target of a new round of discrimination. The legislature enacted new taxes aimed at Chinese miners and passed an immigration tax on the Chinese as well.

Controversy also centered on the status of the Mexican *ranchos*, those vast estates created by the Mexican government that totaled more than 13 million acres (5 million hectares) by 1850. In the early years of statehood, thousands of squatters took up residence on the rancho lands. By the time the legal title to the property was confirmed by federal commissions and courts—a process which often took as long as 17 years—the original occupants were often bankrupt and benefited little from the decision.

Despite the population boom during the gold rush, California remained isolated from the rest of the country until completion of the transcontinental railroad in 1869. In the late 19th century, California's economy became more diversified. The early dependence on gold and silver mining was overcome through the development of large-scale irrigation projects and the expansion of commercial agriculture. The population of southern California boomed in the 1880s, fueled by the success of the new citrus industry, an influx of invalids seeking a warmer climate, and a railroad rate war between the Southern Pacific and the newly completed Santa Fe.

Early 20th Century

During the early 20th century, California's population growth became increasingly urban. Between 1900 and 1920, the population of the San Francisco Bay area doubled, while residents of metropolitan Los Angeles increased fivefold. On 18 April 1906, San Francisco's progress was interrupted by the most devastating earthquake ever to strike California. The quake and the fires that raged for three days killed at least 452 people, razed the city's business section, and destroyed some 28,000 build-

Photo credit: Cory Langley.

Cable cars in San Francisco.

the decade, California ranked first among the states in production of crude oil.

During the 1930s hundreds of thousands of refugees streamed into the state from the dust bowl of the southern Great Plains. The film industry, which offered at least the illusion of prosperity to millions of Americans, continued to prosper during the nationwide economic depression. By 1940 there were more movie theaters in the US than banks, and the films they showed were almost all California products.

During World War II, the enormous expansion of military installations, shipyards, and aircraft plants attracted millions of new residents to California. The war years also saw an increase in the size and importance of ethnic minorities. By 1942, only Mexico City had a larger urban Mexican population than Los Angeles. During the war, more than 93,000 Japanese-Americans in California—most of whom were US citizens and American-born—were interned in "relocation centers" throughout the Far West.

Post–World War II

California continued to grow rapidly during the postwar period, as agricultural, aerospace, and service industries provided new economic opportunities. Politics in the state were influenced by international tensions, and the California legislature expanded the activities of its Fact-Finding Committee on Un-American Activities. Blacklisting became common in the film industry. The early 1950s saw the rise to the US vice-presidency of Richard Nixon,

ings. The survivors immediately set to work to rebuild the city, and completed about 20,000 new buildings within three years. By 1920, the populations of the two urban areas of Los Angeles and San Francisco were roughly equal.

During the first half of the 20th century, California's population growth far outpaced that of the nation as a whole because of the new economic opportunities it offered. In the early 1920s, major discoveries of oil were made in the Los Angeles Basin, and for several years during

California Governors: 1849—2001

1849–1851	Peter Hardeman Burnett	Indep-Dem
1851–1852	John McDougal	Indep-Dem
1852–1856	John Bigler	Democrat
1856–1858	James Neeley Johnson	American
1858–1860	John B. Weller	Democrat
1860	Milton Slocum Latham	Lecompton-Dem
1860–1862	John Gately Downey	Lecompton-Dem
1862–1863	Leland Stanford	Republican
1863–1867	Frederick Ferdinand Low	Union-Rep
1867–1871	Henry Huntly Haight	Democrat
1871–1875	Newton Booth	Republican
1875	Romualdo Pacheco	Republican
1875–1880	William Irwin	Democrat
1880–1883	George Clement Perkins	Republican
1883–1887	George Stoneman	Democrat
1887	Washington Bartlett	Democrat
1887–1891	Robert Whitney Waterman	Republican
1891–1895	Henry Harrison Markham	Republican
1895–1899	James Herbert Budd	Democrat
1899–1903	Henry Tifft Gage	Republican
1903–1907	George Cooper Pardee	Republican
1907–1911	James Norris Gillett	Republican
1911–1917	Hiram Warren Johnson	Republican
1917–1923	William Dennison Stephens	Republican
1923–1927	Friend William Richardson	Republican
1927–1931	Clement Calhoun Young	Republican
1931–1934	James Rolph, Jr.	Republican
1934–1939	Frank Finley Merriam	Republican
1939–1943	Culbert Levy Olson	Democrat
1943–1953	Earl Warren	Republican
1953–1959	Goodwin Jess Knight	Republican
1959–1967	Edmund Gerald Brown, Sr.	Democrat
1967–1975	Ronald Wilson Reagan	Republican
1975–1983	Edmund Gerald Brown, Jr.	Democrat
1983–1991	George Deukmejian	Republican
1991–1999	Peter Barton Wilson	Republican
1999–	Gray Davis	Democrat

Independent Democrat – Indep-Dem
Lecompton Democrat – Lecompton-Dem
Union Republican – Union-Rep

whose early campaigns capitalized on fears of Communism.

At the beginning of 1963, California (according to census estimates) became the nation's most populous state. By 1970, however, California's growth rate had slowed considerably. Economic opportunity gave way to recessions and high unemployment. Pollution of air and water called into question the quality of the California environment. The traditional romantic image of California was overshadowed by reports of mass murders, bizarre religious cults, extremist social and political movements, and racial and campus unrest.

In 1968, Richard Nixon became the first native Californian to be elected a US president. Both Ronald Reagan, governor of the state from 1967 to 1975, and Edmund G. Brown, Jr., elected governor in 1974 and reelected in 1978, were active candidates for the US presidency in 1980. Reagan was the Republican presidential winner that year and in 1984.

1980s–90s

Assisted by the Reagan administration's military build-up, which invested billions of dollars in California's defense industry, the state's economy rebounded in the early and mid-1980s. By the late 1980s and early 1990s, however, a recession and cuts in military spending combined to produce a dramatic economic decline. In 1992, the state's unemployment rate climbed to 10.1%. Jobs in the California aerospace and manufacturing sector dropped by 24%.

California's economic woes were matched by civil disorders. In 1991, an onlooker released a seven-minute videotape which showed a group of Los Angeles police officers beating a black motorist,

Rodney King, with nightsticks, at the conclusion of a high-speed freeway chase. The four officers who had been charged with unnecessary brutality were then acquitted (in a jury trial that took place in a mostly white suburb). The verdict set off riots in South Central Los Angeles that killed 60 people and caused an estimated $1 billion in property damage.

In the late 1980s and early 1990s, California was also hit by two severe earthquakes. The first, which struck the San Francisco area in 1989, caused the collapse of buildings, bridges, and roadways. As many as 270 people were killed and 100,000 houses were damaged. In 1994, an earthquake measuring 6.7 on the Richter scale occurred 20 miles northwest of downtown Los Angeles, leaving 680,000 people without electricity and causing $13–20 million in property damage.

In 1994, anger over illegal immigration led to passage of Proposition 187, which would bar illegal aliens from welfare, education, and nonemergency health services. Passage of the measure prompted immediate challenges in the courts by the opposition, and the issue has not been resolved.

12 STATE GOVERNMENT

The California legislature consists of a 40-member senate and an 80-member assembly. Senators are elected to four-year terms, half of them every two years, and assembly members are elected to two-year terms. Bills, which may be introduced by either house, are referred to committees, and must be read before each house three times. Legislation must be approved by an absolute majority vote of each house, except for appropriations bills, certain urgent measures, and proposed constitutional amendments, which require a two-thirds vote for passage. A governor's veto may be overridden by two-thirds majority votes in both houses.

Constitutional amendments and proposed legislation may also be placed on the ballot through the initiative procedure. For a constitutional amendment, petitions must be signed by at least 8% of the number of voters who took part in the last gubernatorial election; for statutory measures, 5%. In each case, a simple majority vote at the next general election is required for passage.

Officials elected statewide include the governor and lieutenant governor (who run separately), secretary of state, attorney general, controller, treasurer, and superintendent of public instruction. Each serves a four-year term. As chief executive officer of the state, the governor is responsible for the state's policies and programs, appoints department heads and members of state boards and commissions, serves as commander in chief of the California National Guard, may declare states of emergency, and may grant executive clemency to convicted criminals.

The lieutenant governor acts as president of the senate and may assume the duties of the governor in case of the latter's death, resignation, impeachment, inability to discharge the duties of the office, or absence from the state.

13 POLITICAL PARTIES

As the state with the largest number of US representatives (52 in 2000) and electoral votes (54) California plays a key role in national and presidential politics. As of 2000, California had 15,707,307 registered voters, including about 47% Democrat, 36% Republican, and 18% unaffiliated. Even with an advantage in voter registration, however, the Democrats managed to carry California in presidential elections only five times between 1948 and 2000. Also, during the same period only three Democratic governors— Edmund G. "Pat" Brown (in 1958 and 1962), his son, Edmund G. "Jerry" Brown, Jr. (in 1974 and 1978), and the current governor Gray Davis (1999-present) —were elected.

Three times Californians gave their presidential electoral votes to a California Republican, Richard Nixon, though they turned down his bid for governor in 1962. They elected one former film actor, Republican George Murphy, as US senator in 1964, and another actor, Republican Ronald Reagan, as governor in 1966 and 1970 and as president in 1980 and 1984. In the 2000 presidential election, Democrat Al Gore won 53% of the popular vote, while Republican challenger George W. Bush received 42%. Others received 4% of the votes.

Political third parties have had remarkable success in California since the days of the secretive, anti-foreign, anti-Catholic, Native American Party. The latter was called the Know-Nothing party because members were instructed to say they

California Presidential Vote by Political Parties, 1948–2000

Year	California Winner	Democrat	Republican	Progressive	Socialist	Prohibition
1948	*Truman (D)	1,913,134	1,895,269	190,381	3,459	16,926
					Soc. Labor	
1952	*Eisenhower (R)	2,197,548	2,897,310	24,692	273	16,117
1956	*Eisenhower (R)	2,420,135	3,027,668		300	11,119
1960	Nixon (R)	3,224,099	3,259,722		1,051	21,706
1964	*Johnson (D)	4,171,877	2,879,108		489	
					Peace/Freedom	
1968	*Nixon (R)	3,244,318	3,467,664		27,707	
				American	People's	Libertarian
1972	*Nixon (R)	3,475,847	4,602,096	232,554	55,167	980
				Communist		
1976	Ford (R)	3,742,284	3,882,244	12,766	41,731	56,388
				Citizens	Peace/Freedom	
1980	*Reagan (R)	3,039,532	4,444,044	9,687	60,059	17,797
1984	*Reagan (R)	3,922,519	5,467,009	New Alliance	26,297	49,951
1988	*Bush (R)	4,702,233	5,054,917	31,181		70,105
				Ind. (Perot)		
1992	*Clinton (D)	5,121,325	3,630,574	2,296,006	18,597	48,139
					Green (Nader)	
1996	*Clinton (D)	5,119,835	3,828,380	697,847	237,016	73,600
						Libertarian
2000	Al Gore (D)	5,861,203	4,567,429	418,707	28	45,520

*Won US presidential election.

"knew nothing" when asked what they stood for. They elected one of their leaders, J. Neely Johnson, as governor in 1855. The most impressive third-party triumph came in 1912, when the Progressive Party's presidential candidate, Theodore Roosevelt, and his vice-presidential nominee, Governor Hiram Johnson, defeated both the Republican and Democratic candidates among state voters. During the depression year of 1934, the Socialist Party leader and novelist Upton Sinclair won the Democratic nomination for governor on his "End Poverty In California" program. Sinclair received nearly a million votes while losing to Republican Frank Merriam.

Both Senators in 1999 were women: Democrat Barbara Boxer, who won reelection in 1998; and Democrat Dianne Feinstein, elected in 1992 to replace Senator Pete Wilson, who was elected Governor in 1990. Both Feinstein and Wilson won re-election in 1994. In 2000, California's delegation of US Representatives consisted of 32 Democrats and 20 Republicans. After a sixteen-year gap, Democrats regained the governorship in 1998 with the election of Lieutenant-Governor Gray Davis. The Democrats hold 26 state senate seats to the Republicans' 14, while the Democrats controlled the house with 50 seats to the Republicans' 30.

Minority groups of all types are represented in California politics. As of 1992, elected officials included 260 blacks and 682 Hispanics. In 2000, there were 34 women serving in the state legislature and in elective executive office. One of the most prominent black elected officials in the 1970s and 1980s was Los Angeles Mayor Thomas Bradley, who served from 1973–90. Organized groups of homosexuals became involved in San Francisco politics during the 1970s.

14 LOCAL GOVERNMENT

As of 1998, California had 57 counties, about 994 school districts, and 3,006 special districts. There were 471 municipal governments in 1998.

County government is administered by an elected board of supervisors. Government operations are administered by several elected officials, the number varying according to the population of the county. Most counties have a district attorney, assessor, treasurer-tax collector, superintendent of schools, sheriff, and coroner.

Municipalities are governed under the mayor-council, council-manager, or commission system. Most large cities are run by councils of from 5 to 15 members responsible for taxes, public improvements, and the budget. An elected mayor supervises city departments and appoints most city officials.

15 JUDICIAL SYSTEM

California has a complex judicial system and a very large correctional system. The state's highest court is the supreme court, which may review appeals court decisions and superior court cases involving the death penalty. The high court has a chief justice and six associate justices, all of whom serve 12-year terms.

Courts of appeal, organized in six districts, review decisions of superior courts and, in certain cases, of municipal and justice courts. There were 93 district appeals court judgeships in 1999.

Superior courts in each of the 58 county seats have original jurisdiction in felony, juvenile, probate, and domestic relations cases, as well as in civil cases involving more than $15,000. They also handle some tax and misdemeanor cases and appeals from lower courts. Municipal courts, located in judicial districts with populations of more than 40,000, hear misdemeanors (except those involving juveniles) and civil cases involving $15,000 or less. In districts with less than 40,000 population, justice courts have jurisdiction similar to that of municipal courts. All trial court judges are elected to six-year terms.

As of 1999 there were 164,523 prisoners in state and federal prisons in California, an increase of 2.5% from 1998. The State Department of Corrections maintains 32 state prisons and 38 minimum custody facilities in wilderness areas where inmates are trained to fight wildfires. According to the FBI, California's crime rate in 1998 was 4,342.8 crimes per 100,000 population. In that year, 1,418,674 crimes were reported to the police, including 229,883 violent crimes and 1,188,191 crimes against property.

16 MIGRATION

A majority of Californians today are migrants from other states. The first great wave of migration, the Gold Rush beginning in 1848, brought at least 85,000 prospectors by 1850. Many thousands of Chinese were brought in during the latter half of the 19th century to work on farms and railroads. When Chinese immigration was banned by the US Congress in 1882, Japanese migration provided farm labor. By 1940, about 94,000 Japanese lived in California.

During the depression of the 1930s, approximately 350,000 migrants came to California, most of them looking for work. Many thousands of people came there during World War II to take jobs in the growing war industries. After the war, some 300,000 discharged servicemen settled in the state. All told, between 1940 and 1990, California registered a net gain from migration of 12,426,000 people, representing well over half of its population growth during that period. During 1990–98, movement between the states resulted in a net loss of nearly 2.1 million residents, but this was offset by a net gain of 2 million from abroad. As of 1996, nearly 22% of all foreign immigrants in the US were living in California, a higher proportion than in any other state.

Although the 1970s brought an influx of refugees from Indochina, and, somewhat later, from Central America, the bulk of postwar foreign immigration has come from neighboring Mexico. Hundreds of thousands—perhaps even millions—of illegal Mexican immigrants have crossed the border in search of jobs and then, unless they were caught and deported (forcibly returned), stayed on. The federal government estimated in 1996 that there were 2 million illegal immigrants living in California.

In 1996, California admitted 201,529 foreign immigrants (more than any other state and 22% of the US total that year), including 64,238 Mexicans. Counting these state residents for census purposes is extremely difficult, since many of them are unwilling to declare themselves for fear of being identified and deported. As of 1996, California's foreign-born population was estimated at 8 million, or 25% of the state's total.

Intrastate (within California) migration has followed two general patterns: rural to urban until the mid-20th century, and urban to suburban after that. In particular, the percentage of blacks increased in Los Angeles, San Francisco, and San Diego between 1960 and 1970. This occurred as black people settled or remained in the cities while whites moved into the surrounding suburbs. By 1990, 46.4% of all state residents had been born in California.

17 ECONOMY

California leads the 50 states in economic output and total personal income. The state ranks first in the US in such important industries as food products, machinery, electric and electronic equipment, aerospace, dairy production, and beef cattle. California also leads the nation in retail sales, foreign trade, and corporate profits.

The Gold Rush of the mid-19th century made mining the principal economic activity and gave impetus to agriculture and manufacturing. Many unsuccessful miners took up farming or went to work for the big cattle ranches and wheat growers. In the 1870s, California became the most important cattle-raising state and the second-leading wheat producer. Manufacturing outstripped both mining and agriculture to produce goods valued at $258 million by 1900, and ten times that by 1925. Thanks to a rapidly growing work force, industrial output continued to expand during and after both world wars, while massive irrigation projects enabled farmers to make full use of the state's rich soil and favorable climate.

By the late 1970s, one of every four California workers was employed in high-technology industry. California has long ranked first among the states in defense-related manufacturing, and by the mid-1980s, contracts awarded to California firms surpassed the combined totals of New York and Texas.

From its beginnings in the late 18th century, California's wine industry has grown to encompass some 500 wineries. By the early 1980s, they accounted for about 90% of total US production. By the mid-1980s, California had surpassed Chicago to rank second in advertising among the states.

Its highly diversified economy makes California less sensitive to national recessions than most other states. During the first half of the 1980s, the state generally outperformed the national economy. The boom was short-lived, however. Cuts in the military budget in the late 1980s, a decline in Japanese investment, and the national recession in the early 1990s had a devastating impact on the state, particularly on southern California. The aero-

Photo credit: Robert Holmes.

Vineyards in the Carneros District, Napa Valley.

space and construction industries were especially hit hard with job losses.

In 1994, private goods-producing industries accounted for 20% of the state's total economic output, private services-producing industries for 68%, and government for 12%.

18 INCOME

With a per capita (per person) income of $28,163 in 1998, California ranked 15th among the 50 states. Total personal income was $920 billion. The median household income in 1998 was $40,522. Despite California's relatively high average personal income, however, over 16% of the state's residents lived below the federal poverty level in 1998. At the other end of the spectrum, California is justly noted for its large number of wealthy residents, particularly in the Los Angeles, Sacramento, and San Francisco metropolitan areas.

19 INDUSTRY

California is the nation's leading industrial state, ranking first in almost every general manufacturing category: number of establishments, number of employees, total payroll, value of shipments, and new capital spending. California ranks among the leaders in machinery, fabricated metals, agricultural products, food processing, computers, aerospace technology, and many other industries.

Computers and aerospace manufacturers stand out among California's largest publicly owned corporations. Hewlett-Packard, Sun Microsystems, Tandem Computers, Varian Associates, and Silicon Graphics are leading names of the Silicon Valley (Santa Clara County) area just south of San Francisco. Southern California's manufacturing leaders are Rockwell International, Lockheed, Northrop, and Computers Sciences.

California's motion-picture producing industry is based primarily in Los Angeles. A 1999 research report shows the film and TV production industry generating an annual payroll of 13.4 billion, paying $14.6 billion to suppliers, and providing jobs to 475,000 Californians.

20 LABOR

California has the largest work force in the nation and the greatest number of employed workers. In mid-1998, the state's civilian labor force totaled 16.32 million, of whom 5.9% were unemployed.

During the 1960s, a Mexican-American laborer named César Chávez established the National Farm Workers Association (now the United Farm Workers of America). After a long struggle, this union won bargaining rights from grape, lettuce, and berry growers in the San Joaquin Valley. Chávez's group was helped by a secondary boycott against these California farm products throughout the US. As of 1996, there were 162,000 farm laborers in California. About 17.7% of all workers in California belonged to a labor union in 1995.

21 AGRICULTURE

California leads the 50 states in agricultural production, with over 250 crop and livestock commodities. Famous for its specialty crops, California produces practically all the almonds, artichokes, avocados, clovers, dates, figs, kiwifruit, olives, persimmons, pistachios, prunes, raisins, and English walnuts grown commercially in the US.

Nearly one-third of California's total land area was devoted to farming in 1998, when some 89,000 farms comprised about 28.5 million acres (11.5 million hectares). The ten leading cash crops in 1998 were grapes (used for raisins, and especially for wine), greenhouse and nursery products, cotton lint, lettuce, almonds, hay, tomatoes, flowers and foliage, strawberries, and oranges. California leads the nation in agricultural exports.

Irrigation is essential for farming in California, and agriculture consumes 28% of the state's annual water supply. The major irrigation systems include the Colorado River Project, the Central Valley Project, the Feather River Project, and, largest of all, the California Water Project.

22 DOMESTICATED ANIMALS

California is a leading producer of livestock and dairy products. In 1999 there were 5 million cattle and calves valued at $4.1 billion. There were 210,000 hogs and pigs on California farms in 1998, valued at $12.8 million.

In 1997 California was the leading milk producer among the 50 states, with 27.6 billion pounds (12.5 billion kilograms) of milk produced. Milk cows, raised mainly in the southern interior, totaled 1.32 million head in 1997. The state of California ranks first in egg production, and second in honey production.

23 FISHING

The Pacific whaling industry, with its chief port at San Francisco, was important to the California economy in the 19th century, and commercial fishing is still central to the food-processing industry. In 1998, California ranked sixth in the US in commercial fishing, with a catch of 336.1 million pounds (152.4 million kilograms), valued at $110.7 million. In 1998, principal species caught included squid; dungeness crab, 10.6 million pounds (4.8 million kilograms); shrimp, 3.2 million pounds (1.4 million kilograms); salmon, 2.1 million pounds (.9 million kilograms); sablefish, 3.2 million pounds (1.4 million kilograms); and jack mackerel.

Deep-sea fishing is a popular sport. World records for giant sea bass, California halibut, white catfish, and sturgeon have been set in California. In 1998, there were over 2.6 licensed recreational fishers in the state. In 1997, an estimated 905,000 people went fishing off the coast of southern California, and 581,000 fished off the northern coast of the state.

24 FORESTRY

California has more forests than any other state except Alaska. In 1997, forests covered 38.5 million acres (15.6 million hectares). Nearly 41% of the state's forested area is used to produce commercial timber. Forests are concentrated in the northwest-

ern part of the state and in the eastern Sierra Nevada.

About half of the state's forests are protected as national forests and state parks or recreational areas. Although California's giant redwood trees have been preserved in national and state parks since the late 19th century, only about 46% remain of the original 2,000,000 acres (800,000 hectares) of redwoods between Monterey Bay and southern Oregon.

As of 1999, there were 21 national forests with all or part of their acreage in California. Total area within their boundaries amounted to 24.2 million acres (9.8 million hectares), of which 85% is National Forest System land.

25 MINING

According to data compiled by the US Geological Survey, California was the second leading state in the nation in the value of nonfuel minerals produced during 1998, accounting for over 7% of the US total. The value of the nonfuel mineral commodities produced in the state during the year was estimated to be $2.97 billion. The principal minerals produced are portland cement, sand and gravel, boron minerals, and crushed stone. California leads all other states in the production of boron minerals (613,000 metric tons, valued at $440 million) and portland cement (10.6 million metric tons, worth $747 million).

26 ENERGY AND POWER

Petroleum supplies an estimated 42% of the state's energy needs; natural gas, 26%; coal, 1%; nuclear power, 4%; and hydroelectric power, 6%. California ranks sixth among the 50 states in production of electric power, fourth in oil, and tenth in natural gas. Despite its ample energy resources, California is a net importer of electric power because of its heavy industrial, residential, and commercial requirements.

In 1998, electrical output totaled 114.9 billion kilowatt hours. About 42% was generated from hydroelectric plants, 23% from natural gas, less than 1% from oil, 30% from nuclear power plants, and about 5% from geothermal, coal, and other sources.

In 1998, sales of electric power in the state totaled 223.7 billion kilowatt hours, of which 30% went to commercial businesses, 33% to home consumers, 27% to industries, and 10% to other users. Largely because of the mild California climate, utility bills are lower than in many other states. Per capita (per person) energy consumption in California was 241.6 million Btu, 48th among the states.

California's proved oil reserves in 1999 were estimated at more than 3.8 billion barrels, nearly 18% of the US total and third behind Alaska and Texas. In 1999 petroleum production totaled 273 million barrels, representing 13% of the domestic output. Production of natural gas totaled 315.3 billion cubic feet, 1.6% of the US total, and proved reserves were nearly 2.2 trillion cubic feet 1.4% of the national total. Nearly all the coal (90%) consumed for electric power generation is shipped in from other states.

California has been a leader in developing solar and geothermal power as alterna-tives to fossil fuels. State tax credits encourage the installation of solar energy devices in commercial and residential property. Geothermal, wind, and solar energy electricity generation amounted to 5.1 billion kilowatts in 1998, or nearly 4.4% of the total electricity generation for the state. Over 73% of the geothermal, wind, and solar electric capacity nationally comes from California.

California's Energy Crisis

Beginning in 2000, California experienced serious power shortages. There was not enough electricity to supply homes and businesses in the state, so utility companies conserved power by cutting back on electricity for differenct communities. This was called "rolling blackouts" because one town's electricity might be cut back for the morning while the neighboring town would experience power cutbacks in the afternoon. The governor, Gray Davis, was forced to consider government action to help utility companies find enough electricity.

27 COMMERCE

The state's retail sales exceed $91 billion in 1997. Food stores, automobile dealers, general merchandise stores, and eating and drinking places were the leading retail sales sectors. Retail sales in the Los Angeles-Riverside-Orange County area amounted to 48% of the state's total and 5.7% of the national total. Retail sales in the San Francisco-Oakland-San Jose area accounted for 23.4% of the state's retail sales and 2.8% of US retail sales. Wholesale trade sales were $432.9 billion, first in the nation.

Foreign trade is important to the California economy. Goods exported from California were valued at $116 billion in 1998. Leading exports include data-processing equipment, electrical tubes and transistors, scientific equipment, measuring instruments, optical equipment, aircraft parts, and spacecraft. California's leading agricultural export is cotton.

San Francisco and San Jose have been designated as federal foreign-trade zones, where imported goods may be stored duty-free for reshipment abroad, or customs duties avoided until the goods are actually marketed in the US.

28 PUBLIC FINANCE

California's general budget is the largest of all the states in both expenditures and revenues. The state's public finances became the focus of national attention when, on 6 June 1978, California voters approved Proposition 13, a constitutional amendment that reduced local property taxes by more than 50%. As a result of Proposition 13, government employment was reduced by 30,000 as of November 1978 and drastic cuts were made in the state's budget surplus for 1979/80 and future years.

The state budget is prepared by the Department of Finance and presented by the governor to the state legislature for approval. Consolidated state revenues for 1997 totaled $131.1 billion, and state expenditures were $117.2 billion.

California's total public debt exceeded $45.3 billion, or $1,405 per person as of 1997. The total debt amount is second only to New York State's.

29 TAXATION

In the mid-1970s, Californians were paying more in taxes than residents of any other state, but this heavy tax burden was reduced by the passage in 1978 of Proposition 13. The state ranked 12th in federal tax burden per capita (per person) in 1990. In the same year, California's revenues from state taxes and fees totaled more than $44.8 billion. An income tax credit is available for installing solar energy systems in the home.

The state income tax ranges from 0% to 9.3% on net taxable income, with credits available for low-income residents. The state sales tax as of 1997 was 7.25% on retail sales (excepting food for home consumption, prescription medicines, gas, water, electricity, and certain other exempt products). Localities derive most of their revenue from property taxes, which were limited in 1978 by Proposition 13 to 1% of market value, with annual increases in the tax not to exceed 2%. The drastic revision reduced property tax collections by about 57% to an estimated $4.9 billion in the 1978/79 fiscal year.

In 1995, California bore a heavier share of the federal tax burden than any other state, contributing $163 billion in federal taxation. But California also received more federal expenditures than any other state—$152.5 billion, for a net benefit of $10.5 billion.

30 HEALTH

California ranked below the national death rate in 1996 for six of the leading causes of death. Principal causes of deaths and their rates per 100,000 population during 1996 included: heart disease, 214; cancer, 160.2; cerebrovascular diseases, 51.9; pulmonary diseases, 35.8; pneumonia and influenza, 35; and accidents, 29.8. Through 1999, California recorded 115,366 AIDS cases, second only after New York.

In 1998, California's 405 general-care hospitals had 74,482 beds. The average hospital stay costs more in California than the national average. In 1998 there were 9,032 nonfederal licensed physicians per 100,000 population and 63,560 active registered nurses.

Medi-Cal is a statewide program that pays for the medical care of persons who otherwise could not afford it. California has been a leader in developing new forms of health care, including the health maintenance organization (HMO), which provides preventive care, diagnosis, and treatment for which the patient pays a fixed annual premium. In 1998, 22.1% of California's residents did not have health insurance.

31 HOUSING

California ranks high nationwide in the number of housing units (11.7 million in 1996). Between 1960 and 1990, some 6.3 million houses and apartments were built in the state, comprising more than 56% of California housing stock. In 1996, 91,910 housing units were authorized for construction, and 505,200 existing single-family housing units were sold.

The earliest homes in southern California were Spanish colonial structures renowned for their simplicity and harmony with the landscape. The fusion of Spanish adobe structures and traditional American wooden construction appeared in the 1930s, and "California style" houses gained great popularity throughout the West. Adapted from the functional international style of Frank Lloyd Wright and other innovative architects, modern domestic designs emphasizing split-level surfaces and open interiors won enthusiastic acceptance in California. Wright's finest California homes include the Freeman house in Los Angeles and the Millard house in Pasadena.

In 1990, California had 856,165 condominiums, more than any other state except Florida. California also was second to Florida in 1990 in the number of mobile homes, or trailers, at 556,411. The median monthly cost for a mortgaged, owner-occupied housing unit in 1990 was $1,077; the median monthly rent for a housing unit was $620.

32 EDUCATION

California ranks first among the states in enrollment in public schools and in institutions of higher learning.

In 1998, almost 80% of the state's adult population had completed four years of high school. In addition, about 1.96 million Californians were enrolled in

Embarcadero Wharf in San Francisco.

institutions of higher learning, minorities representing 49.3% of total enrollment.

Enrollment in California's public schools was estimated to be 6.1 million in fall 2000. Kindergarten through grade 8 had 4.1 million pupils, and grades 9 through 12 had 1.6 million pupils. Enrollment in private schools in 1997 was 576,047.

Expenditures for public elementary and secondary schools amounted to $4,896 per student in 1995/96 (36th among the states). In 1997, there were 594 Roman Catholic elementary schools with 176,133 pupils and 101 Roman Catholic high schools with 65,768 pupils. In 1996, some 590,000 students participated in

special education programs, at a cost of about $3.4 billion.

The University of California has its main campus at Berkeley and branches at Davis, Irvine, Los Angeles (UCLA), Riverside, San Diego, San Francisco, Santa Barbara, and Santa Cruz. California's 19 state universities include those at Los Angeles, Sacramento, San Diego, San Francisco, and San Jose; state colleges are located at Bakersfield, San Bernardino, and Stanislaus.

Privately endowed institutions with the largest student enrollments are the University of Southern California (USC), with 28,185 students in 1994, and Stanford University (16,049). California has 16

Roman Catholic colleges and universities, including Loyola Marymount University of Los Angeles.

33 ARTS

The arts have always thrived in California. They first appeared in the Franciscan chapels with their religious paintings and church music, later in the art galleries, gas-lit theaters, and opera houses of San Francisco and Los Angeles, and today in seaside artists' colonies, regional theaters, numerous concert halls, and, not least, in the motion-picture studios of Hollywood. The motion-picture industry did not begin in Hollywood—the first commercial films were made in New York City and New Jersey in the 1890s—but within a few decades this Los Angeles suburb had become synonymous with the new art form. In the 1960s, Hollywood replaced New York City as the main center for the production of television programs.

Many gifted composers—including Irving Berlin, George Gershwin, and Kurt Weill—went to Hollywood to write film music. In addition, a number of famed musicians fleeing Europe during the Nazi era, such as composers Igor Stravinsky and Arnold Schoenberg, were longtime residents of the state. Symphony orchestras include the renowned Los Angeles Philharmonic, the San Francisco Symphony, and professional orchestras in Oakland and San Jose. Resident opera companies perform regularly in San Francisco and San Diego. Annual musical events include the Monterey Jazz Festival and summer concerts at the Hollywood Bowl.

California has also played a major role in the evolution of popular music since the 1960s. The "surf sound" of the Beach Boys dominated California pop music in the mid-1960s. By 1967, "acid rock" bands such as the Grateful Dead, the Jefferson Airplane (later Jefferson Starship, and then Starship), and the Doors began to gain national recognition. During the 1970s, California was strongly identified with a group of resident singer-songwriters, including Neil Young, Joni Mitchell, Randy Newman, and Jackson Browne. Los Angeles is a main center of the popular-music industry, with numerous recording studios and branch offices of the leading record companies.

California has nurtured generations of writers, many of whom moved there from other states. In 1864, Mark Twain, a Missourian, came to California as a newspaperman. The writer perhaps most strongly associated with California is Nobel Prize-winner John Steinbeck, a Salinas native. Hollywood's film industry has long been a magnet for writers. San Francisco in the 1950s was the gathering place for a group, later known as the Beats (or "Beat Generation"), that included Jack Kerouac and Allen Ginsberg. The City Lights Bookshop, owned by poet Lawrence Ferlinghetti, was the site of readings by Beat poets during this period.

A California law, effective 1 January 1977, was the first in the nation to provide living artists with royalties on the profitable resale of their work. By 1996, arts associations in California numbered 1,400

'Olympiad 1984' sculpture in front of Stuart Ketchum Hall in Los Angeles.

with 230 local programs for the promotion of the arts.

34 LIBRARIES AND MUSEUMS

As of 1998, California had 171 main public libraries and 516 academic libraries that held a total of 121.5 million volumes. In that same year, the book stock was nearly 61.1 million volumes.

California has three of the largest public library systems in the nation, along with some of the country's finest private collections. The Los Angeles Public Library System had 5.8 million volumes in 1998; the San Diego Public Library, 2.6 million; and the San Francisco Public Library, 2.1 million. Outstanding among academic libraries is the University of California's library at Berkeley, with its Bancroft collection of western Americana.

California has nearly 576 museums and 50 public gardens. Outstanding museums include the California Museum of Science and Industry, Los Angeles County Museum of Art, and Natural History Museum, all in Los Angeles; San Francisco's Museum of Modern Art, Fine Arts Museum, and Asian Art Museum; the San Diego Museum of Man; the California State Indian Museum in Sacramento; the

Norton Simon Museum in Pasadena; and the J. Paul Getty Museum at Malibu.

35 COMMUNICATIONS

The state's first radio broadcasting station, KQW in San Jose, began broadcasting speech and music on an experimental basis in 1912. California stations pioneered in program development with the earliest audience-participation show (1922) and the first "soap opera," *One Man's Family* (1932).

California ranks first in the US in the number of commercial television stations, and second only to Texas in the number of radio stations. In 2000 there were 253 AM and 507 FM radio stations and 138 television stations (including 18 public stations). Los Angeles alone had 15 television stations, including 4 that broadcast in Spanish. Affiliates of the Public Broadcasting System serve Los Angeles, San Francisco, and Sacramento. California has more telephones than any other state. In 1999, 95.7% of the state's occupied housing units had telephones. A total of 1.5 million Internet domain names were registered in the year 2000, the most of any state.

36 PRESS

California's newspapers rank first in number and second in circulation among the 50 states. Los Angeles publishes one of the nation's most influential dailies, the *Los Angeles Times,* and San Francisco has long been the heart of the influential Hearst newspaper chain.

In 1998 there were 66 morning dailies and 27 evening dailies, plus 59 Sunday newspapers. The *Los Angeles Times* is the only California paper whose daily circulation exceeds 1 million. California's leading newspapers, with 1998 daily circulation figures are the *Los Angeles Times* (1,067,540); the *San Francisco Chronicle* (475,324); the *San Diego Union Tribune* (378,112); and the *San Jose Mercury-News* (290,885).

California has more book publishers—about 225—than any state except New York. Among the many magazines published in the state are *Architectural Digest, Bon Appetit, Motor Trend, PC World, Runner's World,* and *Sierra.*

37 TOURISM, TRAVEL, AND RECREATION

California's scenic wonders attract millions of state residents, out-of-state visitors, and foreign tourists each year.

The San Francisco and Los Angeles metropolitan areas offer the most popular tourist attractions. San Francisco's Fisherman's Wharf, Chinatown, and Ghirardelli Square are popular for shopping and dining. Tourists also frequent the city's unique cable cars, splendid museums, Opera House, and Golden Gate Bridge. The Golden Gate National Recreation Area comprises 68 square miles (176 square kilometers) on both sides of the entrance to San Francisco Bay and includes the National Maritime Museum with seven historic ships, and the Muir Woods, located 17 miles (27 kilometers) north of the city.

The Los Angeles area has the state's principal tourist attractions. These include the Disneyland amusement center at Anaheim, and Hollywood, which features visits to motion-picture and television studios and sight-seeing tours of film stars' homes in Beverly Hills. One of Hollywood's most popular spots is Mann's (formerly Grauman's) Chinese Theater, where the impressions of famous movie stars' hands and feet (and sometimes paws or hooves) are embedded in concrete. Southwest of Hollywood, the Santa Monica Mountain National Recreation Area was created by Congress in 1978 as the country's largest urban park, covering 150,000 acres (61,000 hectares).

The rest of the state offers numerous tourist attractions. These include Redwood, Yosemite, and Sequoia national parks—some of the largest and most beautiful parks in the US—and Lake Tahoe, on the Nevada border. The state's 21 national parks had 34.6 million visitors in 1996, and tourism is the third largest employer.

38 SPORTS

There are 35 professional sports teams in California, more than in any other state. The state's five baseball teams are the Los Angeles Dodgers, the San Francisco Giants, the San Diego Padres, the Oakland Athletics, and the Anaheim Angels. Football teams are the Oakland Raiders, the San Francisco 49ers, and the San Diego Chargers. The Los Angeles Lakers, the Los Angeles Clippers, the Golden State Warriors, and the Sacramento Kings play in the National Basketball Association, while the Los Angeles Sparks and Sacramento Monarchs play in the Women's National Basketball Association. In hockey, there are the Los Angeles Kings, the Anaheim Mighty Ducks, and the San Jose Sharks. The Los Angeles Galaxy and San Jose Clash play in Major League Soccer.

Another popular professional sport is horse racing at such well-known tracks as Santa Anita and Hollywood Park. Because of the moderate climate, there is racing practically year round. In 1996, track attendance was over 10.8 million.

California's collegiate teams have been very successful. The University of Southern California's baseball team won five consecutive national championships between 1970 and 1974. Its football team has won the Rose Bowl 20 times, most recently in 1996. The UCLA basketball team has won 10 NCAA titles.

39 FAMOUS CALIFORNIANS

Richard Milhous Nixon (1913–94) is the only native-born Californian ever elected to the presidency. Elected to his first term in 1968, he scored a resounding reelection victory four years later, but within a year his administration was beset by the Watergate scandal. On 9 August 1974, after the House Judiciary Committee had voted articles of impeachment, Nixon became the first president ever to resign the office.

The nation's 31st president, Herbert Hoover (b.Iowa, 1874–1964), moved to California as a young man. Former film actor Ronald Reagan (b.Illinois, 1911) served two terms as state governor (1967–75) before becoming president in 1981.

Elaine L. Chao (1954–) became the first Asian American woman appointed to a President's cabinet in U.S. history. She was confirmed as Secretary of Labor by the United States Senate on January 29, 2001.

He was elected to a second presidential term in 1984.

In 1953, Earl Warren (1891–1974) became the first Californian to serve as chief justice of the US Supreme Court (1953–69). Warren, a native of Los Angeles, was elected three times to the California governorship and served in that office (1943–53) longer than any other person.

Californians have won Nobel Prizes in several categories. Linus Pauling (b.Ore-gon, 1901–94) won the Nobel Prize for chemistry in 1954 and the Nobel Peace Prize in 1962.

The leading figure among the state's newspaper editors and publishers was William Randolph Hearst (1863–1951), whose publishing empire began with the *San Francisco Examiner.* Pioneers of the state's electronics industry include David Packard (b.Colorado, 1912–96) and William R. Hewlett (b.Michigan, 1913). Stephen Wozniak (b.1950) and Steven Jobs (b.1955) were cofounders of Apple Computer. Other prominent business leaders include clothier Levi Strauss (b.Germany, 1830–1902) and cosmetics manufacturer Max Factor (b.Poland, 1877–1938).

California has been home to a great many creative artists. John Steinbeck (1902–68), the only native-born Californian to win the Nobel Prize for literature in 1962. Other native California writers include adventure writer Jack London (1876–1916), novelist and dramatist William Saroyan (1908–81), and novelist-essayist Joan Didion (b.1934). One California-born writer whose life and works were divorced from his place of birth was Robert Frost (1874–1963), a native of San Francisco.

Important composers who have lived and worked in California include native John Cage (1912–92), and immigrants Arnold Schoenberg (b.Austria, 1874–1951) and Igor Stravinsky (b.Russia, 1882–1971). Immigrant painters include landscape artist Albert Bierstadt (b.Germany, 1830–1902),

Former film actor Ronald Reagan (b.Illinois, 1911) served two terms as state governor (1967–75) before becoming president in 1981. He is shown here giving a speech at the Berlin Wall, Brandenburg Gate, in the Federal Republic of Germany on June 12, 1987. Reagan is given credit for helping to end the Cold War.

as well as abstract painter Hans Hofmann (b.Germany, 1880–1966).

Native Californians on the screen include child actress Shirley Temple (Mrs. Charles A. Black, b.1928) and such greats as Marilyn Monroe (Norma Jean Baker, 1926–62). Other longtime residents of the state include John Wayne (Marion Michael Morrison, b.Iowa, 1907–79),

Bette Davis (b.Massachusetts, 1908–89), and Clark Gable (b.Ohio, 1901–60).

California-born athletes have excelled in every professional sport. A representative sampling includes Baseball Hall of Famer Joe DiMaggio (1914–99), along with Richard A. "Pancho" Gonzales (1928–95) and Billie Jean (Moffitt) King (b.1943) in tennis, Frank Gifford (b.1930)

in football, and Mark Spitz (b.1950) in swimming. Robert B. "Bob" Mathias (b.1930) won the gold medal in the decathlon at the 1948 and 1952 Olympic Games.

40 BIBLIOGRAPHY

Green, Carl R. *The California Trail to Gold in American History.* Berkeley Heights, N.J.: Enslow, 2000.

Harder, Dan. *A Child's California.* Portland, Ore.: WestWinds, 2000.

Lommel, Cookie. *James Oglethorpe.* Philadelphia, Penn.: Chelsea House, 2000.

McAuliffe, Emily. *California Facts and Symbols.* New York: Hilltop Books, 1998.

Parker, Janice. *California.* Mankato, Minn.: Weigl, 2000.

Rawls, James J. *Indians of California: The Changing Image.* Norman: University of Oakland, 1984.

Schroeder, Lisa Golden. *California Gold Rush Cooking.* Mankato, Minn.: Blue Earth, 2001.

Stanley, Jerry. *Hurry Freedom: African Americans in Gold Rush California.* New York: Crown, 2000.

Web sites

California Travel & Tourism. Travel & Vacations [Online] Available http://gocalif.ca.gov/ Accessed May 31, 2001.

COLORADO

State of Colorado

ORIGIN OF STATE NAME: From the Spanish word *colorado,* meaning red or reddish brown. The Colorado River often runs red during flood stages.

NICKNAME: The Centennial State.

CAPITAL: Denver.

ENTERED UNION: 1 August 1876 (38th).

SONG: "Where the Columbines Grow."

MOTTO: *Nil sine numine* (Nothing without providence).

COAT OF ARMS: The upper portion of a heraldic shield shows three snow-capped mountains surrounded by clouds; the lower portion has a miner's pick and shovel, crossed. Above the shield are an eye of God and a Roman fasces, symbolizing the republican form of government; the state motto is below.

FLAG: Superimposed on three equal horizontal hands of blue, white, and blue is a large red "C" encircling a golden disk.

OFFICIAL SEAL: The coat of arms surrounded by the words "State of Colorado 1876."

ANIMAL: Rocky Mountain bighorn sheep.

BIRD: Lark bunting.

FISH: Greenback cutthroat trout.

FLOWER: Rocky Mountain columbine.

TREE: Colorado blue spruce.

GEM: Aquamarine.

TIME: 5 AM MST = noon GMT.

1 LOCATION AND SIZE

Located in the Rocky Mountain region of the US, Colorado ranks eighth in size among the 50 states. The state's total area is 104,091 square miles (269,596 square kilometers). Shaped in an almost perfect rectangle, Colorado extends 387 miles (623 kilometers) east-west and 276 miles (444 kilometers) north-south. The total length of Colorado's boundaries is 1,307 miles (2,103 kilometers).

2 TOPOGRAPHY

With an average elevation of 6,800 feet (2,100 meters), Colorado is the nation's highest state. Dominating the state are the Rocky Mountains. Colorado has 54 peaks that are 14,000 feet (4,300 meters) or higher, including Pikes Peak, at 14,110 feet (4,301 meters). The eastern third of the state is part of the western Great Plains and contains Colorado's lowest point, 3,350 feet (1,021 meters). Slightly west of the state's geographic center is the Continental Divide, which separates the Rockies into the Eastern and Western slopes. South of the Front Range, crossing into New Mexico, is the Sangre de Cristo Range. Colorado's western region is mostly mesa country—broad, flat plateaus accented by deep ravines and gorges.

Blue Mesa Reservoir in Gunnison County is Colorado's largest lake. The Colorado River runs southwest from the Rockies to Utah. Five other major river systems originate in Colorado: the South Platte; the North Platte; the Rio Grande; the Arkansas; and the Republican. Eighteen hot springs are still active in Colorado; the largest is at Pagosa Springs.

3 CLIMATE

Colorado has a highland continental climate. Winters are generally cold and snowy; summers are characterized by warm, dry days and cool nights. The average annual temperature statewide ranges from 54°F (12°C) at Lamar and at John Martin Dam to about 32°F (0°C) at the top of the Continental Divide. Bennett recorded the highest temperature in Colorado, 118°F (48°C), on 11 July 1888; the record low was –61°F (–52°C), in Moffat County on 1 February 1985. Annual precipitation ranges from a low of 7 inches (18 centimeters) in Alamosa to a high of 25 inches (64 centimeters) in Crested Butte. The average annual precipitation statewide is 16.5 inches.

4 PLANTS AND ANIMALS

Colorado has a variety of vegetation, distributed among five zones: plains, foothills,

Colorado Population Profile

Total population in 2000:	4,301,261
Population change, 1990–2000:	30.6%
Hispanic or Latino†:	17.1%
Population by race	
One race:	97.2%
White:	82.8%
Black or African American:	3.8%
American Indian/Alaska Native:	1.0%
Asian:	2.2%
Native Hawaiian/Pacific Islander:	0.1%
Some other race:	7.2%
Two or more races:	2.8%

Population by Age Group

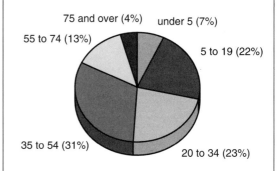

75 and over (4%) under 5 (7%)
55 to 74 (13%)
5 to 19 (22%)
35 to 54 (31%)
20 to 34 (23%)

Top Cities by Population

City	Population	% change 1990–2000
Denver	554,636	18.6
Colorado Springs	360,890	28.4
Aurora	276,393	24.4
Lakewood	144,126	14.0
Fort Collins	118,652	35.2
Arvada	102,153	14.5
Pueblo	102,121	3.5
Westminster	100,940	35.3
Boulder	94,673	13.6
Thornton	82,384	49.7

Notes: †A person of Hispanic or Latino origin may be of any race. NA indicates that data are not available.
Sources: U.S. Census Bureau. Public Information Office. *Demographic Profiles.* [Online] Available http://www.census.gov/Press-Release/www/2001/demoprofile.html. Accessed June 1, 2001. U.S. Census Bureau. *Census 2000: Redistricting Data.* Press release issued by the Redistricting Data Office. Washington, D.C., March, 2001.

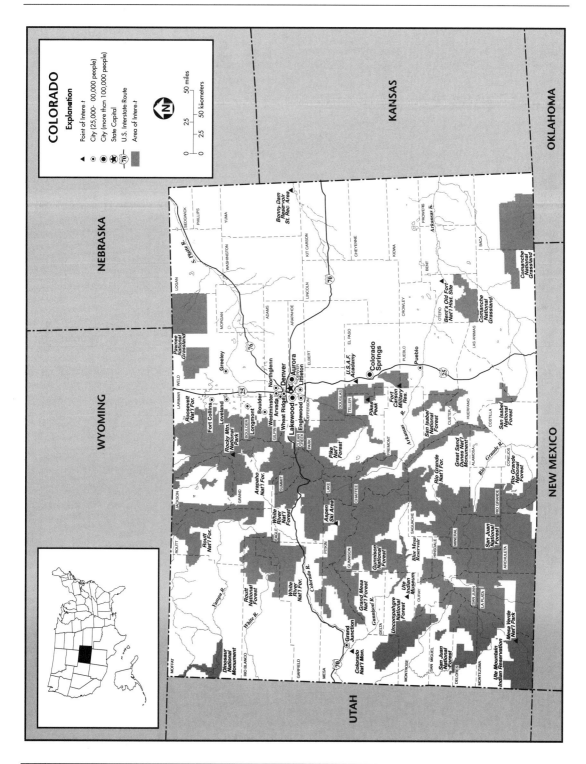

montane, subalpine, and alpine. The plains teem with grasses and as many as 500 types of wildflowers. Arid regions contain two dozen varieties of cacti. Aspen and Engelmann spruce are found up to the timberline.

Colorado has 747 nongame wildlife species and 113 sport-game species. Principal big-game species include the elk, mountain lion, and Rocky Mountain bighorn sheep (the state animal). The lark bunting is the state bird. Colorado has about 100 sport-fish species. In 1997, 17 species were listed as either endangered or threatened: the bald eagle, grizzly bear, wolverine, river otter, and whooping crane are among them.

5 ENVIRONMENTAL PROTECTION

Air pollution, water supply problems, and hazardous wastes head the list of Colorado's current environmental concerns. A motor vehicle emissions inspection system was inaugurated in January 1982 for gasoline-powered vehicles and in January 1985 for diesel-powered vehicles. Cars must use oxygenated fuels and pass tough vehicle emissions controls, and driving is discouraged on high pollution days. The use of woodburning fireplaces is banned in some cities during high pollution days. Some 98% of Colorado's drinking water complies with federal and state standards. There were 17 hazardous waste sites in the state as of 1998.

6 POPULATION

Colorado was the 24th most populous state in 2000. That year, population was estimated at 4.3 million. The population density in 2000 was 41.5 persons per square mile (16 per square kilometer), much less than the national average of 79.6 per square mile (30.7 per square kilometer). The estimated median age that year was 34.3 years (one year younger than the national average). The population in 2005 is projected to be 4.5 million.

Denver is the state's largest city, and 25th largest in the nation in 2000. Its population was 554,636. Populations of other cities in 2000 were Colorado Springs, 360,890; Aurora, 276,393; Lakewood, 144,126; and Fort Collins, 118,652.

7 ETHNIC GROUPS

Once the sole inhabitants of the state, Native Americans in 1997 were estimated at 89,900, or 0.9% of the state's population. There were 303 Eskimos and 67 Aleuts in 1990. The black population in 1997 was estimated at 4.3% (the figure for Denver, however, was about 13%). Hispanic residents numbered 556,000, comprising nearly 14.3% of the population (7th highest rate among the states). There were an estimated 89,900 Asians and Pacific Islanders in 1997 (2.3%), primarily Japanese, Koreans, Vietnamese, Chinese, and Filipinos.

8 LANGUAGES

Colorado English is a mixture of the Northern and Midland dialects. In the southern half of the state, the large Hispanic population has introduced many Spanish words, such as *arroyo* (gulley), into the language. About 2.7 million

Colorado Population by Race

Census 2000 was the first national census in which the instructions to respondents said, "Mark one or more races." This table shows the number of people who are of one, two, or three or more races. For those claiming two races, the number of people belonging to the various categories is listed. The U.S. government conducts a census of the population every ten years.

	Number	Percent
Total population	4,301,261	100.0
One race	4,179,074	97.2
Two races	114,612	2.7
White *and* Black or African American	13,426	0.3
White *and* American Indian/Alaska Native	24,795	0.6
White *and* Asian	16,234	0.4
White *and* Native Hawaiian/Pacific Islander	1,735	—
White *and* some other race	42,383	1.0
Black or African American *and* American Indian/Alaska Native	2,486	0.1
Black or African American *and* Asian	1,518	—
Black or African American *and* Native Hawaiian/Pacific Islander	291	—
Black or African American *and* some other race	3,876	0.1
American Indian/Alaska Native *and* Asian	637	—
American Indian/Alaska Native *and* Native Hawaiian/Pacific Islander	107	—
American Indian/Alaska Native *and* some other race	2,946	0.1
Asian *and* Native Hawaiian/Pacific Islander	1,234	—
Asian *and* some other race	2,534	0.1
Native Hawaiian/Pacific Islander *and* some other race	410	—
Three or more races	7,575	0.2

Source: U.S. Census Bureau. *Census 2000: Redistricting Data.* Press release issued by the Redistricting Data Office. Washington, D.C., March, 2001. A dash (—) indicates that the percent is less than 0.1.

Coloradans—89% of the residents five years old and older—speak only English at home.

9 RELIGIONS

Roman Catholics comprise the single largest religious group in the state, with over 483,000 adherents. The largest Protestant denomination is the United Methodist Church, with 91,310 members. Other denominations include Southern Baptist, 81,627; Presbyterian, 50,831; Lutheran Church–Missouri Synod, 47,262; and Episcopal, 36,119. The Church of Jesus Christ of Latter-day Saints (Mormon) has 70,313 members. According to a 1994 estimate, there are 52,000 Jews in Colorado, nearly all in the Denver area.

10 TRANSPORTATION

As the hub of the Rocky Mountain states, Colorado maintains extensive road and rail systems. As of 1998 there were 3,374 rail miles (5,429 kilometers) of track in the state. Amtrak trains in Colorado had 247,071 riders in 1995. Colorado's extensive network of roads includes 29 mountain passes. As of 1997 there were 13,859 miles (21,976 kilometers) of municipal roads and 71,210 miles (114,463 kilometers) of rural roads. Of the 3.5 million motor vehicles registered in 1997, 1.9 mil-

Cliff Palace, Mesa Verde.

lion were automobiles; 1.59 million, trucks; and 5,721, buses.

A total of 228 public and private airfields served the state in 1996. Denver International Airport replaced the former Stapleton International Airport in 1994 as the state's largest and busiest. In 1996, it handled 16.2 million departing passengers and 288,076 tons of cargo.

11 HISTORY

By AD 800 there were tribes of Pueblos in present-day Colorado, who practiced advanced forms of agriculture and pottery making. From the 11th through the 13th centuries, the Pueblos constructed elabo-

rate apartment-like dwellings in the cliffs of the Colorado canyons and planted their crops both on the mesa tops and in the surrounding valleys.

The explorer Juan de Onate is believed to have traveled into the southeastern area in 1601. In 1706, Juan de Uribarri claimed southeastern Colorado for Spain, joining it with New Mexico. Meanwhile, the French had claimed most of the area east of the Rocky Mountains. In 1763, France formally ceded the Louisiana Territory to Spain, which returned it to the French in 1801. Two years later, as part of the Louisiana Purchase, Colorado east of the

Rockies became US land; the rest of Colorado still belonged to Spain.

Eastern Colorado remained a wilderness for the next few decades, although traders and scouts like Kit Carson did venture into the largely uncharted land, establishing friendly relations with the Indians. Between 1842 and 1853, John C. Frémont led five expeditions into the region, the first three for the US government. Western and southern Colorado came into US possession after the Mexican War (1846–48).

The magnet that drew many Americans to Colorado was the greatly exaggerated report of a gold strike in Cherry Creek (present-day Denver) in July 1858. The subsequent boom led to the founding of such mining towns as Boulder, Colorado City, Central City, and Gold Hill. By 1860, the population exceeded 30,000. A bill to organize the Territory of Colorado was passed by the US Congress on 28 February 1861. Colorado sided with the Union during the Civil War, though some settlers fought for the Confederacy.

The 1860s also saw the most serious conflict between Indians and white settlers in Colorado history. After ceding most of their tribal holdings to the US government, the Cheyenne and Arapaho, unsuccessful at farming, resumed a nomadic lifestyle. They hunted buffalo, raided towns, and attacked travelers along the Overland and Sante Fe trails. On 29 November, US military forces under the command of Colonel John Chivington brutally massacred as many as 200 Native Americans near their reservation in the Arkansas Valley.

Photo credit: EPD Photos

Zebulon Pike was an early explorer of the Colorado region. Colorado's highest point, Pike's Peak, is named in his honor.

Statehood

Colorado entered the Union as the 38th state on 1 August 1876, during the presidency of Ulysses S. Grant. In the early years of statehood, silver strikes at Leadville and Aspen brought settlers and money into Colorado. Rail lines, smelters, and refineries were built, and large coalfields were opened up. The High Plains attracted new farmers, and another new industry—tourism—emerged. As

Colorado Governors: 1886–2001

1886–1879	John Long Routt	Republican	1917–1919	Julius Caldeen Gunter	Democrat
1879–1883	Frederick Walker Pitkin	Republican	1919–1923	Oliver Henry Nelson Shoup	Republican
1883–1885	James Benton Grant	Democrat	1923–1925	William Ellery Sweet	Democrat
1885–1887	Bejamin Harrison Eaton	Republican	1925–1927	Clarence J. Morley	Republican
1887–1889	Alva Adams	Democrat	1927–1933	William Herbert Adams	Democrat
1889–1891	Job Adams Cooper	Republican	1933–1937	Edwin Carl Johnson	Democrat
1891–1893	John Long Routt	Republican	1937	Ray H. Talbot	Democrat
1893–1895	Davis Hanson Waite	Populist	1937–1939	Teller Ammons	Democrat
1895–1897	Albert Wills McIntire	Republican	1939–1943	Ralph L. Carr	Republican
1897–1899	Alva Adams	Democrat	1943–1947	John Charles Vivian	Republican
1899–1901	Charles Spalding Thomas	Democrat	1947–1950	William Lee Knous	Democrat
1901–1903	James B. Orman	Democrat	1950–1951	Walter Walfred Johnson	Democrat
1903–1905	James Hamilton Peabody	Republican	1951–1955	Daniel Isaac J. Thornton	Republican
1905	Alva Adams	Democrat	1955–1957	Edwin Carl Johnson	Democrat
1905	James Hamilton Peabody	Republican	1957–1963	Stephen L. R. McNichols	Democrat
1905–1907	Jesse Fuller McDonald	Republican	1963–1973	John A. Love	Republican
1907–1909	Henry Augustus Buchtel	Republican	1973–1975	John David Vanderhoof	Republican
1909–1913	John Franklin Shafroth	Democrat	1975–1987	Richard David Lamm	Democrat
1913–1915	Elias Milton Ammons	Democrat	1987–1999	Roy Romer	Democrat
1915–1917	George Alfred Carlson	Republican	1999–	Bill Owens	Republican

early as the 1860s, resorts had opened near some of the state's mineral springs.

Colorado's boom years ended with a depression during the early 1890s, when the silver market declined. By the dawn of the 20th century, farmers were returning to the land. The development of the automobile and the advent of good roads opened up more of the mountain areas, bringing a big boom in tourism by the 1920s.

From 1920 to 1940, statewide employment declined, and population growth lagged behind that of the US as a whole. World War II brought military training camps, airfields, and jobs to the state. After the war, the placement of both the North American Air Defense Command and the US Air Force Academy in Colorado Springs helped stimulate the growth of defense, federal research, and aerospace-related industries in the state.

As these and other industries grew, so too did Colorado's population and income. Between 1960 and 1983, the state's population growth rate was more than twice that of the nation as a whole; and between 1970 and 1983, Colorado moved from 18th to 9th rank among the states in income per capita (per person). In the 1970s and early 1980s, Colorado experienced a boom in its oil, mining, and electronics industries. The economy began to shrink, however, in the mid-1980s with the drop in oil prices and the closing of mines. Business starts declined by 23% between 1987 and 1988.

12 STATE GOVERNMENT

Colorado's general assembly, which meets annually, consists of a 35-member senate and 65-member house of representatives. There is no constitutional limit to the length of a session, and the legislature may call special sessions by request of two-thirds of the members of each house.

The executive branch is headed by the governor, who submits the budget and legislative programs to the general assembly, and appoints judges, department heads, boards, and commissions. Elected with the governor is the lieutenant governor, who assumes the governor's duties in the governor's absence.

Bills may originate in either house of the general assembly and become law when passed by majority vote of each house and signed by the governor. A bill may also become law if the governor fails to act on it within 10 days after receiving it. A two-thirds vote in each house is needed to override a gubernatorial veto.

13 POLITICAL PARTIES

The Republicans controlled most statewide offices prior to 1900. Since then, the parties have been more evenly balanced. Of the 2.56 million registered voters in 1998, 31% were Democrats; 37% were Republicans; and 34% were unaffiliated or members of other parties. Following the November 1998 election, the state had two Republican US senators, and four Republican and two Democratic US representatives.

As of 2001, the Democrats control the state senate (17 Republicans to 18 Democrats). The state house, however, is controlled by Republicans (38 Republicans to 27 Democrats). For the first time in 24 years, a Republican, Bill Owens, was elected governor in 1998. In the 2001

Colorado Presidential Vote by Political Parties, 1948–2000

YEAR	COLORADO WINNER	DEMOCRAT	REPUBLICAN	PROGRESSIVE	SOCIALIST	SOC. LABOR
1948	*Truman (D)	267,288	239,714	6,115	1,678	—
					CONSTITUTION	
1952	*Eisenhower (R)	245,504	379,782	1,919	2,181	—
1956	*Eisenhower (R)	263,997	394,479	—	759	3,308
					SOC. WORKERS	
1960	Nixon (R)	330,629	402,242	—	563	2,803
1964	*Johnson (D)	476,024	296,767	—	2,537	—
				AMERICAN IND.		
1968	*Nixon (R)	335,174	409,345	60,813	235	3,016
				AMERICAN		
1972	*Nixon (R)	329,980	597,189	17,269	666	4,361
						LIBERTARIAN
1976	Ford (R)	460,801	584,278	397	1,122	5,338
				STATESMAN	CITIZENS	
1980	*Reagan (R)	368,009	652,264	1,180	5,614	25,744
1984	*Reagan (R)	454,975	821,817	NEW ALLIANCE	—	11,257
1988	*Bush (R)	621,453	728,177	2,491	—	15,482
				IND. (Perot)		
1992	*Clinton (D)	629,681	562,850	366,010	1,608	8,669
					GREEN (Nader)	
1996	Dole (R)	671,152	691,848	99,629	25,070	12,392
2000	*Bush (R)	738,227	883,748	91,434	712	216

* Won US presidential election.

presidential election, Republican George W. Bush carried Colorado with 51% of the vote, while incumbent Democrat Al Gore received 42%. Ben Nighthorse Campbell, the only Native American in Congress, was reelected to a second term as Senator in 1998.

14 LOCAL GOVERNMENT

As of 1998 there were 62 counties (63, including the consolidated city/county of Denver), 269 municipal governments, cities, towns, and designated places, and 176 school districts. The administrative and policymaking body in each county is the board of county commissioners. Other county officials include the county clerk, treasurer, assessor, sheriff, coroner, superintendent of schools, surveyor, and attorney.

Statutory cities are those whose structure is defined by the state constitution. Power is delegated by the general assembly to either a council-manager or mayor-council form of government. Towns, which generally have fewer than 2,000 residents, are governed by a mayor and a six-member board of trustees.

Denver, the only city in Colorado that is also a county, exercises the powers of both levels of government. It is run by a mayor and city council. A city auditor, independently elected, serves as a check on the mayor.

15 JUDICIAL SYSTEM

The supreme court, the highest court in Colorado, consists of seven justices elected on a nonpartisan ballot. The next highest court, the court of appeals, consists of ten judges and is confined to civil matters.

County courts hear minor civil disputes and misdemeanors. Appeals from the Denver county courts are heard in Denver's superior court. Municipal courts throughout the state handle violations of municipal ordinances. Colorado's FBI Crime Index crime rate in 1998 was 4,487.5 per 100,000 people. There were 15,045 inmates in state and federal prisons in 1999.

16 MIGRATION

Since the end of World War II, net migration into the state has been substantial, amounting to over 880,000 between 1950 and 1990. During 1990–98, net domestic migration added 359,000 residents. The largest increase has been in the Denver metropolitan area. A number of migrant workers, mostly Mexican Americans, work seasonally in the western orchards and fields. Colorado had a net gain of 46,800 from international migration during 1990–97. In 1990, native Coloradans made up 43.3% of the population.

17 ECONOMY

With its abundant reserves of coal, natural gas, and other minerals—and the economic potential of its vast oil-shale deposits—Colorado is a major mining state, although the mineral industry's share of the state economy has declined throughout this century. Trade is the leading source of employment, while manufacturing (fourth in employment) is the principal contributor to the gross state product. The US government employs

Photo credit: Denver Metro Convention & Visitors Bureau.

Denver skyline and the city park.

over 93,000 people, making it a driving force in Colorado's economy. Tourism has also expanded in all areas of the state.

18 INCOME

In 1998, Colorado ranked seventh among the 50 states in per capita (per person) income, with $29,994. Total disposable personal income in 1996 reached $81.3 billion. About 9.3% of all Coloradans were living below the federal poverty level in 1998.

19 INDUSTRY

Colorado is the main manufacturing center of the Rocky Mountain states; the value of shipments by manufacturers was $42 billion in 1997. The major industries are food and food products, manufacturing, service industries, retail trade, and transportation equipment.

High-technology research and manufacturing grew notably in Colorado during the 1980s and early 1990s. Storage Technology in Louisville is the largest high-tech company with headquarters in the state, but many large out-of-state companies—including Apple Computer, IBM, Hewlett-Packard, Eastman Kodak, Digital Equipment, and MCI Telecommunications—have divisions there.

20 LABOR

In mid-1998, Colorado's civilian labor force was 2.25 million, with an unemployment rate of 3.3%. Colorado's leading areas of employment in 1998 were services (30.2%); wholesale and retail trade (24.4%); government jobs (15.7%); and manufacturing (10.1%). About 9.1% of all employees were union members in 1998.

21 AGRICULTURE

Colorado ranked 16th among the 50 states in agricultural income in 1999, at $4.4 billion. As of 1998, there were about 29,500 farms and ranches covering about 32.5 million acres (13 million hectares). Colorado's 1998 agricultural output (and national rankings) included dry beans, 2.8 million hundredweight (4th); sugar beets, 1.3 million tons (7th); barley, 9.4 million bushels (6th); and wheat, 103 million bushels (8th). In 1998, Colorado produced 548,350 tons of fresh market vegetables, 1,440 tons of vegetables for processing, 65 million pounds of commercial apples, and 20 million pounds (9 million kilograms) of peaches.

22 DOMESTICATED ANIMALS

A leading sheep-producing state, Colorado is also a major area for cattle and other livestock. At one time, cattle production accounted for over half of Colorado's agricultural receipts. In 1999 there were over 3.1 million head of cattle and calves, valued at $1.8 billion. Colorado had an estimated 870,000 hogs and pigs in 1998, valued at $42.6 million.

23 FISHING

There is practically no commercial fishing in Colorado. Warm-water lakes lure the state's 769,846 sport anglers with perch, black bass, and trout, while walleyes are abundant in mountain streams. In 1998, federal hatcheries distributed 10 million trout for restoration or conservation purposes within the state.

24 FORESTRY

Although approximately 21.3 million acres (8.6 million hectares) of forested lands are located in Colorado, commercial forestry is not a major element of the state's economy.

25 MINING

According to the US Geological Survey estimates, the value of 1998 nonfuel mineral production was about $604 million. In 1997, Colorado mined 32.4 million metric tons of sand and gravel; 10.2 million metric tons of crushed stone; 24,000 metric tons of dimension stone; and 290,000 metric tons of clay. As of 1998, Colorado was the second leading producer of molybdenum, ranked 26th in total nonfuel mineral production.

26 ENERGY AND POWER

An abundant supply of coal, oil, and natural gas makes Colorado a major energy-producing state. During 1998, 35.5 billion kilowatt hours of electricity were generated in Colorado, about 93% of that in coal-fired plants. Petroleum production in 1999 was 18.5 million barrels; natural gas production was 696.3 billion cubic feet (19.7 billion cubic meters).

Colorado's coal output was 29.6 million short tons in 1998. Colorado holds the major portion of the nation's proved oil shale reserves. Because of its ample sunshine, Colorado is also well suited to solar energy development.

27 COMMERCE

Colorado is the leading wholesale and retail distribution center for the Rocky Mountain states. Sales from wholesale trade totaled $63 billion in 1997, and retail sales totaled $42 billion. Foreign exports in 1998 included nearly $5.2 billion in goods.

28 PUBLIC FINANCE

In 1992 Colorado's citizens passed a constitutional amendment, entitled the Taxpayer's Bill of Rights (TABOR), that restricts state expenditures, based on population growth and inflation. The amendment also requires a vote of the people for any new or increased taxes. Revenues for the 1997 general fund budget were $12.78 billion, and expenditures were $10.86 billion. Colorado's outstanding debt totaled $3.4 billion or $875 per capita.

29 TAXATION

As of 1998, Colorado's state income tax had a flat rate of 4.63%. The state also imposed a 3% sales and 2.9% use tax, along with taxes on cigarettes, alcoholic beverages, racing, fossil fuel production, motor fuel sales, and insurance premiums. Colorado municipalities are also allowed to levy sales and use taxes. In

Photo credit: © Corel Corporation.

A view of the mountains in Rocky Mountain National Park.

1997, state taxes amounted to $1,359 per person, 44th lowest among the states.

30 HEALTH

Death rates for heart disease, cancer, and cerebrovascular diseases are far below the US norm, while those for accidents are slightly higher. The suicide rate of 15.4 per 100,000 is higher than the US rate of 11.3. In 1998, Colorado had 69 accredited hospitals, with 9,179 beds. The average cost per inpatient day in a hospital is $1,240. The state had 234 nonfederal physicians per 100,000 population in 1997. About 15% of Colorado's population does not have health insurance.

31 HOUSING

In October 1999, there were an estimated 1.7 million year-round housing units, an increase of about 30% from 1980. In 1998, 51,200 new privately-owned housing units were authorized. The Denver-Boulder area is Colorado's primary region of housing growth, with some 23,300 housing units completed in 1996. In 1990, the median home value was $82,700.

32 EDUCATION

Colorado residents are better educated than the average American. According to the 1998, 34% of the adult population of Colorado had completed four years of college, ranking first among the 50 states. Almost 89.6% of all adult Coloradans were high school graduates.

In 1997, Colorado's public elementary and secondary schools had 687,167 pupils. There were 36,397 elementary and secondary school teachers in 1996, with an average salary of $36,271. Expenditures for public elementary and secondary schools amounted to $5,051 per student in 1995/96 (34th among the states). More than 252,245 students were enrolled in 35 colleges and universities in 1997. These include the Colorado School of Mines; the University of Colorado (Boulder), the largest university in the state; Colorado State University; and the University of Denver. The US Air Force Academy is located in Colorado Springs.

33 ARTS

Arts organizations include the Colorado Springs Symphony and Colorado Opera Festival of Colorado Springs; the Central City Opera House Association; and the Four Corners Opera Association in Durango.

34 LIBRARIES AND MUSEUMS

Public libraries in the state hold nearly 10.5 million volumes and circulate more than 35 million. The largest system is the Denver Public Library with 1.9 million volumes in 27 branches. The leading academic library is at the University of Colorado at Boulder, with over 2.8 million volumes.

Colorado has 174 museums and historic sites. One of the most prominent museums in the West is the Denver Art Museum, with its large collection of Native American, South Seas, and Oriental art. Another major art museum is the Colorado Springs Fine Arts Center, specializing in southwestern and western American art.

35 COMMUNICATIONS

Over 96% of the state's occupied housing units had telephones as of 1999. Of the 206 radio stations in operation in 2000, 80 were AM and 126 were FM. A total of 109,775 Internet domain names were registered in Colorado in 2000.

36 PRESS

As of 1998, there were 20 morning dailies, 9 afternoon dailies, and 16 Sunday papers. The leading newspapers were the *Rocky*

Silent film star Lon Chaney (1883–1930) was born in Colorado Springs. A master of disguise, he was known as "The Man of a Thousand Faces." Chaney is pictured here as he appeared in The Miracle Man *(1919). His realistic portrayal of a cripple won him critical acclaim. He went on to play Quasimodo in* The Hunchback of Notre Dame *(1923) and the acid-scarred musician in the horror classic* The Phantom of the Opera *(1925).*

Mountain News, with a circulation of 331,978 in the mornings and 432,931 on Sundays; and the *Denver Post,* 341,554 mornings and 484,657 Sundays.

37 TOURISM, TRAVEL, AND RECREATION

Annually, travel and tourism generate over $6 billion in expenditures in the state. Vail and Aspen are popular ski resort centers. Colorado has over 25 ski areas. Skiing is in season from mid-November through late March. The US Air Force Academy near Colorado Springs is a popular tourist attraction, as is nearby Pikes Peak.

Besides its many museums, parks, and rebuilt Larimer Square district, Denver's main attraction is the US Mint. All nine national forests in Colorado are open for camping, as are the state's two national parks: Rocky Mountain and Mesa Verde.

38 SPORTS

There are five major league professional sports teams in Colorado, all in Denver: the Broncos of the National Football League, the Nuggets of the National Basketball Association, the Colorado Rockies of Major League Baseball, the Avalanche of Major League Hockey, and the Colorado Rapids of Major League Soccer. The Buffaloes of the University of Colorado produced some excellent football teams in the late 1980s and early 1990s and were named national Champions in 1990 (with Georgia Tech).

39 FAMOUS COLORADANS

Fort Collins was the birthplace of Byron R. White (b.1917), an associate justice of the US Supreme Court since 1962. Gary Hart (b.Kansas, 1936) was a senator and a presidential candidate in 1984 and 1988. Early explorers of the Colorado region include Zebulon Pike (b.New Jersey, 1779–1813). Willard F. Libby (1909–80), won the Nobel Prize for chemistry in 1960. Colorado's most famous sports personality is Jack Dempsey (1895–1983), who held the world heavyweight boxing crown from 1919 to 1926.

40 BIBLIOGRAPHY

Athearn, Robert G. *The Coloradans*. Albuquerque: University of New Mexico Press, 1982.

Ayer, Eleanor H. *Colorado*.New York: Benchmark Books, 1997. Aylesworth, Thomas G. *The Southwest: Colorado, New Mexico, Texas*. New York: Chelsea House, 1996.

Blashfield, Jean F. *Colorado*. New York: Children's Press, 1999.

Harling, Michael. *Peter Forsberg*. New York: Greystone, 2000.

McAuliffe, Emily. *Colorado Facts and Symbols*. New York: Hilltop Books/Grolier, 1998.

Thompson, Kathleen. *Colorado*. Austin, Tex.: Raintree Steck-Vaughn, 1996.

Shuter, Jane. *Mesa Verde*. Chicago: Heinemann, 2000.

Ubbelohde, Carol, Maxine Benson, and Duane A. Smith. *A Colorado History*. 5th ed. Boulder: Pruett, 1982.

Websites

Colorado Travel and Tourism Authority. The Official Website of Colorado Tourism. [Online] Available http://www.colorado.com/ Accessed May 31, 2001.

State of Colorado. Colorado's Kids Page. [Online] Available http://www.state.co.us/kids/index.html Accessed May 31, 2001.

CONNECTICUT

State of Connecticut

ORIGIN OF STATE NAME: From the Mahican word *quinnehtukqut,* meaning "beside the long tidal river."

NICKNAME: The Constitution State (also: the Nutmeg State).

CAPITAL: Hartford.

ENTERED UNION: 9 January 1788 (5th).

SONG: "Yankee Doodle."

MOTTO: *Qui transtulit sustinet* (He who transplanted still sustains).

COAT OF ARMS: On a rococo shield, three grape vines, supported and bearing fruit, stand against a white field. Beneath the shield is a streamer bearing the state motto.

FLAG: The coat of arms appears on a blue field.

OFFICIAL SEAL: The three grape vines and motto of the arms surrounded by the words *Sigillum reipublicæ Connecticutensis* (Seal of the State of Connecticut).

ANIMAL: Sperm whale.

BIRD: American robin.

FLOWER: Mountain laurel.

TREE: White oak.

MINERAL: Garnet.

INSECT: European praying mantis.

SHIP: *USS Nautilus.*

TIME: 7 AM EST = noon GMT.

1 LOCATION AND SIZE

Located in New England in the northeastern US, Connecticut ranks 48th in size among the 50 states. The state's area is 5,018 square miles (12,997 square kilometers). Connecticut has an average length of 90 miles (145 kilometers) east-west, and an average width of 55 miles (89 kilometers) north-south. It has a boundary length of 328 miles (528 kilometers) and a shoreline of 253 miles (407 kilometers).

2 TOPOGRAPHY

Connecticut is divided into four main geographic regions: the Central Lowlands, formed by the Connecticut and Quinnipiac river valleys; the Eastern Highlands; the Western Highlands, an extension of the Green Mountains in the northwest; and the Coastal Lowlands, with good harbors at Bridgeport, New Haven, New London, Mystic, and Stonington. Mt. Frissell, near the Massachusetts border, is the highest point in the state at 2,380 feet (725 meters).

Connecticut has more than 6,000 lakes and ponds. The main river is the Connecticut, New England's longest river at 407 miles (655 kilometers). This waterway divides the state roughly in half before emptying into Long Island Sound. Other principal rivers include the Thames, Housatonic, and Naugatuck.

3 CLIMATE

Connecticut has a generally temperate climate, with mild winters and warm summers. The January mean temperature is 27°F (–3°C) and the July mean is 70°F (21°C). Coastal areas have warmer winters and cooler summers than the interior. The highest recorded temperature in Connecticut was 106°F (41°C) in Danbury on 15 July 1995; the lowest, –32°F (–36°C) in Falls Village on 16 February 1943. The annual rainfall is about 44 to 48 inches (112 to 122 centimeters) and is evenly distributed throughout the year. The state receives some 25 to 60 inches (64 to 150 centimeters) of snow each year.

4 PLANTS AND ANIMALS

Connecticut has an impressive variety of vegetation zones. Along the shore of Long Island Sound are tidal marshes with salt grasses. On slopes fringing the marshes are black grass, switch grass, and march elder. Vegetation in the swamp areas includes various ferns, abundant cattails, and skunk cabbage. The state's hillsides and uplands support a variety of flowers and plants, including mountain laurel (the state flower), pink azalea, and Queen Anne's lace. Endangered species in the state include showy lady's slipper, ginseng, showy aster, nodding pogonia, goldenseal, climbing fern, and chaffseed.

The impact of human settlement on Connecticut wildlife has been profound, however. Only the smaller mammals—the

Connecticut Population Profile

Total population in 2000:	3,405,565
Population change, 1990–2000:	3.6%
Hispanic or Latino†:	9.4%
Population by race	
One race:	97.8%
White:	81.6%
Black or African American:	9.1%
American Indian/Alaska Native:	0.3%
Asian:	2.4%
Native Hawaiian/Pacific Islander:	—
Some other race:	4.3%
Two or more races:	2.2%

Population by Age Group

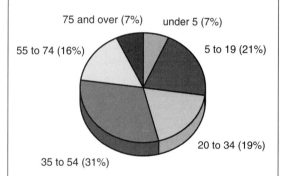

75 and over (7%) under 5 (7%)
55 to 74 (16%) 5 to 19 (21%)
20 to 34 (19%)
35 to 54 (31%)

Top Cities by Population

City	Population	% change 1990–2000
Bridgeport	139,529	–1.5
New Haven	123,626	–5.2
Hartford	121,578	–13.0
Stamford	117,083	8.4
Waterbury	107,271	–1.6
Norwalk	82,951	5.9
Danbury	74,848	14.1
New Britain	71,538	–5.2
West Hartford	63,589	5.8
Greenwich	61,101	4.6

Notes: †A person of Hispanic or Latino origin may be of any race. NA indicates that data are not available.
Sources: U.S. Census Bureau. Public Information Office. *Demographic Profiles.* [Online] Available http://www.census.gov/Press-Release/www/2001/demoprofile.html. Accessed June 1, 2001. U.S. Census Bureau. *Census 2000: Redistricting Data.* Press release issued by the Redistricting Data Office. Washington, D.C., March, 2001.

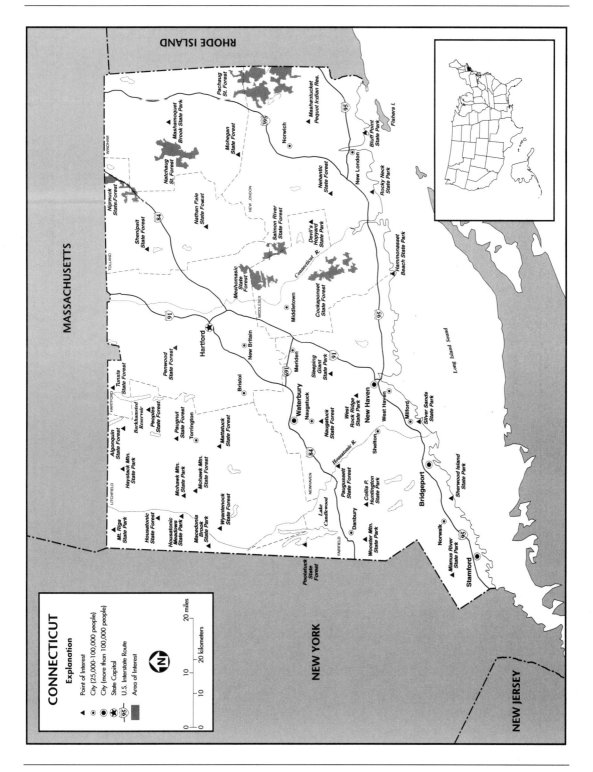

CONNECTICUT

Explanation

▲ Point of Interest
⊙ City (25,000–100,000 people)
◉ City (more than 100,000 people)
✪ State Capital
—95— U.S. Interstate Route
Area of Interest

0   10   20 miles
0   10   20 kilometers

MASSACHUSETTS

RHODE ISLAND

NEW YORK

NEW JERSEY

Long Island Sound

Pachaug St. Forest
Mashamoquet Brook State Park
Mohegan State Forest
Natchaug St. Forest
Nipmuck State Forest
Mashantucket Pequot Indian Res.
Norwich
Nehantic State Forest
Bluff Point State Park
Fishers I.
New London
Rocky Neck State Park
Shenipsit State Forest
Nathan Hale State Forest
Salmon River State Forest
Devil's Hopyard State Park
Hammonasset Beach State Park
Meshomasic State Forest
Cockaponset State Forest
Middletown
Connecticut R.
Penwood State Forest
Hartford
New Britain
Meriden
Sleeping Giant State Park
Tunxis State Forest
Barkhamsted Reservoir
Peoples State Forest
Paugnut State Forest
Algonquin State Forest
Bristol
Waterbury
Naugatuck
West Rock Ridge State Park
New Haven
West Haven
Milford
Silver Sands State Park
Haystack Mtn. State Park
Mohawk Mtn. State Park
Mohawk Mtn. State Forest
Mattatuck State Forest
Torrington
Paugussett State Forest
Shelton
Housatonic R.
Mt. Riga State Park
Housatonic Meadows State Park
Housatonic State Forest
Macedonia Brook State Park
Wyantenock State Forest
Collis P. Huntington State Park
Bridgeport
Sherwood Island State Park
Lake Candlewood
Danbury
Wooster Mtn. State Park
Pootatuck State Forest
Norwalk
Mianus River State Park
Stamford

WINDHAM
NEW LONDON
TOLLAND
MIDDLESEX
HARTFORD
LITCHFIELD
NEW HAVEN
FAIRFIELD

woodchuck, gray squirrel, cottontail, eastern chipmunk, porcupine, raccoon, and striped skunk—remain common. Freshwater fish are abundant, and aquatic life in Long Island Sound even more so. Common birds include the robin (the state bird), blue jay, song sparrow, wood thrush, and many species of waterfowl.

The threatened or endangered wildlife listed in 1997 by the Department of Interior include five kinds of turtles, the American peregrine falcon, and bald eagle.

5 ENVIRONMENTAL PROTECTION

The Department of Environmental Protection is responsible for protecting natural resources and controlling water, air, and land pollution in the state. In 1997, about 75% of the state's 900 miles (1,400 kilometers) of rivers met the federal government's "swimmable-fishable" standards. In 1994 Connecticut and New York adopted a plan to manage Long Island Sound, which in the past had served as an industrial waste dump.

In the early 1980s, ozone levels were among the highest in the US. However, the number of days the ozone standard is exceeded has fallen since the 1970s. The vehicles emission program established by the state in January 1983 reduced carbon monoxide and hydrocarbon pollution.

In 1998, the state had 14 hazardous waste sites. During 1986–96, annual landfill garbage declined from 1,400 pounds (630 kilograms) to 300 pounds (135 kilograms) per person.

6 POPULATION

The 2000 census total for Connecticut was over 3.4 million. The state had a population gain of 3.6% for the entire decade of the 1990s, compared with a US population growth of 13.1%. About 7% of the population was under five years of age in 2000 (compared with the national rate of 6.8%). Some 7% of the population was 75 or older (5.9% for the entire US).

The 2005 population is projected at 3.3 million. Connecticut's population density in 2000 was 702.9 persons per square mile (271.4 persons per square kilometer), considerably higher than the national average of 79.6 per square mile (30.7 per square kilometer). About 79.1% of all Connecticut residents lived in urban areas and 20.9% in rural areas. Major cities with their 2000 populations are Bridgeport, 139,529; New Haven, 123,626; Hartford, 121,578; Stamford, 117,083; and Waterbury, 107,271.

7 ETHNIC GROUPS

Connecticut has large populations of second-generation European descent. The biggest groups came from Italy, Ireland, Poland, and Quebec, Canada. Most of these immigrants clustered in the cities of New Haven, Hartford, Bridgeport, and New London.

In 1997, the black population was estimated at 300,000, about 9.2% of the state total. According to 1997 federal estiamates, there were also about 259,000 residents of Hispanic origin, primarily Puerto Ricans. In addition Connecticut

Connecticut Population by Race

Census 2000 was the first national census in which the instructions to respondents said, "Mark one or more races." This table shows the number of people who are of one, two, or three or more races. For those claiming two races, the number of people belonging to the various categories is listed. The U.S. government conducts a census of the population every ten years.

	Number	Percent
Total population	3,405,565	100.0
One race	3,330,717	97.8
Two races	70,473	2.1
White *and* Black or African American	11,725	0.3
White *and* American Indian/Alaska Native	7,652	0.2
White *and* Asian	7,343	0.2
White *and* Native Hawaiian/Pacific Islander	538	—
White *and* some other race	24,391	0.7
Black or African American *and* American Indian/Alaska Native	3,439	0.1
Black or African American *and* Asian	945	—
Black or African American *and* Native Hawaiian/Pacific Islander	665	—
Black or African American *and* some other race	9,008	0.3
American Indian/Alaska Native *and* Asian	365	—
American Indian/Alaska Native *and* Native Hawaiian/Pacific Islander	41	—
American Indian/Alaska Native *and* some other race	668	—
Asian *and* Native Hawaiian/Pacific Islander	465	—
Asian *and* some other race	2,738	0.1
Native Hawaiian/Pacific Islander *and* some other race	490	—
Three or more races	4,375	0.1

Source: U.S. Census Bureau. *Census 2000: Redistricting Data.* Press release issued by the Redistricting Data Office. Washington, D.C., March, 2001. A dash (—) indicates that the percent is less than 0.1.

had an estimated 7,900 Native Americans and 76,300 Asians and Pacific Islanders.

8 LANGUAGES

Connecticut English is basically that of the Northern dialect, but features of the eastern New England subdialect occur east of the Connecticut River. Almost 2.6 million Connecticuters (85% of the population five years old and older) speak only English at home. Other languages spoken at home, and the number of people who speak them, include Spanish, 167,007; Italian, 71,309; French, 53,586; Polish, 40,306; and Portuguese, 24,936.

9 RELIGIONS

Since World War I, Roman Catholics have been the most numerous religious group in the state. As of 1990, there were 1,374,747 Roman Catholics and 557,439 known members of Protestant denominations. Leading groups included Congregationalists (United Church of Christ), 135,231; Episcopalians, 78,804; and United Methodists, 56,372. In 1994, the state's estimated Jewish population was 98,000.

10 TRANSPORTATION

As of 1996, Amtrak operated about 18 trains through the state, serving 12 sta-

Photo credit: Connecticut Department of Economic Development.

Mystic Seaport, whaling museum.

tions with a total of 927,805 riders. Local bus systems provide intracity transportation. Intercity bus service (not subsidized by the state or the federal government) is provided in 31 municipalities by 28 companies.

Connecticut has an extensive system of expressways, state highways, and local roads, totaling 20,675 miles (33,145 kilometers) in 1997. Over 99% of the roads are either paved or hard-surfaced. As of 1997 there were 1.96 million automobiles, 686,847 trucks, and 9,486 buses registered in the state.

Most of Connecticut's waterborne traffic is handled through the two major ports of New Haven and Bridgeport, which collectively handled 14 million tons of cargo in 1998 and at the shallow-draft terminals in Norwalk and Stamford.

In 1996 Connecticut had 55 airports. The principal air terminal is Bradley International Airport at Windsor Locks, 14 miles (23 kilometers) north of Hartford. Served by nine major airlines and nine commuter lines, Bradley handled 5.3 million passengers during 1996.

11 HISTORY

By the early 17th century, Connecticut had between 6,000 and 7,000 Native Americans organized into 16 tribes. Because of their fear of the warlike Pequot along the shore and of the Mohawk to the west, most of Connecticut's other Native Americans sought the friendship of English newcomers in the 1630s. The impact of English settlers on Connecticut's friendly tribesmen was devastating, however. The Native Americans lost their land, were made dependents in their own territory, and were ravaged by such European diseases as smallpox and measles. By the 1770s, Connecticut's Native American population was less than 1,500.

The early English settlers were part of a great migration of some 20,000 English Puritans between 1630 and 1642. In 1639, the Puritan settlements at Windsor, Wethersfield, and Hartford joined together to form the Connecticut Colony. A separate Puritan colony established at New Haven in 1638 joined them in 1665. Connecticut functioned throughout the colonial period much like an independent republic. It was the only American colony that generally did not follow English legal and legislative practices.

With its Puritan roots and historic autonomy, Connecticut was a patriot stronghold during the American Revolution. The state's most famous Revolutionary War figure was Nathan Hale, executed as a spy by the British in New York City in 1776. On 9 January 1788, Connecticut became the fifth state to ratify the Constitution. Connecticut strongly disagreed with the foreign policy of Presidents Thomas Jefferson and James Madison and opposed the War of 1812, even refusing to allow its militia to leave the state.

Long before the Civil War, Connecticut was stoutly antislavery. Connecticut had a number of antislavery societies whose members routed escaped slaves to Canada via the Underground Railroad. Some 55,000 Connecticut men served in the Civil War, suffering more than 20,000 casualties. The contributions by Connecticut industries to the war effort signaled the state's emergence as a manufacturing giant. Its industrial development was helped by abundant waterpower, an elaborate transportation network, and, most important, the technological and marketing expertise of the people.

1900–1945

The state's textile industry ranked sixth in the nation in 1900, with an annual output of $50 million. By 1904, Connecticut's firearms industry was producing more than one-fourth of the total value of all firearms manufactured by nongovernment factories in the US. These great strides in manufacturing transformed Connecticut from a rural, agrarian society in the early 1800s to an increasingly urban state.

The state's contribution to the Allied forces in World War I more than equaled its Civil War effort. About 66,000 Connecticuters served in the armed forces, and by 1917–18, four-fifths of Connecticut's industry was involved in defense production. During the 1920s, the state became a national leader in the production of specialty parts for the aviation, automotive, and electric power industries.

The stock market crash of 1929 and the subsequent depression of the 1930s hit highly industrialized Connecticut hard. By

Connecticut Governors: 1769–2001

Years	Governor	Party
1769–1784	Jonathan Trumbull	
1784–1786	Matthew Griswold	
1786–1796	Samuel Huntington	Federalist
1796–1797	Oliver Wolcott, Sr.	Federalist
1797–1809	Jonathan Trumbull	Federalist
1809–1811	John Treadwell	Federalist
1811–1812	Roger Griswold	Federalist
1812–1817	John Cotton Smith	Federalist
1817–1827	Oliver Wolcott, Jr.	Dem-Rep
1827–1831	Gideon Thomlinson	Dem-Rep
1831–1833	John Samuel Peters	Nat-Rep
1833–1834	Henry Waggaman Edwards	Democrat
1834–1835	Samuel Augustus Foot	Whig
1835–1838	Henry Waggaman Edwards	Democrat
1838–1842	William Wolcott Ellsworth	Whig
1842–1844	Chauncey Fitch Cleveland	Democrat
1844–1846	Roger Sherman Baldwin	Whig
1846–1847	Isaac Toucey	Democrat
1847–1849	Clark Bissell	Whig
1849–1850	Joseph Trumbull	Whig
1850–1853	Thomas Hart Seymour	Democrat
1853–1854	Charles Hobby Pond	Democrat
1854–1855	Henry Dutton	Whig
1855–1857	William Thomas Minor	American
1857–1858	Alexander Hamilton Holley	Republican
1858–1866	William Alfred Buckingham	Republican
1866–1867	Joseph Roswell Hawley	Republican
1867–1869	James Edward English	Democrat
1869–1970	Marshall Jewell	Republican
1870–1871	James Edward English	Democrat
1871–1873	Marshall Jewell	Republican
1873–1877	Charles Roberts Ingersoll	Democrat
1877–1879	Richard Dudley Hubbard	Democrat
1879–1881	Charles Bartlett Andrews	Republican
1881–1883	Hobart B. Bigelow	Republican
1883–1885	Thomas MacDonald Waller	Democrat
1885–1887	Henry Baldwin Harrison	Republican
1887–1889	Phineas Chapman Lounsbury	Republican
1889–1893	Morgan Gardner Bulkeley	Republican
1893–1895	Luzon Burritt Morris	Democrat
1895–1897	Owen Vincent Coffin	Republican
1897–1899	Lorrin Alamson Cooke	Republican
1899–1901	George Edward Lounsbury	Republican
1901–1903	George Payne McLean	Republican
1903–1905	Abiram Chamberlain	Republican
1905–1907	Henry Roberts	Republican
1907–1909	Rollin Simmons Woodruff	Republican
1909	George Leavens Lilley	Republican
1909–1911	Frank Bentley Weeks	Republican
1911–1915	Simeon Eben Baldwin	Democrat
1915–1921	Marcus Hensey Holcomb	Republican
1921–1923	Everett John Lake	Republican
1923–1925	Charles Augustus Templeton	Republican
1925	Hiram Bingham	Republican
1925–1931	John Harper Trumbull	Republican
1931–1939	Wilbur Lucius Cross	Democrat
1939–1941	Raymond Earl Baldwin	Republican
1941–1943	Robert Augustine Hurley	Democrat
1943–1946	Raymond Earl Baldwin	Republican
1946–1947	Charles Wilbert Snow	Democrat
1947–1948	James Lukens McConaughy	Republican
1948–1949	James Coughlin Shannon	Republican
1949–1951	Chester Bliss Bowles	Democrat
1951–1955	John Davis Lodge	Republican
1955–1961	Abraham Alexander Ribicoff	Democrat
1961–1971	John Noel Dempsey	Democrat
1971–1975	Thomas Joseph Meskill	Republican
1975–1980	Ella Tambussi Grasso	Democrat
1980–1991	William Atchinson O'Neill	Democrat
1991–1995	Lowell Palmer Weicker, Jr.	Republican
1995–	John G. Rowland	Republican

Democratic Republican – Dem-Rep
National Republican – Nat-Rep

the spring of 1932, the state's unemployed totaled 150,000 and cities such as Bridgeport fell deeply in debt. Connecticut was pulled out of the unemployment doldrums in 1939, when the state's factories were once again stimulated by defense contracts. During World War II, Connecticut's factories turned out submarines, Navy Corsair fighter aircraft, helicopters, 80% of all ball bearings manufactured in the US, and many thousands of small arms. Approximately 220,000 Connecticut men and women served in the US armed forces.

Post-World War II

Since 1945, Connecticut has seen substantial population growth, economic diversification with a greater proportion of service industries, the expansion of middle-class suburbs, and an influx of black and Hispanic migrants to the major cities. Urban renewal projects in Hartford and New Haven have resulted in expanded office and recreational facilities, but not much desperately needed new housing. A major challenge facing Connecticut in the

1980s was once again how to handle the social and economic integration of this incoming wave of people and industries.

Connecticut became the nation's wealthiest state during the 1980s, achieving the highest per capita (per person) income in 1986. The state's prosperity came in part from the expansion of the military budget, as 70% of Connecticut's manufacturing sector was defense related. The end of the Cold War, however, brought cuts in military spending which reduced the value of defense-related contracts in Connecticut from $6 billion in 1989 to $4.2 billion in 1990. Department of Defense spending per capita fell from $1,800 in the 1980s to $1,289 in 1992. By 1992, manufacturing jobs had declined by 25% while jobs in such service industries as retail, finance, insurance, and real estate increased by 23%. The total number of jobs, however, dropped by 10%.

In the 1980s and early 1990s, Connecticut witnessed an increasing contrast between the standard of living enjoyed by urban and suburban residents, blacks and whites, and the wealthy and the poor. In 1992, the median family income in many of the state's suburbs was nearly twice that of families living in urban areas.

12 STATE GOVERNMENT

The state legislature is called the general assembly, consisting of a 36-member senate and 151-member house of representatives. Legislators are elected to both

Connecticut Presidential Vote by Political Parties, 1948–2000

YEAR	CONNECTICUT WINNER	DEMOCRAT	REPUBLICAN	PROGRESSIVE	SOCIALIST
1948	Dewey (R)	423,297	437,754	13,713	6,964
1952	*Eisenhower (R)	481,649	611,012	1,466	2,244
1956	*Eisenhower (R)	405,079	711,837	—	—
1960	*Kennedy (D)	657,055	565,813	—	—
1964	*Johnson (D)	826,269	390,996	—	—
				AMERICAN IND.	
1968	Humphrey (D)	621,561	556,721	76,660	—
					AMERICAN
1972	*Nixon (R)	555,498	810,763	—	17,239
					US LABOR
1976	Ford (R)	647,895	719,261	7,101	1,789
				LIBERTARIAN	CITIZENS
1980	*Reagan (R)	541,732	677,210	8,570	6,130
				CONN-ALLIANCE	COMMUNIST
1984	*Reagan (R)	569,597	890,877	1,274	4,826
				LIBERTARIAN	NEW ALLIANCE
1988	*Bush (R)	676,584	750,241	14,071	2,491
					IND. (Perot)
1992	*Clinton (D)	682,318	578,313	5,391	348,771
1996	*Clinton (D)	735,740	483,109	5,788	139,523
					REFORM
2000	Gore (D)	816,015	561,094	64,452	4,713

* Won US presidential election.

houses for two-year terms. Elected members of the executive branch are the governor and lieutenant governor (who run jointly and must each be at least 30 years of age), secretary of state, treasurer, comptroller, and attorney general. All are elected for four-year terms and may be reelected.

A bill becomes law when approved by both houses of the general assembly and signed by the governor. If the governor fails to sign it within 5 days when the legislature is in session, or within 15 days when it has adjourned, the measure also becomes law. A bill vetoed by the governor may be overridden by a two-thirds vote of the members of each house.

13 POLITICAL PARTIES

Connecticut's Democrats have held power in most years since the mid-1950s. As of 2000, there were 1.9 million registered voters: Democratic Party was 38%; Republican, 26%; and Independent, 37%. In the November 2000 elections, Democrat Al Gore carried the state with 56% of the popular vote; Republican George W. Bush won 38%. Following the November 2000 elections, Connecticut's delegation of US Representatives consisted of four Democrats and two Republicans. Senator-Joseph Lieberman was chosen as the Democratic Vice-presidental candidate by Al Gore in the 2000 presidential election.

In 1998, Republican John G. Rowland was reelected governor. As of 2001, the Democrats control the state senate (15 Republicans to 21 Democrats). The state house is also controlled by Democrats (51 Republicans to 100 Democrats).

14 LOCAL GOVERNMENT

As of 1997, Connecticut had 8 counties and 30 municipal governments. Counties in Connecticut have been geographical subdivisions without governmental functions since county government was abolished in 1960.

Connecticut's cities generally use the council-manager or mayor-council forms of government. The council-manager system provides for an elected council that determines policy, enacts local legislation, and appoints the city manager. The mayor-council system employs an elected chief executive with extensive appointment power and control over administrative agencies.

In most towns, an elected, three-member board of selectmen heads the administrative branch. The town meeting, in which all registered voters may participate, is the legislative body. Boroughs are generally governed by an elected warden, and borough meetings exercise major legislative functions.

15 JUDICIAL SYSTEM

Connecticut's judicial system has undergone significant streamlining in recent years, with the abolition of municipal, circuit, and juvenile courts. Currently, the Connecticut judicial system consists of the supreme court, appeals court, superior court, and probate courts.

The supreme court comprises the chief justice, five associate justices, and two senior associate justices. The high court hears cases on appeal, primarily from the appeals court but also from the superior

Photo credit: Connecticut Department of Economic Development.

State capitol building, Hartford.

court in certain special instances, such as the review of a death sentence, reapportionment, election disputes, invalidation of a state statute, or censure of a probate judge.

The superior court, the sole general trial court, has the authority to hear all legal controversies except those over which the probate courts have exclusive jurisdiction. The superior court sits in 12 state judicial districts and is divided into trial divisions for civil, criminal, and family cases. Connecticut had an inmate population of 18,360 in 1999. The total crime rate in 1998 was 3,786 per 100,000.

16 MIGRATION

After World War II, the rush of middle-class whites (many from neighboring states) to Connecticut suburbs, fueled in part by the "baby boom" that followed the war, was accompanied by the flow of minority groups to the cities. All told, Connecticut had a net increase from migration of 561,000 between 1940 and 1970, followed by a net loss of 113,000 from 1970 to 1990. During 1990–98, interstate migration resulted in a net loss of 217,000, while immigration from abroad added 68,000.

17 ECONOMY

Connecticut's most important economic pursuit is manufacturing. In the 1980s, Connecticut became a leader in the manufacture of aircraft engines and parts, bearings, hardware, submarines, helicopters, typewriters, electronic instrumentation, electrical equipment, guns and ammunition, and optical instruments.

Because defense production has traditionally been important to the state, the economy has fluctuated with the rise and fall of international tensions. Connecticut has lessened its dependence on the defense sector somewhat by attracting nonmilitary domestic and international firms to the state. Between 1984 and 1991, manufacturing employment declined 22.4%, while nonmanufacturing jobs rose by 11.6%. By the early 1990s, manufacturing accounted for 20% of employment, compared to 50% in 1950.

However, the state was hit hard by cuts in military spending in the late 1980s and early 1990s. In 1992, 70% of manufacturing was still defense-related. Pratt and Whitney, the jet engine maker, and General Dynamics Electric Boat Division, manufacturer of submarines, announced in 1992 that they would lay off a total of 16,400 workers over the next six years.

18 INCOME

Connecticut ranked first among the states in per person income in 1998, at $37,338. The median household income was $44,978 in 1998. Only 9.9% of all state residents were living below the federal poverty level in 1998.

19 INDUSTRY

Six main groups of industries drive the state's economy: aerospace and advanced manufacturing; communications, information and education; financial services; health and biomedical; business services; and tourism and entertainment.

The state's value of shipments of manufactured goods totaled $49 billion in 1997. Leading industrial and service corporations with headquarters in Connecticut include General Electric, United Technologies, GTE, Xerox, and American Brands. In 1997, 22 Connecticut-based firms appeared on *Fortune* magazine's list of the 500 biggest industrial companies in the US.

20 LABOR

The state's civilian labor force in mid-1998 was approximately 1.71 million, of whom 3.4% were unemployed. Some 17.5% of all workers were union members in 1998.

21 AGRICULTURE

Agriculture is no longer of much economic importance in Connecticut. The number of farms declined from 22,241 in 1945 to 4,100 in 1998. In 1999, cash receipts from all agricultural sales totaled $297 million. Connecticut produced 3.5 million pounds (1.6 million kilograms) of tobacco in 1996. The state ranked fifth in mushroom production and eighth in pears in 1995. Other principal crops are hay, greenhouse and nursery products, potatoes, sweet corn, tomatoes, apples, and peaches.

22 DOMESTICATED ANIMALS

In 1999 there were 64,000 cattle on Connecticut farms, valued at $54.4 million. During 1997, dairy farmers produced 502 million pounds (236 million kilograms) of milk. Egg production that year was valued at $45.7 million.

23 FISHING

Commercial fishing does not play a major role in the economy. In 1998, the value of commercial landings was $34.4 million for a catch of 17.6 million pounds (7.9 million kilograms) of edible finfish and shellfish. Connecticut had 173,052 sport fishing license holders in 1998.

24 FORESTRY

By the early 20th century, the forests that covered 95% of Connecticut in the 1630s were mostly destroyed. Woodland recovery has been stimulated since the 1930s by an energetic reforestation program. More than half of the state's 1.8 million acres (0.7 million hectares) of forestland is wooded with new growth. State wood-

The Hartford Insurance Company headquarters is located in Hartford.

lands include 91 state parks and 30 state forests covering some 168,000 acres (69,055 hectares).

25 MINING

The value of nonfuel mineral production in Connecticut in 1998 was estimated by the US Geological Survey to be nearly $105 million. Crushed stone and construction sand and gravel are the state's two leading mineral commodities produced. Other commodities include clays, industrial sand, and dimension stone.

26 ENERGY AND POWER

In 1997, Connecticut's fuel bill was $7.25 billion, of which 50% was for petroleum products, 13% for natural gas, and less than 1% for coal and nuclear fuel. In 1994, prices were 69% higher than the national average for natural gas, 47% higher for electricity, and about 12% higher for petroleum products.

Production of electricity was 15.1 billion kilowatt hours in 1998. The use of coal to generate electric power declined from 85% of the total fuel used in 1965 to 10% in 1998, as a result of the increased utilization of nuclear energy and oil. As of 1999, Connecticut had two nuclear reactors. Having no petroleum or gas resources of its own, Connecticut must rely primarily on imported oil.

27 COMMERCE

Considering its small size, Connecticut is a busy commercial state. In 1997, retail trade sales amounted to $36 billion. The estimated value of Connecticut's goods exported abroad was $7.3 billion in 1998. Transport equipment, nonelectrical machinery, electronic equipment, and instruments account for most of the state's foreign sales.

28 PUBLIC FINANCE

In 1991, the state of Connecticut underwent a major reorganization of its finances, including the enactment of a personal income tax at a rate of 4.5%. Also included in the revenue restructuring was a drop in the sales tax rate from 8% to 6% and a reduction in the corporate tax rate from 13.8% to 11.5%. By 1996, the state marked its fifth straight year of a budget surplus in excess of $160 million.

Revenues for 1997 were $14.52 million; expenditures were $13.83 billion. In 1997 Connecticut's outstanding debt totaled $17.05 billion or $5,214 per person (3d highest ratio among the states).

29 TAXATION

Connecticut's state taxes totaled $8.15 billion, or $2,491 per person (third highest rate among the states). Principal taxes are a 6% sales and use tax, a corporation business tax, and a motor fuels tax of 25 cents per gallon. Other state taxes are levied on cigarettes, alcoholic beverages, and theater admissions. Property taxes are the main source of local revenue. In 1995, local taxes totaled $4.6 billion, or about $1,409 per person.

30 HEALTH

Connecticut is one of the healthiest states in the US. The two leading causes of death are heart disease and cancer. Death rates for cerebrovascular diseases, accidents and adverse effects, motor vehicle accidents, and suicide were below their respective national rates in 1998. In 1998, Connecticut had 33 community hospitals, with 6,949 beds. Hospital expenses in 1998 averaged $1,518.90 per day and $7,915.30 per stay, well above the US average. In 1998, 12.6% of the state's population did not have health insurance.

31 HOUSING

In 1999 there were nearly 1.4 million housing units in Connecticut. There were 11,900 new housing units authorized in 1998; new housing construction was valued at 1.4 billion that year. As of 1990, year-round housing units in Connecticut had a median monthly mortgage and owner cost of $1,096 and a median monthly rent of $598.

32 EDUCATION

As of 1998, 83.7% of adult state residents were high school graduates, and 31.4% had completed four or more years of college. As of fall 1997, Connecticut's public schools had 535,164 students enrolled. Expenditures for public elementary and

Mark Twain's house, Nook Farm Museum.

secondary schools amounted to $8,246 per student in 1995/96 (4th among the states). The state's private preparatory schools include Choate Rosemary Hall, Taft, Westminster, Loomis Chaffee, and Miss Porter's.

Public institutions of higher education include the University of Connecticut at Storrs, with 22,466 students in 1994; four divisions of the Connecticut State University; 12 regional community colleges; and 5 state technical colleges. Connecticut's 23 private four-year colleges and universities had 55,767 students in 1994. Among the oldest institutions is Yale University in New Haven, founded in 1701.

33 ARTS

Art museums in Connecticut include the Wadsworth Atheneum in Hartford, the oldest (1842) free public art museum in the US; the Yale University Art Gallery and the Yale Center for British Art in New Haven; the New Britain Museum of American Art; and the Lyman Allyn Museum of Connecticut College in New London.

Professional theaters include the American Shakespeare Festival Theater in Stratford, the Long Wharf Theater and the Yale Repertory Theater in New Haven, the Hartford Stage Company, and the Eugene O'Neill Memorial Theater Center in Waterford.

The state's foremost metropolitan orchestras are the Hartford and New Haven symphonies. Professional opera is presented by the Stamford State Opera and by the Connecticut Opera in Hartford. Prominent dance groups include the Connecticut Dance Company in New Haven, the Hartford Ballet Company, and the Pilobolus Dance Theater in the town of Washington.

34 LIBRARIES AND MUSEUMS

As of 1994, Connecticut had 194 public libraries. The leading public library is the Connecticut State Library (Hartford), which houses over 1 million bound volumes and over 2,451 periodicals, and which also serves as the official state historical museum.

Connecticut's most distinguished academic collection is the Yale University library system (9 million volumes) in New Haven, headed by the Sterling Memorial Library and the Beinecke Rare Book and Manuscript Library. In all, Connecticut libraries held 13.5 million volumes in 1998 and had a combined circulation of 26.1 million.

Connecticut has more than 162 museums, in addition to its historic sites. The Peabody Museum of Natural History at Yale in New Haven includes an impressive dinosaur hall. Connecticut's historical sites include the Henry Whitfield House in Guilford (1639), said to be the oldest stone house in the US, and Noah Webster's birthplace in West Hartford.

35 COMMUNICATIONS

As of 1999, 96.5% of the state's occupied housing units had telephones. In 2000, Connecticut had 40 AM and 59 FM radio stations, and 15 television stations. There were educational television stations in Bridgeport, Hartford, and Norwich. In 2000, 109,775 domain names were registered on the Internet.

36 PRESS

The *Hartford Courant*, founded in 1764, is generally considered to be the oldest US newspaper in continuous publication.

The leading Connecticut dailies in 1998 were the *Courant*, with an average morning circulation of 211,041 (Sundays, 303,399), and the *New Haven Register*, with an average evening circulation of 100,061 (Sundays, 112,318). Statewide, in 1998 there were 13 morning newspapers, 8 evening newspapers, and 12 Sunday newspapers. In 1997, Connecticut also had 57 weekly newspapers. Leading periodicals are *American Scientist, Connecticut Magazine, Fine Woodworking, Golf Digest,* and *Tennis.*

37 TOURISM, TRAVEL, AND RECREATION

Tourism has become an increasingly important part of the state economy in recent decades. Popular tourist attractions include the Mystic Seaport restoration and its aquarium, the Mark Twain House and state capitol in Hartford, and the Yale campus in New Haven. Outstanding events include the Harvard-Yale regatta held each June on the Thames River in New London.

38 SPORTS

Connecticut's only major league professional team, the National Hockey League's Hartford Whalers, moved to North Carolina after the 1996/97 season. New Haven has a minor league hockey franchise, the Red Sox. Auto racing takes place at Lime Rock Race Track, in Salisbury.

Connecticut schools, colleges, and universities provide amateur athletic competitions, highlighted by Ivy League football games on autumn Saturdays at the Yale Bowl in New Haven.

39 FAMOUS CONNECTICUTERS

Connecticut cannot claim any US president or vice-president as a native son, although Al Gore chose Connecticut Senator, Joseph Lieberman, as his running mate in the 2000 Presidental race. Two Connecticut natives have served as chief justice of the US: Oliver Ellsworth (1745–1807) and Morrison R. Waite (1816–88). Other prominent federal officeholders were Dean Acheson (1893–1971), secretary of state; and Abraham A. Ribicoff (1910–98), secretary of health, education, and welfare. Connecticut senator Lowell P. Weicker, Jr. (b.France, 1931) was brought to national attention by his work during the Watergate hearings in 1973.

Ella Tambussi Grasso (1919–81), elected in 1974 and reelected in 1978, was the first woman governor in the US who did not succeed her husband in the post.

Photo credit: EPD Photos.

Nathan Hale, Revolutionary War hero, proclaimed "I only regret that I have but one life to lose for my country" as British soldiers prepared to hang him as a spy.

Shapers of US history include Jonathan Edwards (1703–58), a Congregationalist minister who sparked the 18th-century religious revival known as the Great Awakening; Connecticut's most revered Revolutionary War figure, Nathan Hale (1755–76), who was executed for spying behind British lines; radical abolitionist John Brown (1800–1859); and Henry Ward Beecher (1813–87), a religious leader and abolitionist.

Connecticuters prominent in US cultural development include painter John Trumbull (1756–1843); Noah Webster (1758–1843), who compiled the *American Dictionary of the English Language* (1828); and Harriet Beecher Stowe (1811–96), who wrote one of the most widely read books in history, *Uncle Tom's Cabin* (1852). Mark Twain (Samuel L. Clemens, b.Missouri, 1835–1910) was living in Hartford when he wrote *The Adventures of Huckleberry Finn* (1885).

Charles Ives (1874–1954) was one of the nation's most distinguished composers. A renowned voice in modern poetry, Wallace Stevens (b.Pennsylvania, 1879–1955), wrote most of his work while employed as a Hartford insurance executive.

James Merrill (b.New York, 1926–95) was a poet whose works won the National Book Award (1967) and many other honors.

Among the premier inventors born in Connecticut were Eli Whitney (1765–1825), inventor of the cotton gin; Samuel Colt (1814–62), inventor of the six-shooter; and Edwin H. Land (1909–91), inventor of the Polaroid Land Camera.

Other prominent Americans born in Connecticut include circus promoter Phineas Taylor "P. T." Barnum (1810–91), pediatrician Benjamin Spock(1903–98), actress Katharine Hepburn (b.1909), soprano Eileen Farrell (b.1920), and consumer-advocate Ralph Nader (b.1934), who was the Green Party candidate for president in 2000. Connecticut Senator Joseph I. Lieberman (b.1942), unsuccessful vice presidential running mate of Democrat Al Gore in 2000, was the first Jewish American ever to run for a national office.

40 BIBLIOGRAPHY

Aylesworth, Thomas G. *Southern New England: Connecticut, Massachusetts, Rhode Island*. New York: Chelsea House, 1996.

Bachman, Ben. *Upstream: A Voyage on the Connecticut River*. Boston: Houghton Mifflin, 1985.

Boyle, Doe. *Fun with the Family in Connecticut: Hundreds of Ideas for Day Trips with the Kids*. Guilford, Conn.: Globe Pequot Press, 2000.

Connecticut. Mankato, Minn.: Capstone, 1997.

Lieberman, Joseph I. *In Praise of Public Life*. New York: Simon & Schuster, 2000.

McAuliffe, Emily. *Connecticut Facts and Symbols*. New York: Hilltop Books, 1999.

McNair, Sylvia. *Connecticut*. Chicago: Children's Press, 1999.

Thompson, Kathleen. *Connecticut*. Austin, Tex.: Raintree Steck-Vaughn, 1996.

Whitehurst, Susan. *The Colony of Connecticut*. New York: PowerKids, 2000.

Web sites

State of Connecticut. ConneCT-About Connecticut. [Online] Available http://www.state.ct.us/about.htm Accessed May 31, 2001.

State of Connecticut. ConneCT State of Connecticut Website. [Online] Available http://www.state.ct.us/index.asp Accessed May 31, 2001.

DELAWARE

State of Delaware

ORIGIN OF STATE NAME: Named for Thomas West, Baron De La Warr, colonial governor of Virginia; the name was first applied to the bay.

NICKNAMES: The First State; the Diamond State.

CAPITAL: Dover.

ENTERED UNION: 7 December 1787 (1st).

SONG: "Our Delaware."

COLORS: Colonial blue and buff.

MOTTO: Liberty and Independence.

COAT OF ARMS: A farmer and a rifleman flank a shield that bears symbols of the state's agricultural resources—a sheaf of wheat, an ear of corn, and a cow. Above is a ship in full sail; below, a banner with the state motto.

FLAG: Colonial blue with the coat of arms on a buff-colored diamond; below the diamond is the date of statehood.

OFFICIAL SEAL: The coat of arms surrounded by the words "Great Seal of the State of Delaware 1793, 1847, 1907." The three dates represent the years in which the seal was revised.

BIRD: Blue hen chicken.

FISH: Weakfish.

FLOWER: Peach blossom.

TREE: American holly.

ROCK: Sillimanite.

INSECT: Ladybug.

TIME: 7 AM EST = noon GMT.

1 LOCATION AND SIZE

Located on the eastern seaboard of the US, Delaware ranks 49th in size among the 50 states. The state's total area is 2,044 square miles (5,295 square kilometers). Delaware extends 35 miles (56 kilometers) east-west at its widest; its maximum north-south extension is 96 miles (154 kilometers). Delaware's boundary length is 200 miles (322 kilometers).

2 TOPOGRAPHY

Delaware lies entirely within the Atlantic Coastal Plain except for its northern tip, which is part of the Piedmont Plateau. The state's highest elevation is 442 feet (135 meters). The rolling hills and pastures of the north give way to marshy regions in the south, with sandy beaches along the coast. Delaware's mean elevation, 60 feet (18 meters), is the lowest in the US. The Nanticoke, Choptank, and Pocomoke rivers flow westward into Chesapeake Bay. Other rivers flow into Delaware Bay.

3 CLIMATE

Delaware's climate is temperate and humid. The average annual temperature

---

in Wilmington ranges from 31°ғ (–1°c) in January to 76°ғ (24°c) in July. Both the record low and high temperatures for the state were established at Millsboro: –17°ғ (–27°c) on 17 January 1893, and 110°ғ (43°c) on 21 July 1930. The average annual precipitation is 41 inches (104 centimeters).

4 PLANTS AND ANIMALS

Common trees include black walnut, hickory, and sweetgum. Shadbush and sassafras are found chiefly in southern Delaware. Mammals native to the state include the white-tailed deer, muskrat, and common cottontail. The quail, robin, and cardinal are native birds. Of the 9 endangered animal species, two are the southern bald eagle and the Delmarva Peninsula fox squirrel.

5 ENVIRONMENTAL PROTECTION

The traffic of oil tankers into the Delaware Bay represents an environmental hazard. The Coastal Zone Act of 1971 restricts industrial development, oil drilling, and tanker movement along Delaware's coastline. In 1979 the act was amended to allow offshore oil drilling and development. The state's municipal governments have constructed three municipal landfills to handle solid waste.

6 POPULATION

Delaware ranked 45th among the 50 states in 2000, with a population of 783,600; the population density was 401 persons per square mile (154.8 persons per

Delaware Population Profile

Total population in 2000:	783,600
Population change, 1990–2000:	17.6%
Hispanic or Latino†:	4.8%
Population by race	
One race:	98.3%
White:	74.6%
Black or African American:	19.2%
American Indian/Alaska Native:	0.3%
Asian:	2.1%
Native Hawaiian/Pacific Islander:	—
Some other race:	2.0%
Two or more races:	1.7%

Population by Age Group

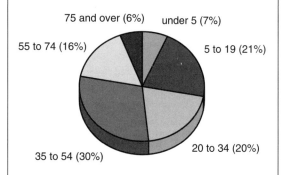

75 and over (6%)
under 5 (7%)
55 to 74 (16%)
5 to 19 (21%)
35 to 54 (30%)
20 to 34 (20%)

Top Cities by Population

City	Population	% change 1990–2000
Wilmington	72,664	1.6
Dover	32,135	16.3
Newark	28,547	13.7
Milford	6,732	11.5
Seaford	6,699	17.8
Middletown	6,161	60.7
Elsmere	5,800	–2.3
Smyrna	5,679	8.6
New Castle	4,862	0.5
Georgetown	4,643	24.4

Notes: †A person of Hispanic or Latino origin may be of any race. NA indicates that data are not available.
Sources: U.S. Census Bureau. Public Information Office. *Demographic Profiles.* [Online] Available http://www.census.gov/Press-Release/www/2001/demoprofile.html. Accessed June 1, 2001. U.S. Census Bureau. *Census 2000: Redistricting Data.* Press release issued by the Redistricting Data Office. Washington, D.C., March, 2001.

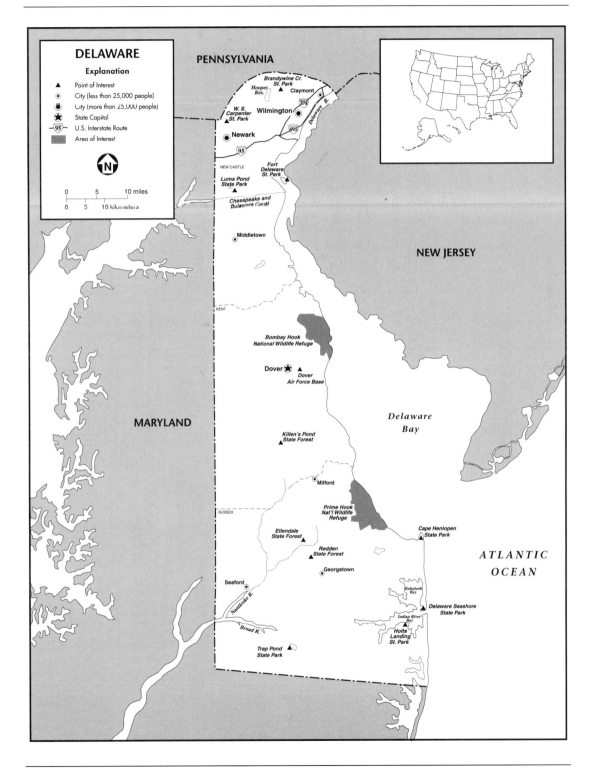

Photo credit: Delaware Tourism Office.

Liberty bell in front of Legislative Hall in Dover, Delaware's state capital.

24,000, or 3.3% of the total population, is of Hispanic origin.

8 LANGUAGES

English in Delaware is basically North Midland, with Philadelphia features in Wilmington and the northern portion. Over 575,000 Delawareans speak only English at home. Other languages spoken at home (and number of speakers) include Spanish (15,302), and German (4,206).

9 RELIGIONS

There are about 116,000 Catholics and an estimated 9,500 Jews in Delaware. The leading Protestant groups are the United Methodist Church, 61,091; the Episcopal Church, 13,307; and the Presbyterian Church, 15,401. The first Methodist services conducted in America were held in Delaware in the late 18th century. The African Methodist Episcopal Church was also founded by slaves and ex-slaves from Delaware.

square kilometer), significantly higher than the national average of 79.6 persons per square mile (30.7 per square kilometer). The largest cities in 2000 were Wilmington, with 72,664; and Dover, the capital, with 32,135.

7 ETHNIC GROUPS

Black Americans constitute Delaware's largest racial minority, at an estimated 140,000 in 1997 and comprising about 19.2% of the population (the 10th highest rate among the states). An estimated

10 TRANSPORTATION

As of 1998, there were 261 rail miles (420 kilometers) of track, which carried nearly 14.1 million tons of freight. The state had 5,722 miles (9,207 kilometers) of public highways, roads, and streets. The Lewes–Cape May Ferry provides auto and passenger service between southern Delaware and New Jersey. New Castle is Delaware's chief port. Much of the oil imported into the United States is transported by tanker on the Delaware River. Greater Wilmington Airport is the largest and busiest civilian airport.

Delaware Population by Race

Census 2000 was the first national census in which the instructions to respondents said, "Mark one or more races." This table shows the number of people who are of one, two, or three or more races. For those claiming two races, the number of people belonging to the various categories is listed. The U.S. government conducts a census of the population every ten years.

	Number	Percent
Total population	783,600	100.0
One race	770,567	98.3
Two races	12,131	1.5
White *and* Black or African American	3,145	0.4
White *and* American Indian/Alaska Native	1,605	0.2
White *and* Asian	1,645	0.2
White *and* Native Hawaiian/Pacific Islander	78	—
White *and* some other race	2,372	0.3
Black or African American *and* American Indian/Alaska Native	890	0.1
Black or African American *and* Asian	338	—
Black or African American *and* Native Hawaiian/Pacific Islander	82	—
Black or African American *and* some other race	1,282	0.2
American Indian/Alaska Native *and* Asian	72	—
American Indian/Alaska Native *and* Native Hawaiian/Pacific Islander	5	—
American Indian/Alaska Native *and* some other race	176	—
Asian *and* Native Hawaiian/Pacific Islander	75	—
Asian *and* some other race	325	—
Native Hawaiian/Pacific Islander *and* some other race	41	—
Three or more races	902	0.1

Source: U.S. Census Bureau. *Census 2000: Redistricting Data.* Press release issued by the Redistricting Data Office. Washington, D.C., March, 2001. A dash (—) indicates that the percent is less than 0.1.

11 HISTORY

At the time of the first European contact, the Leni-Lenape people occupied northern Delaware, while several tribes, including the Nanticoke and Assateague, inhabited southern Delaware. Permanent settlements were made by the Swedes in 1638 at Wilmington and by the Dutch in 1651 at New Castle. The Dutch conquered the Swedes in 1655, and were in turn conquered in 1664 by the English, who placed Delaware under the control of William Penn.

In the War for Independence, Delaware troops fought so well that they gained the nickname "Blue Hen's Chicken," after a famous breed of now-extinct fighting gamecocks.

On 7 December 1787, Delaware became the first state to ratify the federal Constitution. Although Delaware had not abolished slavery, it remained loyal to the Union during the Civil War. However, white Delawareans manipulated registration laws to deny blacks voting rights until 1890. Delaware refused ratification of the three "Civil War" constitutional amendments (abolition of slavery, equal protection, voting rights for black men) until 1901.

Delaware Governors: 1775—2001

1775–1777	John McKinly	
1777	Thomas McKean	
1777–1778	George Read	
1778–1782	Caesar Rodney	
1782–1783	John Dickinson	
1783	John Cook	
1783–1786	Nickolas Van Dyke	
1786–1789	Thomas Collins	
1789	Jehu Davis	
1789–1796	Joshua Clayton	Federalist
1796–1797	Gunning Bedford, Sr.	Federalist
1797–1801	Daniel Rogers	Federalist
1801	Richard Bassett	Federalist
1801–1802	James Sykes	Federalist
1802–1805	David Hall	Dem-Rep
1805–1808	Nathaniel Mitchell	Federalist
1808–1811	George Truitt	Federalist
1811–1814	Joseph Haslet	Dem-Rep
1814–1817	Daniel Rodney	Federalist
1817–1820	John Clark	Federalist
1820–1821	Jacob Stout	Federalist
1821–1822	John Collins	Dem-Rep
1822–1823	Caleb Rodney	Dem-Rep
1823	Joseph Haslet	Dem-Rep
1823–1824	Charles Thomas	Dem-Rep
1824–1827	Samuel Paynter	Federalist
1827–1830	Charles Polk	Federalist
1830–1833	David Hazzard	Anti–Republican
1833–1836	Caleb Prew Bennett	Jackson Democrat
1836–1837	Charles Polk	Federalist
1837–1840	Cornelius Parsons Comegys	Whig
1841–1845	William B. Cooper	Whig
1845–1846	Thomas Stockton	Whig
1846	Joseph Maull	Whig
1846–1847	William Temple	Whig
1847–1851	William Tharp	Democrat
1851–1855	William Henry Harrison Ross	Democrat

1855–1859	Peter Foster Causey	Whig
1859–1863	William Burton	Democrat
1863–1865	William Cannon	Unionist
1865–1871	Gove Saulsbury	Democrat
1871–1875	James Ponder	Democrat
1875–1879	John P. Cochran	Democrat
1879–1883	John Wood Hall	Democrat
1883–1887	Charles Clark Stockley	Democrat
1887–1891	Benjamin Thomas Briggs	Democrat
1891–1895	Robert John Reynolds	Democrat
1895	Joshua Hopkins Marvel	Republican
1895–1897	William T. Watson	Democrat
1897–1901	Ebe Walter Tunnell	Democrat
1901–1905	John Hunn	Republican
1905–1909	Preston Lea	Republican
1909–1913	Simeon Selby Pennewill	Republican
1913–1917	Charles R. Miller	Republican
1917–1921	John Gillis Townsend, Jr.	Republican
1921–1925	William Du Hamel Denney	Republican
1925–1929	Robert P. Robinson	Republican
1929–1937	Clayton Douglass Buck	Republican
1937–1941	Richard Cann McMullen	Democrat
1941–1949	Walter W. Bacon	Republican
1949–1953	Elbert Nostrand Carvel	Democrat
1953–1960	James Caleb Boggs	Republican
1960–1961	David Penrose Buckson	Republican
1961–1965	Elbert Nostrand Carvel	Democrat
1965–1969	Charles Laymen Terry, Jr.	Democrat
1969–1973	Russell Wilbur Peterson	Republican
1973–1977	Sherman Willard Tribbitt	Democrat
1977–1985	Pierre Samuel du Pont IV	Republican
1985–1992	Michael Newbald Castle	Republican
1993	Dale Edward Wolf	Republican
1993–2001	Thomas Richard Carper	Democrat
2001-	Ruth Ann Minner	Democrat

Democratic Republican – Dem-Rep

The key event in the state's early economic history was the completion of a railroad between Philadelphia and Baltimore through Wilmington in 1838. Foreign immigration contributed to the state's growth, largely from the British Isles and Germany in the mid-19th century and from Italy, Poland, and Russia in the early 20th century. In the early 1900's, E. I. du Pont de Nemours and Co., founded near Wilmington in 1802 as a gunpowder manufacturer, made the city famous as a center for the chemical industry.

During the 1950s, Delaware's population grew by an unprecedented 40%. Although many neighborhood schools became racially integrated during the 1950s, massive busing was instituted by court order in 1978 to achieve a racial balance in schools throughout northern Delaware. This court order was lifted in 1995.

The 1980s ushered in a period of dramatic economic improvement. Some of Delaware's prosperity came from a 1981 state law that raised interest rate limits and lowered taxes for large financial institutions. More than thirty banks established themselves in Delaware, and the state also succeeded in attracting foreign companies. Two industrial parks were built in Sussex, Delaware's southernmost county, and a third complex in the center of the state.

Although business has grown in Delaware, urban and rural poverty are still present. Delaware's teenage pregnancy rate is one of the highest in the country, while its welfare benefits are lower than any other mid-Atlantic state with the exception of West Virginia. Delaware's unemployment rate, however, has consistently been lower than the national average since the early 1980s.

12 STATE GOVERNMENT

Delaware's legislative branch is the general assembly, consisting of a 21-member senate and a 41-member house of representatives. Delaware's major elected executives include the governor and lieutenant governor (elected separately), treasurers, and attorney general.

13 POLITICAL PARTIES

Since the 1930s, the two major parties have been relatively evenly matched. As of 1999, 199,101 voters were registered as members of the Democratic party, comprising 42% of the total number of registered voters, while 163,313, or 34%, were registered as Republicans. There were 111,357 voters registered as independents or with minor parties.

In November 2000, Delaware gave the Democratic candidate, Al Gore, 55% of the vote. Republican George W. Bush received 42%. Democrat Ruth Ann Minner won election to the governor's office in 2000, becoming the 1st female governor in the state's history. Democrat Thomas Carper was elected Senator in 2000. Republican Michael Castle won reelection in 2000 to remain Delaware's sole US Representative.

Delaware Presidential Vote by Major Political Parties, 1948–2000

YEAR	DELAWARE WINNER	DEMOCRAT	REPUBLICAN
1948	Dewey (R)	67,813	69,588
1952	*Eisenhower (R)	83,315	90,059
1956	*Eisenhower (R)	79,421	98,057
1960	*Kennedy (D)	99,590	96,373
1964	*Johnson (D)	122,704	78,078
1968	*Nixon (R)	89,194	96,714
1972	*Nixon (R)	92,283	140,357
1976	*Carter (D)	122,596	109,831
1980	*Reagan (R)	105,700	111,185
1984	*Reagan (R)	101,656	152,190
1988	*Bush (R)	108,647	139,639
1992**	*Clinton (D)	126,054	102,313
1996**	*Clinton (D)	140,355	99,062
2000	Al Gore (D)	180,068	137,288

* Won US presidential election.

**Independent Ross Perot received 59,213 votes in 1992 and 28,719 votes in 1996.

14 LOCAL GOVERNMENT

Delaware is divided into three counties. In New Castle, voters elect a county executive and a county council; in Sussex, the members of the elective county council choose a county administrator. Kent operates under an elected levy court. Most of

Delaware's 57 municipalities elect a mayor and council.

15 JUDICIAL SYSTEM

Delaware's highest court is the supreme court, composed of a chief justice and four associate justices. Other state courts include the court of chancery and the superior court. The court of chancery handles all corporate cases and is one of the busiest of such courts in the US due to Delaware's high concentration of incorporated businesses. In 1998, Delaware had a total crime rate of 5,363.2 per 100,000.

16 MIGRATION

Delaware enjoyed a net gain from migration of 122,000 persons between 1940 and 1970. Between 1970 and 1990, however, there was a net migration of only about 25,000, and 29,000 during 1990–98. Half of all residents in 1990 were born within the state.

17 ECONOMY

Since the 1930s, and particularly since the mid-1970s, Delaware has been one of the nation's most prosperous states. Although manufacturing—primarily the chemical and automotive industries—is the major contributor to the state's economy, it is only the third largest employer after services and trade. Tourism also plays a major role in the state's economy.

18 INCOME

Average personal income per capita (per person) in Delaware was $29,383 in 1998, tenth highest among the 50 states. Median household income was $42,000 in 1998. In the same year, some 9.5% of the state's residents were living below the federal poverty level.

19 INDUSTRY

Wilmington is called the "Chemical Capital of the World," largely because of E. I. du Pont de Nemours and Co., the chemical industry giant that was the nation's 16th largest industrial corporation in 1999. Important manufactured products, in addition to chemicals and transportation equipment, include apparel, processed meats and vegetables, paper, printing and publishing, scientific instruments, and plastic products.

20 LABOR

The civilian labor force totaled 392,000 in mid-1998. Some 15,000 Delawareans were unemployed, for an unemployment rate of 3.8%. Some 13.6% of all workers were union members in 1998.

21 AGRICULTURE

Though small by national standards, Delaware's agriculture is efficient and productive. In 1999, Delaware's farm industry income was $718 million with crops accounting for $153.1 of the total. The major field crops are corn, soybeans, barley, wheat, melons, potatoes, mushrooms, lima beans, and green peas. Production in 1998 included corn for grain, 15.5 million bushels; soybeans, 7.1 million bushels; wheat, 3.7 million bushels; and barley, 1.8 million bushels.

A dock worker watches as the cargo of a ship is unloaded at the Port of Wilmington.

22 DOMESTICATED ANIMALS

Livestock and livestock products account for about 75% of Delaware's farm income. Production of broilers in 1998 accounted for 72% of the state's farm receipts. Some 10,100 dairy cows produced 153 million pounds (69.4 million kilograms) of milk in 1997.

23 FISHING

Fishing, once an important industry in Delaware, has declined in recent decades. The total commercial landings in 1998 were 7.9 million, worth $5.8 million.

24 FORESTRY

Delaware has 389,000 acres (159,000 hectares) of forestland. Sussex County has large areas of southern yellow pine, nearly all of it (96%) privately owned.

25 MINING

The value of nonfuel mineral production in Delaware in 1998 was about $11.2 million. However, the Delaware Geological

Photo credit: Delaware Tourism Office.

The skyline of Wilmington, the largest city in Delaware.

Survey estimates the nonfuel mineral industry generates a total of $30 million per year. An estimated 2.24 million metric tons of construction sand and gravel were produced in 1998. Delaware also produces magnesium compounds for use in chemical and pharmaceutical production.

26 ENERGY AND POWER

In 1998, production of electric power reached 6.3 billion kilowatt hours. Most power is supplied by coal- and oil-fired plants. Delaware has no coal or oil resources of its own, and no nuclear reactors.

27 COMMERCE

Annual sales from wholesale trade in Delaware total over $13 billion, while retail establishments have sales of almost $8.6 billion. In 1998, over $2.2 billion worth of products made in the state were exported.

28 PUBLIC FINANCE

Delaware's annual state budget is prepared by the Office of the Budget and submitted by the governor to the general assembly for amendment and approval. State revenues for 1997 were $ 4.21 million; expenditures were $ 3.4 billion.

At the close of fiscal 1997, the outstanding debt of Delaware state and local governments was more than $3.43 billion, or $4,691 per capita (6th highest ratio of any state).

29 TAXATION

Delaware's state tax revenues come primarily from taxes on personal and corporate income, inheritance and estates, motor fuels, cigarettes, betting, and alcoholic beverages. There is no state sales tax. Delaware's state taxes totaled $1.74 billion in 1997, or about $2,383 per person (the 5th highest rate among the states). Delaware paid $4.4 billion in federal taxes in 1995 and received $3.2 billion in federal expenditures—or, for every $1 Delaware paid it received back about 73¢ from the federal government.

30 HEALTH

Delaware has lower death rates than the nation as a whole for heart diseases, cerebrovascular diseases, motor vehicle accidents, and suicide, but higher for chronic liver and lung diseases. Delaware's six community hospitals had 1,977 beds in 1998. The average expense of a community hospital for care was $1,224.70 per inpatient day. Over 14.7% of the population did not have health insurance in 1998.

31 HOUSING

In October 1999 there were about 326,000 housing units in Delaware. In 1990, the median value of a home in Delaware was $100,100, and the median rent for a housing unit was $495 per month.

32 EDUCATION

Nearly 85.2% of adult Delawareans were high school graduates in 1998. In 1997, 111,960 students were enrolled in public schools, and 44,890 students were enrolled in higher education. Delaware has two public four-year institutions: the University of Delaware (Newark), and Delaware State College (Dover).

33 ARTS

The restored Grand Opera House in Wilmington, Delaware's Center for the Performing Arts, is the home of the Delaware Symphony and the Delaware Opera Guild.

34 LIBRARIES AND MUSEUMS

Delaware had 30 public libraries in 1995, with 1.3 million books and a circulation of 3 million. The University of Delaware's Hugh M. Morris Library (Newark) is the largest academic library in the state. Notable among the state's 27 museums are the Hagley Museum, the Delaware History Museum, the Winterthur Museum, and the Delaware Art Museum, all in Wilmington. The Delaware State Museum is in Dover.

35 COMMUNICATIONS

In 1999, about 95.7% of Delaware's housing units had telephones. The state had 10 AM and 20 FM radio stations and 3 television stations in 2000. A total of 19,351 domain names were also registered in the same year.

36 PRESS

The *Wilmington Morning News* and the *Wilmington Evening Journal* merged to form the *News Journal* in 1989. The paper's daily circulation is 125,401 (149,519 on Sunday).

37 TOURISM, TRAVEL, AND RECREATION

Rehoboth Beach on the Atlantic Coast bills itself as the "Nation's Summer Capital" because of the many federal officials and foreign diplomats who summer there. Fishing, clamming, crabbing, boating, and swimming are the main recreational attractions.

Photo credit: EPD Photos

John Dickinson (b.Maryland, 1732–1808) was known as the "Penman of the Revolution." He was elected a representative to Congress from Delaware in 1779 and assisted in framing the constitution of Delaware in 1792. He died in Wilmington.

38 SPORTS

Delaware has two major horse-racing tracks: Harrington and Dover Downs, which also has a track for auto racing. The combined attendance at thoroughbred and trotter horse races in 1996 was over 539,000. The Dover 500 is an annual NASCAR event.

39 FAMOUS DELAWAREANS

Three Delawareans have served as US secretary of state: Louis McLane (1786–1857), John M. Clayton (1796–1856), and Thomas F. Bayard (1828–98). Eleuthère I. du Pont (b.France, 1771–1834) founded the company that bears his name. Delaware authors include Henry Seidel Canby (1878–1961), critic; and novelist Anne Parrish (b.Colorado, 1888–1957). Dr. Henry J. Heimlich (b.1920), developer of the anti-choking "Heimlich maneuver," is also from Delaware. Actors from Delaware include Judge Reinhold (b.1958) and Valerie Bertinelli (b. 1960).

40 BIBLIOGRAPHY

Blashfield, Jean F. *Delaware*. New York: Children's Press, 2000.

Fradin, Dennis B. *The Delaware Colony*. Chicago: Children's Press, 1992.

Kule, Elaine A. *Delaware Facts and Symbols*. Mankato, Minn.: Hilltop Books, 2001.

Miller, Jay. *The Delaware*. Chicago: Children's Press, 1994.

Schuman, Michael. *Delaware*. New York: Benchmark Books, 2000.

Whitehurst, Susan. *The Colony of Delaware*. New York: PowerKids Press, 2000.

Williams, William Henry. *Slavery and Freedom in Delaware, 1639–1865*. Wilmington, Del.: SR Books, 1996.

Web sites

State of Delaware. Delaware's Kids' Page. [Online] Available http://www.state.de.us/kidspage/ Accessed May 31, 2001.

State of Delaware. State of Delaware Web Site. [Online] Available http://www.delaware.gov/ Accessed May 31, 2001.

FLORIDA

State of Florida

ORIGIN OF STATE NAME: Named in 1513 by Juan Ponce de León, who landed during *Pascua Florida,* the Easter festival of flowers.

NICKNAME: The Sunshine State.

CAPITAL: Tallahassee.

ENTERED UNION: 3 March 1845 (27th).

SONG: "Old Folks at Home" (also known as "Swanee River").

POET LAUREATE: Dr. Edmund Skellings.

MOTTO: In God We Trust.

FLAG: The state seal appears in the center of a white field, with four red bars extending from the seal to each corner; the flag is fringed on three sides.

OFFICIAL SEAL: In the background, the sun's rays shine over a distant highland; in the foreground are a sabal palmetto palm, a steamboat, and an Indian woman scattering flowers on the ground. The words "Great Seal of the State of Florida" and the state motto surround the whole.

ANIMAL: Florida panther.

MARINE MAMMALS: Manatee, dolphin.

BIRD: Mockingbird.

FISH: Largemouth bass (freshwater), Atlantic sailfish (saltwater).

FLOWER: Orange blossom.

TREE: Sabal palmetto palm.

GEM: Moonstone.

STONE: Agatized coral.

SHELL: Horse conch.

BEVERAGE: Orange juice.

TIME: 7 AM EST = noon GMT; 6 AM CST = noon GMT.

1 LOCATION AND SIZE

Located in the extreme southeastern US, Florida is the second-largest state east of the Mississippi River and ranks 22d in size among the 50 states. The total area of Florida is approximately 58,664 square miles (151,939 square kilometers). Florida extends 361 miles (581 kilometers) east-west; its maximum north-south extension is 447 miles (719 kilometers). The state comprises a peninsula surrounded by ocean on three sides, with a panhandle of land in the northwest.

Offshore islands include the Florida Keys, extending form the state's southern tip into the Gulf of Mexico. The total boundary length of Florida is 1,799 miles (2,895 kilometers).

2 TOPOGRAPHY

Florida is a huge plateau, much of it barely above sea level. No point in the state is more than 70 miles (113 kilometers) from salt water. Most of the panhandle region is gently rolling country, much like that of southern Georgia and Alabama, with large swampy areas cutting in from the Gulf coast. Peninsular Florida, which contains extensive swampland, has a relatively elevated central section of rolling country, dotted with lakes and springs. Its east coast is shielded from the Atlantic by a string of sandbars. The west coast is cut by numerous bays and inlets, and near its southern tip are the Ten Thousand Islands, a mass of mangrove-covered islets. Southwest of the peninsula lies Key West, the southernmost point of the US mainland.

Almost all the southeastern peninsula and the entire southern end are covered by the Everglades, the world's largest sawgrass swamp, with an area of approximately 4,000 square miles (10,400 square kilometers). To the west and north of the everglades is Big Cypress Swamp, covering about 2,100 square miles (5,400 square kilometers).

Lake Okeechobee, in south-central Florida, is the largest of the state's approximately 30,000 lakes, ponds, and sinks. Although quite shallow, it has a surface area of about 700 square miles (1,800 square kilometers), making it the fourth-largest natural lake located entirely within the US. Crystal River, in Citrus County, has the largest average flow of all inland springs, 878 cubic feet (24.8 cubic meters) per second.

Florida has more than 1,700 rivers, streams, and creeks; the longest river is the St. Johns, which empties into the Atlantic.

Florida Population Profile

Total population in 2000:	15,982,378
Population change, 1990–2000:	19.0%
Hispanic or Latino†:	16.8%
Population by race	
One race:	97.6%
White:	78.0%
Black or African American:	14.6%
American Indian/Alaska Native:	0.3%
Asian:	1.7%
Native Hawaiian/Pacific Islander:	0.1%
Some other race:	3.0%
Two or more races:	2.4%

Population by Age Group

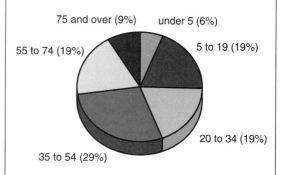

75 and over (9%)
under 5 (6%)
55 to 74 (19%)
5 to 19 (19%)
20 to 34 (19%)
35 to 54 (29%)

Top Cities by Population

City	Population	% change 1990–2000
Jacksonville	735,617	8.5
Miami	362,470	1.1
Tampa	303,447	7.7
St. Petersburg	248,232	3.9
Hialeah	226,419	17.0
Orlando	185,951	11.4
Fort Lauderdale	152,397	2.0
Tallahassee	150,624	17.2
Hollywood	139,357	12.7
Pembroke Pines	137,427	52.4

Notes: †A person of Hispanic or Latino origin may be of any race. NA indicates that data are not available.
Sources: U.S. Census Bureau. Public Information Office. *Demographic Profiles.* [Online] Available http://www.census.gov/Press-Release/www/2001/demoprofile.html. Accessed June 1, 2001. U.S. Census Bureau. *Census 2000: Redistricting Data.* Press release issued by the Redistricting Data Office. Washington, D.C., March, 2001.

ALABAMA

GEORGIA

ATLANTIC OCEAN

ESCAMBIA | SANTA ROSA | OKALOOSA | WALTON | HOLMES | JACKSON

Blackwater River State For. ▲

Florida Caverns State Park ▲

Eglin A.F. Base ▲

Pensacola

Gulf Islands National Seashore

St. Andrews State Recreational Area

WASHINGTON

BAY

CALHOUN

GULF

LIBERTY

Apalachicola Nat'l For.

FRANKLIN

GADSDEN

LEON

Tallahassee ★

WAKULLA

St. Marks National Wildlife Ref.

JEFFERSON | MADISON | HAMILTON

TAYLOR

SUWANNEE

LAFAYETTE

DIXIE

GIL-CHRIST

Osceola Nat'l For.

BAKER

COLUMBIA

UNION

NASSAU

Fort Clinch State Park

Jacksonville ⊙

DUVAL

CLAY

Lower Suwannee Nat'l Wildlife Ref.

Manatee Springs State Park ▲

LEVY

BRADFORD

ALACHUA

Gainesville ⊙

Ocala Nat'l For.

ST. JOHNS

PUTNAM

FLAGLER

MARION

Daytona Beach

CITRUS

SUMTER

LAKE

VOLUSIA

Gulf of Mexico

HERNANDO

PASCO

Lake Louisa State Park ▲

POLK

Seminole

ORANGE

Orlando ●

OSCEOLA

Cape Canaveral Air Force Station

Melbourne

Palm Bay

PINELLAS

Clearwater ⊙

Largo ⊙

St. Petersburg ⊙

HILLSBOROUGH

Lakeland ⊙

Tampa ●

MANATEE

Sarasota ⊙

Avon Park A.F. Range ▲

HARDEE

Highlands Hammock State Park ▲

HIGHLANDS

OKEECHOBEE

BREVARD

INDIAN RIVER

ST. LUCIE

Port St. Lucie ⊙

DE SOTO

SARASOTA

CHARLOTTE

Brighton Seminole Indian Res. ▲

Lake Okeechobee

GLADES

HENDRY

MARTIN

PALM BEACH

West Palm Beach ⊙

LEE

Cape Coral ⊙

Big Cypress National Preserve

Arthur R. Marshall Loxahatchee National Wildlife Refuge

Boca Raton ⊙

Pompano Beach ⊙

Coral Springs ⊙

Sunrise ⊙

Plantation ⊙

Fort Lauderdale ●

COLLIER

BROWARD

Pembroke Pines ⊙

Hollywood ●

Hialeah ●

Miami Beach ⊙

Miami ●

MONROE

DADE

Everglades National Park

Florida Bay

Florida Keys

FLORIDA

Explanation

▲ Point of Interest

⊙ City (50,000-100,000 people)

● City (more than 100,000 people)

★ State Capital

🛡95 U.S. Interstate Route

▨ Area of Interest

Ⓝ

| 0 | 25 | 50 miles |

| 0 | 25 | 50 kilometers |

Other major rivers are the Suwannee and the Apalachicola. Jim Woodruff Lock and Dam, built on the Apalachicola in 1957, created Lake Seminole, most of which is in Georgia. More than 4,500 islands ring the mainland. Best known are the Florida Keys, of which Key Largo—about 29 miles (47 kilometers) long and less than 2 miles (3 kilometers) wide—is the largest.

3 CLIMATE

A mild, sunny climate is one of Florida's most important natural resources, making it a major tourist center and a retirement home for millions of transplanted northerners. Average annual temperatures range from 65°F to 70°F (18°C to 21°C) in the north, and from 74°F to 77°F (23°C to 25°C) in the southern peninsula and on the Keys. The record high temperature 109°F (43°C), was registered at Monticello on 29 June 1931; the record low, –2°F (–19°C), at Tallahassee on 13 February 1899.

Photo credit: Orlando/Orange County Convention & Visitors Bureau, Inc.

Citrus fruit ripening under the Florida sun. Citrus groves are scattered throughout Central Florida.

At Jacksonville, the average annual precipitation is 53 inches (135 centimeters), with an average of 116 days of precipitation a year. More than half the annual rainfall generally occurs between June and September; periods of extremely heavy rainfall are common. Florida's long coastline makes it highly vulnerable to hurricanes and tropical storms, which may approach from either the Atlantic or the Gulf coast, bringing winds of up to 150 miles per hour (240 kilometers per hour).

4 PLANTS AND ANIMALS

Generally, Florida has seven floral zones: flatwoods, scrublands, grassy swamps, savannas, salt marshes, hardwood forests (hammocks), and pinelands. North Florida's native plants include longleaf and other pines, oaks, and cypresses. One giant cypress, called "the Senator," is thought to be 3,500 years old. The state is known for its wide variety of palms. Dense mangrove thickets grow along the lower coastal regions, and northern hardwood forests include varieties of rattan, magnolia, and oak. All species of cacti and orchids are regarded as threatened, as are most types of ferns and palms. Endangered species (54) include the Chapman rhododendron, key tree–cactus, and Harper's beauty.

Florida once claimed more than 80 land mammals. Today the white-tailed deer, wild hog, and gray fox can still be found in the wild. Such small mammals as the raccoon, squirrel, and cottontail and marsh rabbits remain common. The mockingbird was named the state bird in 1927. Among game birds are the bobwhite quail, wild turkey, and at least 30 duck species. The Arctic tern stops in Florida during its remarkable annual migration between the North and South poles.

Common Florida reptiles are the diamondback rattler and various water snakes. Turtle species include mud, green, and loggerhead, and various lizards abound. More than 300 native butterflies have been identified. The peninsula is famous for its marine life: scores of freshwater and saltwater fish, rays, shrimps, live coral reefs, and marine worms.

The state's unusually long list of threatened and endangered wildlife (39 species) includes the American crocodile, American alligator, shortnose sturgeon, West Indian manatee, Florida panther, Key Largo woodrat, Everglade kite, and Bahama swallowtail butterfly.

5 ENVIRONMENTAL PROTECTION

Throughout the 20th century, a rapidly growing population, the expansion of agriculture, and the exploitation of such resources as timber and minerals have put severe pressure on Florida's natural environment.

The state agency principally responsible for safeguarding the environment is the Department of Environmental Protection (DEP), created in 1993 by the merger of the Departments of Natural Resources and Environmental Protection. Its Division of State Lands has purchased more than 1.2 million acres (500,000 hectares) of environmentally important land.

Contamination and depletion of groundwater and control of storm water are the state's most serious environmental problems. Major contaminants include the pesticide ethylene dibromide (EDB). Florida has one of the nation's largest programs to clean groundwater contaminated by leaking underground storage tanks.

Contamination of groundwater is not the state's only water problem. Salt water from the Atlantic and the Gulf of Mexico has begun seeping into the layers of porous limestone that hold Florida's reserves of fresh water, as increased demand for water has reduced the subterranean runoff of fresh water into these bodies.

In 1960, the only undersea park in the US, the John Pennekamp Coral Reef State Park, was established in a 75-square mile (194-square-kilometer) sector off the Atlantic coast of Key Largo. This is an effort to protect a portion of the beautiful reefs, rich in tropical fish and other marine life, that adjoin the Keys.

6 POPULATION

Florida, the most populous state in the southeastern US, is also one of the fastest-growing of the 50 states. In 1960, it was the tenth most populous state; by 1980, it ranked seventh; and by 2000, it ranked fourth, with a population of nearly 16 mil-

Florida Population by Race

Census 2000 was the first national census in which the instructions to respondents said, "Mark one or more races." This table shows the number of people who are of one, two, or three or more races. For those claiming two races, the number of people belonging to the various categories is listed. The U.S. government conducts a census of the population every ten years.

	Number	Percent
Total population	15,982,378	100.0
One race	15,606,063	97.6
Two races	359,000	2.2
White *and* Black or African American	38,429	0.2
White *and* American Indian/Alaska Native	43,940	0.3
White *and* Asian	37,068	0.2
White *and* Native Hawaiian/Pacific Islander	3,389	—
White *and* some other race	131,473	0.8
Black or African American *and* American Indian/Alaska Native	7,182	—
Black or African American *and* Asian	8,427	0.1
Black or African American *and* Native Hawaiian/Pacific Islander	4,852	—
Black or African American *and* some other race	65,492	0.4
American Indian/Alaska Native *and* Asian	1,577	—
American Indian/Alaska Native *and* Native Hawaiian/Pacific Islander	222	—
American Indian/Alaska Native *and* some other race	3,733	—
Asian *and* Native Hawaiian/Pacific Islander	2,234	—
Asian *and* some other race	9,531	0.1
Native Hawaiian/Pacific Islander *and* some other race	1,451	—
Three or more races	17,315	0.1

Source: U.S. Census Bureau. *Census 2000: Redistricting Data.* Press release issued by the Redistricting Data Office. Washington, D.C., March, 2001. A dash (—) indicates that the percent is less than 0.1.

lion. US Census Bureau projections indicate that Florida will have a population of 16.3 million by 2005.

Of the 1990 population, 90.8% lived in metropolitan areas; the average population density in 2000 was 296.4 persons per square mile (about 114.4 persons per square kilometer), much higher than the national average of 79.6 persons per square mile (30.7 per square kilometer). Florida has one of the oldest populations of the 50 states with the median age at 38.7, higher than the national average of 35.3. In 2000, 57% of the population was over the age of 35.

The most populous city in Florida is Jacksonville, the 14th-largest city in the US in 2000. Its population that year was 735,617. Miami is Florida's second-largest city, with a 2000 population of 362,470. Other cities and their 2000 populations are Tampa, 303,447; St. Petersburg, 248,232; Hialeah, 226,419; and Orlando, 185,951. Tallahassee, the state capital, had a population of 150,624 in 2000.

7 ETHNIC GROUPS

Florida's population consists mainly of whites of northern European heritage, blacks, and Hispanics. The largest group of first- and second-generation residents are Cubans, who represented 4% of Florida's population in 1990. The state also has the highest number of foreign-born Nicaraguans, and is second behind New York as a residence of individuals from Jamaica, Colombia, Haiti, and Trinidad & Tobago. There were an estimated 2.1 million individuals of Hispanic origin in 1997, 6th highest (by percentage) among the states. The 1990 census counted 541,011 Cubans, 174,445 Puerto Ricans, and 134,161 Mexicans. An estimated 4.1% of the state's population was Cuban-born in 1996. The black population, as estimated in 1997, was 2.25 million, or almost 15.4%.

The 1990 census reported a population of 42,619 Native Americans from 34 tribes; the 1997 estimate was 54,600. Asians and Pacific Islanders were estimated to number 253,000 in 1997. In 1990 there were 37,531 Filipinos, 28,787 Chinese, 22,240 Asian Indians, 14,586 Vietnamese, 15,401 Japanese, 14,722 Koreans, and 3,075 Hawaiians.

8 LANGUAGES

Massive migration from the North Central and North Atlantic areas, including a large number of speakers of Yiddish, has affected the previously rather uniform Southern speech of much of the state. Borrowing from the Spanish of the expanding number of Cubans and Puerto Ricans in the Miami area has had a further effect. Indian place-names in Florida include Okeechobee, Apalachicola, Kissimmee, Sarasota, Pensacola, and Hialeah.

About 10 million Floridians (83%) speak only English at home. Other languages spoken at home included Spanish (1,447,000); French (194,000); German (81,000); Italian (70,000); and Yiddish (27,000).

9 RELIGIONS

Protestant denominations claim the majority of church members in Florida. The largest Protestant denominations are the Southern Baptist Convention, with 786,000 members; United Methodist Church, 462,000; Presbyterian Church (USA), 202,000; Episcopal Church, 120,000; Assembly of God, 134,000; and Lutheran Church–Missouri Synod, 68,000. The Roman Catholic population of Florida numbers 1,598,000. The state also has a sizable Jewish population, estimated at 638,000 in 1994. A Greek Orthodox community is centered in Tarpon Springs.

10 TRANSPORTATION

As of 1998, there were a total of 2,927 rail miles (4,710 kilometers) of track in Florida, operated by 15 railroads. As of 1997, Florida had 114,572 miles (184,346 kilometers) of public roads. Florida had 10.8 million registered motor vehicles in 1997. The Overseas Highway down the Keys includes the 7 Mile Bridge, which is actually only 6.8 miles long, and is one of 44 bridges that connect the Keys to the mainland.

Inland waterways in Florida include the southernmost section of the Atlantic Intracoastal Waterway and the easternmost section of the Gulf Intracoastal Waterway. Both are navigable, federally maintained coastal channels for commercial vessels and pleasure craft. Florida has several commercially important ports. By far the largest port is Tampa, which handled 53 million tons of cargo in 1998, making it the 11th busiest port in the US. Other major ports include Jacksonville, Port Everglades in Ft. Lauderdale, Pensacola, and Miami.

Florida is the third-ranking state in terms of aircraft, pilots, and airline passengers. During 1995, more than 47 million passengers took off from Florida's 19 commercial service airports. Florida's busiest airport is Miami International, which boarded 11.9 million passengers in 1996.

11 HISTORY

By about 2000 BC, Native Americans in north Florida had an agricultural and hunting economy organized around village life. The southern groups did not practice agriculture until about 450 BC, when they began to plant corn in villages around Lake Okeechobee. As they spread over Florida and adjusted to widely different local conditions, the various tribes fell into six main divisions, with numerous subgroups and distinctive cultural traits. When Europeans arrived in the early 16th century, they found nearly 100,000 Native Americans, including the Apalachee, Timucua, Tocobaga, Calusa, and Tequesta tribes.

The Spaniards sought to Christianize the Native Americans and settle them around missions to grow food, supply labor, and help defend the province. The impact of the Europeans on the native population was, on the whole, disastrous. They died of European-introduced diseases, were killed in wars with whites or with other Indians, or moved away. When the Spanish departed Florida in 1763, the remaining 300 of the original 100,000 Native Americans left with them.

As early as 1750, small groups of Creek tribes from Georgia and Alabama began to move into the north Florida area vacated by the previous tribes. Called Seminole, the Creek word for runaway or refugee, these groups numbered only 5,000 when Florida became part of the US. However, pressures on the US president and Congress to remove the Seminole intensified after runaway black slaves began seeking refuge with them. When the Seminole resisted being removed to present-day Oklahoma (after first being confined to reservations) the result was the longest and most costly of Indian wars, the Seminole War of 1835–42. The warfare and the succeeding forced migration left fewer than 300 Seminole in Florida.

European Settlement

The history of the twice-repeated annihilation of Florida Indians is, at the same time, the history of white settlers' rise to power in Florida. Sailing from Puerto Rico in search of the fabled island of Bimini, Juan Ponce de León sighted Florida on 27 March 1513. Ponce de León claimed the land for Spain and named it La Florida, for *Pascua Florida,* the Easter festival of flowers.

In 1562, Jean Ribault, with a small expedition of French Huguenots, arrived at the St. Johns River, east of present-day Jacksonville, and claimed Florida for

France. Another group of French Huguenot settlers built nearby Fort Caroline two years later. In the summer of 1565, the Spaniard Pedro Menéndez de Avilés marched overland to take Fort Caroline by surprise, killing most of the occupants. St. Augustine was the first permanent European settlement in the US. It served primarily, under Spanish rule, as a military outpost, maintained to protect the wealth of New Spain. In 1763, when Spain ceded Florida to England in exchange for Cuba, about 3,000 Spaniards departed from St. Augustine and 800 from Pensacola, leaving Florida to the Seminole.

British Florida reached from the Atlantic to the Mississippi River and became two colonies, East and West Florida. There, settlers established farms and plantations and moved steadily toward economic and political self-sufficiency (although these settlers did not join the American Revolution). In 1781, Spain attacked and captured Pensacola. Two years later, Britain ceded both Floridas back to Spain. During the second Spanish era, English influence remained strong. Florida west of the Perdido River was taken over by the US in 1810, as part of the Louisiana Purchase (1803).

Statehood

Present-day Florida was ceded to the US in 1821, in settlement of $5 million in claims by US citizens against the Spanish government. At this time, General Andrew Jackson, who three years earlier had led a punitive expedition against the Seminole, came back to Florida as military governor. In 1824 Tallahassee, in the wilderness of north-central Florida, was selected as Florida's capital. Middle Florida, as the Tallahassee region was then called, rapidly became an area of slave-owning cotton plantations and was for several decades the fastest-growing part of the territory. Floridians drew up a state constitution in 1838–39. But, being proslavery, Florida had to wait until 1845 to enter the Union, when it was paired with the free state of Iowa under the Missouri Compromise.

In 1861, Florida seceded from the Union and joined the Confederacy. Some 15,000 whites (one-third of whom died) served in the Confederate army, and 1,200 whites and almost as many blacks joined the Union army. Bitterness and some violence accompanied Republican Reconstruction government in 1868–76. The conservative Bourbon Democrats then governed for the rest of the century. The Spanish-American War in 1898, during which Tampa became the port of embarkation for an expedition to Cuba, stimulated the economy and advertised the state nationwide.

Twentieth Century

Feverish land speculation brought hundreds of thousands of people to Florida in the first half of the 1920s. Cresting in 1925, the real estate boom was already over in 1926, when a devastating hurricane struck Miami, burying all hope of recovery. The Florida depression that began in 1926 was compounded by the national depression that hit late in 1929. The state joined the federal government in assuming responsibility for relief and recovery. The state's first paper mill

Florida Governors: 1845–2001

1845–1849	William Dunn Moseley	Democrat	1921–1925	Cary Augustus Hardee	Democrat
1849–1853	Thomas Brown	Whig	1925–1929	John Wellborn Martin	Democrat
1853–1857	James E. Broome	Democrat	1929–1933	Doyle Elam Carlton	Democrat
1857–1861	Madison Stark Perry	Democrat	1933–1937	David Sholtz	Democrat
1861–1865	John Milton	Democrat	1937–1941	Frederick Preston Cone	Democrat
1865	A. K. Allison	Confederate	1941–1945	Spessard Lindsey Holland	Democrat
1865	William Marvin	Dem-Prov	1945–1949	Willard Fillmore Caldwell	Democrat
1865–1868	David Shelby Walker	Conservative	1949–1953	Fuller Warren	Democrat
1868–1872	Harrison Reed	Republican	1953	Dananiel Thomas McCarty	Democrat
1873–1874	Ossian Bintley Hart	Republican	1953–1955	Charley Eugene Johns	Democrat
1874–1877	Marcellus Lovejoy Stearns	Republican	1955–1961	Thomas LeRoy Collins	Democrat
1877–1881	George Franklin Drew	Democrat	1961–1965	Cecil Farris Bryant	Democrat
1881–1885	William Dunnington Bloxham	Democrat	1965–1967	William Haydon Burns	Democrat
1885–1889	Edward Alysworth Perry	Democrat	1967–1971	Claude Roy Kirk, Jr.	Republican
1889–1893	Francis Philip Fleming	Democrat	1971–1979	Reuben O'Donovan Askew	Democrat
1893–1897	Henry Laurens Mitchell	Democrat	1979–1987	Daniel Robert Graham	Democrat
1897–1901	William Dunnington Bloxham	Democrat	1987	John Wayne Mixon	Democrat
1901–1905	William Sherman Jennings	Democrat	1987–1991	Robert Martinez	Republican
1905–1909	Napoleon Bonaparte Broward	Democrat	1991–1999	Lawton Mainor Chiles, Jr.	Democrat
1909–1913	Albert Waller Gilchrist	Democrat	1999–	Jeb Bush	Republican
1913–1917	Park Trammell	Democrat			
1917–1921	Sidney Johnston Catts	Prohibitionist		Democrat Provisional – Dem-Prov	

opened in the same year, revolutionizing the forest industry.

The 1940s opened with recovery and optimism, arising from the stimulus of production for World War II. New army and navy installations and training programs brought business growth. The number of army and navy airfield flying schools increased from 5 to 45. Families of thousands of trainees visited the state. Florida was on the eve of another boom. Between 1940 and 1990, migration would bring Florida's population ranking from 27th in the nation up to 4th, with more than 12.8 million people.

In 1986, Florida absorbed 1,000 arrivals a day. Until the early 1980s, many of those migrants were 65 years of age or over. In the mid-1980s, however, the majority of newcomers were younger—25 to 44 years old. They came in search of the opportunities provided by Florida's growing and diversifying economy. The management of growth in Florida has dominated state politics in the postwar era, centering on conflicts between developers and those who seek to preserve the natural beauty of the state.

Racial and ethnic relations have become another central issue. There have been efforts to reapportion (reorganize) Florida's 23 Congressional districts and the Legislature's 40 Senate and 120 House seats. The reorganization has been complicated by battles between blacks and Hispanics over the number and character of minority districts. Tensions between the two groups led to violence in 1989 when a Hispanic police officer shot and killed a black motorcyclist. Riots broke out in the mostly black Overton section of Miami and continued for three days. Six people died and 27 stores were set on fire.

In August 1992, Hurricane Andrew caused over $10 billion in damages in south Florida, primarily in and around Homestead.

12 STATE GOVERNMENT

Florida's legislature consists of a 40-member senate and a 120-member house of representatives. Senators serve four-year terms, with half the senate being elected every two years. Representatives serve two-year terms. The maximum length of a regular session is 60 calendar days, unless it is extended by a three-fifths vote of each house.

The governor is elected for a four-year term; a two-term limit is in effect. The lieutenant governor is elected on the same ticket as the governor. A six-member cabinet—consisting of the secretary of state, attorney general, comptroller, insurance commissioner and treasurer, commissioner of agriculture, and commissioner of education—is independently elected.

Each cabinet member heads an executive department. The governor appoints the heads of ten departments and shares supervision of seven additional departments with the cabinet. The governor and cabinet also share management of or membership in several other state agencies. These provisions make Florida's elected cabinet one of the strongest such bodies in any of the 50 states.

Passage of legislation requires a majority vote of those present and voting in both houses. A bill passed by the legislature becomes law if it is signed by the governor. The governor may veto legislation and, in general appropriations bills, may veto individual items. The governor's vetoes may be overridden by a two-thirds

Florida Presidential Vote by Political Parties, 1948–2000

YEAR	FLORIDA WINNER	DEMOCRAT	REPUBLICAN	STATES' RIGHTS DEMOCRAT	PROGRESSIVE
1948	*Truman (D)	281,988	194,280	89,755	11,620
1952	*Eisenhower (R)	444,950	544,036		
1956	*Eisenhower (R)	480,371	643,849		
1960	Nixon (R)	748,700	795,476		
1964	*Johnson (D)	948,540	905,941		
				AMERICAN IND.	
1968	*Nixon (R)	676,794	886,804	624,207	
1972	*Nixon (R)	718,117	1,857,759		
				AMERICAN	
1976	*Carter (D)	1,636,000	1,469,531	21,325	
					LIBERTARIAN
1980	*Reagan (R)	1,417,637	2,043,006	IND. (Anderson)	30,457
1984	*Reagan (R)	1,448,816	2,730,350	189,099	744
				NEW ALLIANCE	
1988	*Bush (R)	1,656,701	2,618,885	6,665	19,796
				IND. (Perot)	
1992	Bush (R)	2,072,798	2,173,310	1,053,067	15,079
1996	*Clinton (D)	2,546,870	2,244,536	483,870	23,965
				REFORM	
2000	*Bush (R)	2,912,253	2,912,790	17,484	97,488

* Won US presidential election.

vote of the legislators present in each house.

[13] POLITICAL PARTIES

Aided from 1889 to 1937 by a poll tax, which effectively prevented the majority of the state's mostly Republican blacks from voting, the Democrats won every governor's election but one from 1876 through 1962. By the time Republican Claude R. Kirk, Jr. won the governorship in 1966, Florida had already become, for national elections, a two-party state, although Democrats retained a sizable advantage in party registration.

As of 1994, the state had 3,318,565 registered Democrats, comprising 51% of the total number of registered voters, and 2,672,968 registered Republicans, or 41%. Eight percent of the registered voters, numbering 523,292, are unaffiliated. In addition to the Democratic and Republican parties, organized groups include the Citizens and Libertarian parties.

Republican Jeb Bush, brother of President George W. Bush, was elected governor in 1998. Democrat Robert Graham was reelected to the Senate in 1998. Florida's US House delegation in 2001 had fifteen Republicans and eight Democrats. The state senate contained 15 Democrats and 25 Republicans, and the state house of representatives had 43 Democrats and 77 Republicans. In the 2000 presidential election, Floridians gave 49% of the vote to Republican George W. Bush and 49% to Democrat Al Gore in one of the closest presidential races in history. George W. Bush was the winner in Florida by a narrow margin.

Photo credit: AP Photo/Wilfredo Lee.

The eyes of the nation turned to Florida in the final hours of the 2000 presidential elections. When the polls closed, initial results showed Republican George W. Bush ahead of Democrat Al Gore by less than 2000 votes. Gore asked for a recount and the Bush margin of victory began to dwindle as the recount went on and on and on, first by machine, and then by hand.

Broward County canvassing board member Judge Robert Rosenberg is shown here on November 24, 2000, training a magnifying glass on a disputed ballot looking for indentations that might show the "intent of the voter."

Ultimately, the controversy made its way to the Supreme Court of the United States. The Court ruled that the standards used in the hand count were inconsistent and therefore unconstitutional. The Court's controversial decision effectively decided the election in favor of Bush.

14 LOCAL GOVERNMENT

In 1997, Florida had 66 counties, 394 municipalities, 95 school districts, and 526 special districts. Generally, legislative authority within each county is vested in a five-member elected board of county commissioners. Counties may generally enact any law not inconsistent with state law. Municipalities are normally incorporated and chartered by an act of the state legislature. Except where a county charter specifies otherwise, municipal ordinances override county laws. Municipal governments may provide a full range of local services. Consolidated city/county governments are found in Miami (Dade County) and Jacksonville (Duval County).

15 JUDICIAL SYSTEM

The state's highest court is the supreme court, a panel of seven justices that sits in Tallahassee. The supreme court has appeals jurisdiction only. Below the supreme court are five district courts of appeal. District courts hear appeals of lower court decisions and may review the actions of executive agencies.

The state's principal trial courts are its 20 circuit courts, which have original jurisdiction in many types of cases, including civil suits involving more than $15,000, felony cases, and all cases involving juveniles. Circuit courts may also hear appeals from county courts if no constitutional question is involved.

Each of Florida's 66 counties has a county court with original jurisdiction in misdemeanor cases, civil disputes involving $15,000 or less, and traffic-violation cases. Florida has one of the highest crime rates in the US. In 1996, the total crime rate was 7,497.4 per 100,000. As of 1997, a total of 64,565 persons were serving prison sentences in institutions run by state and federal correctional authorities in Florida.

16 MIGRATION

Florida is populated mostly by migrants. In 1990, only 30.5% of all state residents were Florida-born, compared with 61.8% for the US as a whole. Only Nevada had a lower proportion of native residents. Migration from other states accounted for more than 85% of Florida's population increase in the 1970s. From 1985 to 1990, net migration gains added another 1,461,550 new residents. During 1990–98, the net gain from interstate migration was over 1 million.

In the 20th century, US immigrants to Florida have come, for the most part, from the Northeast and Midwest, often to escape harsh northern winters, and a large proportion of the migrants have been retirees and other senior citizens. Although the state has had a significant Cuban population since the second half of the 19th century, the number of immigrants surged after the Cuban revolution of 1959. From December 1965 to April 1973, an airlift agreed to by the Cuban and US governments landed a quarter of a million Cubans in Miami. In 1996, there were an estimated 590,000 Cuban-born Floridians.

Haitian "boat people" have arrived in Florida in significant numbers—often reaching the southern peninsula in packed,

Photo credit: Orlando/Orange County Convention & Visitors Bureau, Inc.

Kennedy Space Center–Spaceport USA is NASA's site for shuttle and other launches.

barely seaworthy small craft. The number of ethnic Haitians in Florida was reported at 105,495 in 1990. As of 1996, an estimated 2.2 million Floridians (15%) were foreign-born. In 1996, 79,461 foreign immigrants were admitted into Florida, including 22,217 Cubans, 7,748 Haitians, 4,996 Jamaicans, and 3,510 Colombians. During 1990–98, international migration resulted in a net gain of 552,775. The federal government estimated in 1996 that there were 350,000 illegal immigrants living in Florida.

17 ECONOMY

Tourists and winter residents with second homes in Florida contribute billions of dollars annually to the state economy and make retailing and construction particularly important economic areas. However, this dependence on spending by visitors and part-time dwellers also makes the economy—and especially the housing industry—highly sensitive to recession. The economic downturn of the early 1980s hit Florida harder than the US generally. New housing starts, for example, which fell by about 2% in the US from 1981 to 1982, dropped by more than 20% in Florida during the same period.

An extremely low level of unionization among Florida workers encouraged growth in manufacturing in the 1970s and early 1980s—but may also help explain Floridians' below-average income levels.

The arms build-up during the early 1980s helped to expand Florida's aerospace and electronics industries. Even in 1991, after reduction of the military budget, Florida ranked seventh nationally in the value of Department of Defense contracts awarded. Miami is said to have one of the largest "underground economies" in the US, a reference both to the sizable inflow of cash from illicit drug trafficking and to the large numbers of Latin American immigrants working for low, unreported cash wages.

Florida's private goods-producing industries contribute 15% to the state's total economic output, while private services-producing industries account for 72%. Government contributes 13%.

18 INCOME

In 1998, Florida's per capita (per person) income was $26,845, 20th among the 50 states. In 1998, 13.9% of all Floridians lived below the federal poverty level. In 1994, the West Palm Beach area ranked second highest in per capita personal income (at $33,518) of all metropolitan areas in the nation.

19 INDUSTRY

Florida is not a center of heavy industry, and many of its manufacturing activities are related to agriculture and exploitation of natural resources. Leading industries include food processing, electric and electronic equipment, transportation equipment, and chemicals.

Florida ranks second only to California in both employment and number of firms engaged in the manufacture of guided missiles and space vehicles. Some 10% of all US aircraft engines and engine parts are manufactured in Florida. Nearly 20% of the nation's boat manufacturers are located in the state. Laser research and development began in the 1950s by Martin–Marietta in Orlando. Since then, the greater Orlando area has grown to have the third-highest concentration of electro-optics and laser manufacturers in the US. In 2000, there were 14 Fortune 500 companies headquartered in the state.

20 LABOR

Florida's civilian labor force was 7.2 million in mid-1998. There was an unemployment rate of 4.3%.

Reflecting the importance of tourism to Florida's economy, a higher proportion of the state's workers are employed in the trade and service industries than for the US as a whole. Those two sectors together accounted for about 62% of employment in 1998. The proportion of workers in manufacturing is a little over half the US average.

Some 6.7% of all workers were union members in 1998. There were 131 labor unions operating in Florida in 1997. The state has a right-to-work law, and workers are not required to join a union.

21 AGRICULTURE

Florida's most important agricultural products, and the ones for which it is most famous, are its citrus fruits. Florida continues to supply the vast majority of orange juice consumed in the US. Florida produced 76% of the nation's oranges and grapefruits in 1998. The state is also an important producer of other fruits, vegetables, sugarcane, and soybeans.

The total value of Florida's crops in 1999 exceeded $457 billion, second highest among the 50 states. Total farm marketings, including livestock marketings and products, totaled $7 billion in 1999 (seventh in the US). There were about 45,000 farms covering some 10.6 million acres (4.3 million hectares) in 1998. This total represented nearly 30% of the state's entire land area.

The orange crop totaled 244 million 90-pound (41-kilogram) boxes in 1997/98. The grapefruit crop was 49.5 million 85-pound (39-kilogram) boxes; tangerines, 5.2 million 95-pound (43-kilogram) boxes; and tangelos and temple oranges, 5.1 million 90-pound (41-kilogram) boxes. There are 50 factories in Florida where citrus fruits are processed into canned or chilled juice, frozen or pasteurized concentrate, or canned fruit sections. Production of frozen orange juice concentrate totaled 2.4 billion gallons (4.5 billion liters) in the 1996 season. Citrus by-products include citrus molasses, alcohol, wines, preserves, and citrus seed oil.

Florida is one of the country's leading producers of vegetables. Florida's tomato and vegetable growers, who had at one time enjoyed a near monopoly of the US winter vegetable market, began in the late 1970s to face increasing competition from Mexican growers. Lower-priced Mexican produce had captured about half the market by 1980. Other important fresh fruits and vegetables produced in the state include strawberries, watermelons, sweet corn, bell peppers, and cucumbers. About two-thirds of all farm laborers are hired hands.

Florida's major field crop is sugarcane, which enjoyed a sizable production increase in the 1960s and 1970s, following the cutoff of imports from Cuba. In 1998, Florida's sugarcane production was 17 million tons. Florida's second-largest field crop is peanuts (2.2 million pounds/99.7 million kilograms) in 1998. Cotton, hay, corn, tobacco, soybeans, and wheat are other important field crops.

22 DOMESTICATED ANIMALS

Florida is an important cattle-raising state. Most of the beef cattle are sold to out-of-state feedlots. In 1999, Florida had nearly 2 million cattle, valued at $936 million. Other types of livestock raised commercially are hogs, sheep, rabbits, and poultry. Florida's 160,000 dairy cows produced 2.5 billion pounds (1.1 billion kilograms) of milk in 1997.

The raising of thoroughbred horses and the production of eggs and honey are also major industries. Florida ranks third in the US in number of thoroughbreds, surpassed only by Kentucky and California.

23 FISHING

Florida's extensive shoreline and numerous inland waterways make sport fishing a major recreational activity. Commercial fishing is also economically important. In 1998, Florida's commercial fish catch was 114.4 million pounds (52 million kilo-

Canoeing in Orange County, Florida.

grams), with a value of $188.5 million. The most important commercial species of shellfish are shrimp, spiny lobster, and crabs. Valuable finfish species include grouper, swordfish, and snapper. In 1997, Florida had 28 Atlantic and 460 Gulf coast processing and wholesale plants.

Both freshwater and saltwater fishing are important sports. Tarpon, sailfish, and redfish are some of the major saltwater sport species. Largemouth bass, panfish, sunfish, catfish, and perch are leading freshwater sport fish. Florida had over one million licensed sport fishers in 1998. Coastal marine fishing requires no license; in 1997 an estimated 2.6 million people participated in recreational marine fishing off the Gulf coast, and 1.9 million off the Atlantic coast.

24 FORESTRY

About 47% of Florida's land area—16.2 million acres (6.6 million hectares)—was forested in 1997. The most common tree is the pine, which occurs throughout the state but is most abundant in the north. The most important forestry product is pulpwood for paper manufacturing. Lumber production in 1995 was 805 million board feet, 769 million board feet of softwoods, and 36 million board feet of hardwoods.

Practically all of Florida's natural forest had been cleared by the mid-20th century.

The forests existing today are thus almost entirely the result of reforestation. Since 1928, more than 5.6 billion seedlings have been planted in the state. Four national forests—Apalachicola, Ocala, Osceola, and Choctawatchee—covered 1.2 million acres (495,600 hectares) in Florida, and state forests, 1.5 million acres in 1997.

25 MINING

Florida's estimated nonfuel mineral production in 1998 was valued at $1.96 billion. The state ranks sixth in US mineral production. Florida continued to lead the nation in phosphate rock, mineral sands, and peat output, and ranked among the top three states in crushed stone and masonry cement production.

The state is a world leader in phosphate rock production and leads the nation in heavy-mineral output. Phosphate rock was the leading mineral commodity, in terms of value, accounting for over 50% of the estimated value. Crushed stone, sales of which were estimated at $449 million, was the second leading mineral commodity. Portland and masonry cement ranked third; sand and gravel and clays rounded out the top five commodities in terms of reportable value.

26 ENERGY AND POWER

In 1997, 3.6 trillion Btu (0.8 billion kilocalories) of energy was consumed in Florida. Per capita (per person) energy use in 1997 was 246.2 million Btu (5.93 million kilocalories). Florida's mild climate and abundant sunshine offer great potential for solar energy development, but this potential has not been extensively exploited. In 1998, electric energy production was 169.4 billion kilowatt hours. In 1998, 24% of electricity produced came from residual fuel oil, 39% from coal, 18% from nuclear power, and 19% from natural gas. Hydroelectricity and distillate fuels totaled less than 0.1%. There are five nuclear power plants in the state.

In 1999, the state produced 4.8 million barrels of crude oil, and proven reserves are 71 million barrels. Natural gas production in 1998 was 5.7 million cubic feet (162 million cubic meters). Proven natural gas reserves are 88 billion cubic feet (2.6 billion cubic meters) in 1998.

27 COMMERCE

Wholesale trade in 1997 totaled $195 billion. According to the 1992 US Census of Retail Trade, the state ranked fourth in retail sales, at $118.7 billion, or 6.3% of the national total. The fashionable shops lining Palm Beach's Worth Avenue make it one of the nation's most famous shopping streets. At least 27% of retail trade are in the 10,502 restaurants, cafeterias, bars, and similar establishments—a reflection, in part, of the importance of the travel business in Florida's economy.

The value of all exports sent from Florida was over $28 billion in 1997. Duty-free goods for reshipment abroad pass through Port Everglades, Miami, Orlando, Jacksonville, Tampa, and Panama City— free-trade zones established to bring international commerce to the state. Florida is a popular entry point for marijuana,

Photo credit: Florida Department of Commerce, Division of Tourism.

St. Petersburg, Florida.

cocaine, and other illicit drugs being smuggled into the US from Latin America.

28 PUBLIC FINANCE

The largest expenditure items are education, health and social concerns, general government, and transportation. By prohibiting borrowing to finance operating expenses, Florida's constitution requires a balanced budget. The total revenues for 1997 were $41.43 billion; expenditures were $37.46 billion.

The total indebtedness of Florida state and local governments in 1997 exceeded $16 billion. The state debt outstanding at the end of 1997 was $1,093 per capita (per person).

29 TAXATION

Florida ranked 39th among the 50 states in per capita (per person) state taxation in 1997 with a tax burden of $1,439 per capita. The 6% sales and use tax is the largest single source of state revenue, but property taxes make up the bulk of local receipts. The state constitution prohibits a personal income tax. In 1995, local taxes amounted to $13.34 billion, with 80% coming from property taxes.

The state sales tax applies to most retail items, as well as to car and hotel room rentals and theater admissions. The use tax is levied on wholesale items brought into Florida for sale. Other taxes include those on gasoline and other motor fuels, cigarettes, alcoholic beverages, drivers' licenses and motor vehicles, and parimutuel betting. In 1995, Floridians paid nearly $51.7 billion in federal income taxes.

30 HEALTH

Reflecting the population's age distribution (28% over age 55), Florida has a relatively low birth rate and a high death rate. Florida exceeds the national rate in deaths from heart disease, cancer, cerebrovascular disease, accidents, and suicide. The leading causes of death are cardiovascular disease and cancer. The former accounted for 41% of all deaths in the state. Cancer claimed just over 24% of the total. Age–adjusted rates are a better measure of the incidents of disease and death.

In 1998 there were 204 hospitals in Florida. The total number of beds available was 49,231; admissions totaled 1.9 million. As of 1996, the total number of nonfederal physicians in the state was 39,715, or about 277 for every 100,000 residents. The average expense for a hospital stay was $5,883; per inpatient day, $1,056, in 1998. Over 17.5% of Floridians did not have health insurance, in the same year.

31 HOUSING

In October 1999, there were an estimated 5.8 million housing units in Florida. Multifamily housing ranges from beachfront luxury high-rises along the Gold Coast to dilapidated residential hotels in the South Beach section of Miami Beach. In 1990, the median monthly cost for an owner-occupied housing unit with a mortgage was $718; for a unit without a mortgage,

it was $186. That year, the median rent for a housing unit was $481.

Some 16% of all housing units are condominiums, a higher proportion than any other state except Hawaii. Large retirement communities, often containing thousands of condominium units, are commonplace in Dade, Broward, and Palm Beach counties. Florida also leads the nation in the number of mobile homes or trailers, which represent nearly 13% of all housing units.

In 1998, 148,600 new housing units were authorized for construction. The total value of new housing authorized in that year was $14.1 billion.

32 EDUCATION

In 1998, 81.9% of Floridians 25 years of age or older were high school graduates; 22.5% had four or more years of college. There were 2.29 million students enrolled in public schools during 1997. The High School Competency Test measures communication and math skills of 11th-grade students. In 1996, 77% of students who took the test passed the communications part and 75% passed the mathematics section. Expenditures for public elementary and secondary schools amounted to $5,355 per student in 1995/96 (27th among the states).

Florida has nine state universities, with a total fall 1994 enrollment of 155,232. The largest is the University of Florida (Gainesville), followed by the University of South Florida (Tampa). Also part of the state university system are special university centers, such as the University of Flor-

The 72,000-seat Florida Citrus Bowl in Orlando.

ida's Institute of Food and Agricultural Science. The state's 29 community colleges have an enrollment of more than 326,000. Almost two-thirds of the community college students attended on a part-time basis. Of Florida's 76 private institutions of higher education, by far the largest is the University of Miami (Coral Gables).

33 ARTS

Regional and metropolitan symphony orchestras include the Florida Philharmonic (Miami), Florida Orchestra (Tampa), Jacksonville Symphony, and the Florida West Coast Symphony (Sarasota). Opera companies include the Florida Grand Opera (Miami) and the Sarasota Opera. State theater companies are based in Boca Raton, Gainesville, Miami, and Sarasota. Museums and performing arts centers include the John and Mabel Ringling Museum of Art (Sarasota), the Norton Gallery (West Palm Beach), the Miami Art Museum, Orlando Museum of Art, Philharmonic Center for the Arts (Naples), Tampa Bay Performing Arts Center, and the Kravis Center for the Performing Arts (West Palm Beach).

34 LIBRARIES AND MUSEUMS

Florida had 9 multi-county library systems and 40 county systems in 1999, and circulation totaled 72.8 million. The State Library in Tallahassee housed 661,849 volumes, in the same year. The largest university library in the state is that of the

University of Florida (Gainesville), with holdings of more than 3.2 million volumes in 1996.

Florida has 278 museums, galleries, and historical sites, as well as numerous public gardens. The estates and homes of a number of prominent former Florida residents are now open as museums, including the homes of Ernest Hemingway and John James Audubon in Key West, Thomas Edison's house in Fort Myers, John and Mabel Ringling's estate in Sarasota, the Palm Beach home of Henry Morrison Flagler, and James R. Deering's estate in Miami.

The largest historic restoration in Florida is in St. Augustine, where several blocks of the downtown area have been restored to their 18th-century likeness under the auspices of the Historic St. Augustine Preservation Board. The Metrozoo-Miami has an average annual attendance of 650,000.

35 COMMUNICATIONS

As of 1999, 92.6% of Florida's occupied housing units had telephones. In 2000, the state had 217 AM stations and 310 FM, and 105 TV stations. A total of 471,645 domain names were registered in 2000 on the Internet.

36 PRESS

The oldest newspaper still publishing is the *Jacksonville Times-Union* (now *Florida Times-Union*), which first appeared in February 1883. In 1998, there were 38 morning papers, 5 evening papers, and 36 Sunday papers. The leading English-language dailies and their daily circulations in 1998 were the *Miami Herald* (349,114); the *St. Petersburg Times* (344,784); the *Ft. Lauderdale Sun-Sentinel* (272,258); and the *Orlando Sentinel* (258,959).

In 1997 fifteen black newspapers and 4 Spanish-language newspapers were also published in Florida. There were 30 book publishers in Florida in 1997, including Academic Press and University Presses of Florida.

37 TOURISM, TRAVEL, AND RECREATION

Tourism is a mainstay of the state's economy. In 1999 nearly 59 million visitors spent over $46 billion in the state. In 1999, the state had 4,717 licensed hotels and motels. Florida's biggest tourist attractions are its sun, sand, and surf. A major tourist attraction is Walt Disney World, a huge amusement park near Orlando. Both Busch Gardens (Tampa) and Sea World of Florida (Orlando) report average annual attendances of 3 million. Other major attractions are the Kennedy Space Center at Cape Canaveral and the St. Augustine historic district.

Nine parks and other facilities in Florida operated by the National Park Service draw millions of visitors annually. The most popular destination is the Gulf Islands National Seashore, located near Pensacola, followed by the Canaveral National Seashore. Fishing and boating are major recreational activities. Off-track betting, horse-racing, dog-racing, jai alai, and bingo are all legalized forms of gaming. In 1996, dog-racing attendance was over 3.8 million and thoroughbred horse-racing attendance was over 2.2 million.

38 SPORTS

Florida has 13 major league professional sports teams: the Miami Dolphins, Tampa Bay Buccaneers, and Jacksonville Jaguars of the National Football League; the Miami Heat and the Orlando Magic of the National Basketball Association; the Tampa Bay Lightning and Florida Panthers of the National Hockey League; the Florida Marlins and Tampa Bay Devil Rays of Major League Baseball; and the Miami Fusion and Tampa Bay Mutiny of Major League Soccer; and the Miami Sol and Orlando Miracle of the Women's National Basketball Association. Several professional baseball teams also have spring training facilities in Florida.

Several tournaments on both the men's and women's professional golf tours are played in Florida. In auto racing, the Daytona 500 is a top race on the NASCAR circuit. Three of the major collegiate football bowl games are played in the state: the Orange Bowl in Miami, the Gator Bowl in Jacksonville, and the Florida Citrus Bowl in Orlando.

39 FAMOUS FLORIDIANS

Florida produced one of the major US military figures of World War II, General Joseph Warren Stilwell (1883–1946), dubbed "Vinegar Joe" for his strongly stated opinions. Janet Reno (b.1938), Attorney General of the United States in the Clinton presidency, was born in Miami.

Photo credit: EPD Photos/National Archives.

Florida native General Daniel James, Jr. (1920–78), known as "Chappie," was the first black four-star general in the US.

In the 1880s, Henry Morrison Flagler (b.New York, 1830–1913) began to acquire and build railroads down the length of Florida's east coast and to develop tourist hotels, helping to create one of the state's major present-day industries.

Well-known Florida authors include James Weldon Johnson (1871–1938), perhaps best known for his 1912 novel *Autobiography of an Ex-Colored Man* and Marjorie Kinnan Rawlings (b.Washington, D.C., 1895–1953) wrote the Pulitzer Prize-winning *The Yearling* (1938), the poignant story of a 12-year-old boy on the Florida frontier in the 1870s.

40 BIBLIOGRAPHY

Blaustein, Daniel. *The Everglades and the Gulf Coast*. New York: Benchmark Books, 2000.

Dregni, Michael, ed. *Our Florida: A Heritage of the Sunshine State in Stories and Photos*. Stillwater, Minn.: Voyageur Press, 2000.

Hurston, Zora Neale. *Their Eyes Were Watching God*. New York: J.B. Lippincott, 1937.

London, Jonathan. *Panther: Shadow of the Swamp*. Cambridge, Mass.: Candlewick, 2000.

McAuliffe, Emily. *Florida Facts and Symbols*. New York: Hilltop Books, 1999.

Rawlings, Marjorie Kinnan. *The Yearling*. New York: Scribner, 1938.

Somervill, Barbara A. *Florida*. New York: Children's Press, 2001.

Sullivan, Ann. *Florida*. Mankato, Minn.: Weigl, 2000.

Web sites

Florida Department of State. Florida Government Information Locator. [Online] Available http://dlis.dos.state.fl.us/fgils Accessed May 31, 2001.

Florida Department of State. Florida Kids Home Page. [Online] Available http://dhr.dos.state.fl.us/kids/ Accessed May 31, 2001.

GEORGIA

ORIGIN OF STATE NAME: Named for King George II of England in 1732.

NICKNAME: The Empire State of the South (also Peach State).

CAPITAL: Atlanta.

ENTERED UNION: 2 January 1788 (4th).

SONG: "Georgia" and "Georgia on My Mind."

MOTTO: Wisdom, Justice, Moderation.

COAT OF ARMS: Three columns support an arch inscribed with the word "Constitution;" intertwined among the columns is a banner bearing the state motto. Right of center stands a soldier with a drawn sword, representing the aid of the military in defending the Constitution. Surrounding the whole are the words "State of Georgia 1776."

FLAG: On January 30, 2001, a new flag featuring the Georgia state seal in gold surrounded by 13 white stars was adopted. A gold ribbon below the seal features small images of the three historical flags of Georgia and current and past version of the United States flag.

OFFICIAL SEAL: OBVERSE: same as the coat of arms. REVERSE: a sailing vessel and a smaller boat are offshore; on land, a man and horse plow a field, and sheep graze in the background. The scene is surrounded by the words "Agriculture and Commerce 1776."

BIRD: Brown thrasher.

FISH: Largemouth bass.

FLOWER: Cherokee rose.

WILDFLOWER: Azalea.

TREE: Live oak.

GEM: Quartz.

INSECT: Honeybee.

FOSSIL: Shark tooth.

TIME: 7 AM EST = noon GMT.

1 LOCATION AND SIZE

Located in the southeastern US, Georgia is the largest state east of the Mississippi River, and ranks 21st in size among the 50 states. The total area of Georgia is 58,910 square miles (152,576 square kilometers). Georgia extends 254 miles (409 kilometers) east-west; the maximum north-south extension is 320 miles (515 kilometers). The Sea Islands extend the length of the Georgia coast. The state's total boundary length is 1,039 miles (1,672 kilometers).

2 TOPOGRAPHY

The Blue Ridge Mountains end in northern Georgia, where Brasstown Bald, at 4,784 feet (1,458 meters), is the highest point in the state. The central region is characterized by the rolling hills of the Piedmont Plateau. The piedmont area ends in a ridge of sand hills running across the state from Augusta to Columbus. The coastal plain of southern Georgia, thinly populated except for towns at the mouths of inland rivers, ends in marshlands along the Atlantic Ocean. Lying offshore are the Sea Islands.

Two great rivers rise in the northeast: the Savannah and the Chattahoochee. The two largest rivers of central Georgia are the Ocmulgee and Oconee. Clark Hill Reservoir and Hartwell Reservoir are huge lakes created by dams on the Savannah River. Artificial lakes on the Chattahoochee River include Lake Seminole, Walter F. George Reservoir, and Lake Harding.

3 CLIMATE

The Chattahoochee River divides Georgia into separate climatic regions. The mountain region to the northwest is colder than the rest of Georgia, averaging 39°F (4°C) in January and 78°F (26°C) in July. The state experiences mild winters, ranging from a January average of 44°F (7°C) in the piedmont to 54°F (12°C) on the coast. Summers are hot in the piedmont and on the coast, with July temperatures averaging 80°F (27°C) or above. The record high is 113°F (45°C) at Greenville on 27 May 1978; the record low is –17°F (–27°C), registered in Floyd County on 27 January 1940.

Rainfall averages 50 inches (127 centimeters) annually in the lowlands, increasing to 75 inches (191 centimeters) in the mountains; snow falls occasionally in the interior. Tornadoes are an annual threat in mountain areas, and Georgia beaches are exposed to hurricane tides.

Georgia Population Profile

Total population in 2000:	8,186,453
Population change, 1990–2000:	26.4%
Hispanic or Latino†:	5.3%
Population by race	
One race:	98.6%
White:	65.1%
Black or African American:	28.7%
American Indian/Alaska Native:	0.3%
Asian:	2.1%
Native Hawaiian/Pacific Islander:	0.1%
Some other race:	2.4%
Two or more races:	1.4%

Population by Age Group

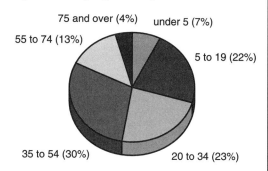

75 and over (4%)
under 5 (7%)
55 to 74 (13%)
5 to 19 (22%)
35 to 54 (30%)
20 to 34 (23%)

Top Cities by Population

City	Population	% change 1990–2000
Atlanta	416,474	5.7
Augusta-Richmond	199,775	347.5
Columbus	186,291	3.9
Savannah	131,510	–4.4
Athens-Clarke	101,489	121.9
Macon	97,255	–8.8
Roswell	79,334	65.5
Albany	76,939	–1.5
Marietta	58,748	33.1
Warner Robins	48,804	11.6

Notes: †A person of Hispanic or Latino origin may be of any race. NA indicates that data are not available.
Sources: U.S. Census Bureau. Public Information Office. *Demographic Profiles.* [Online] Available http://www.census.gov/Press-Release/www/2001/demoprofile.html. Accessed June 1, 2001. U.S. Census Bureau. *Census 2000: Redistricting Data.* Press release issued by the Redistricting Data Office. Washington, D.C., March, 2001.

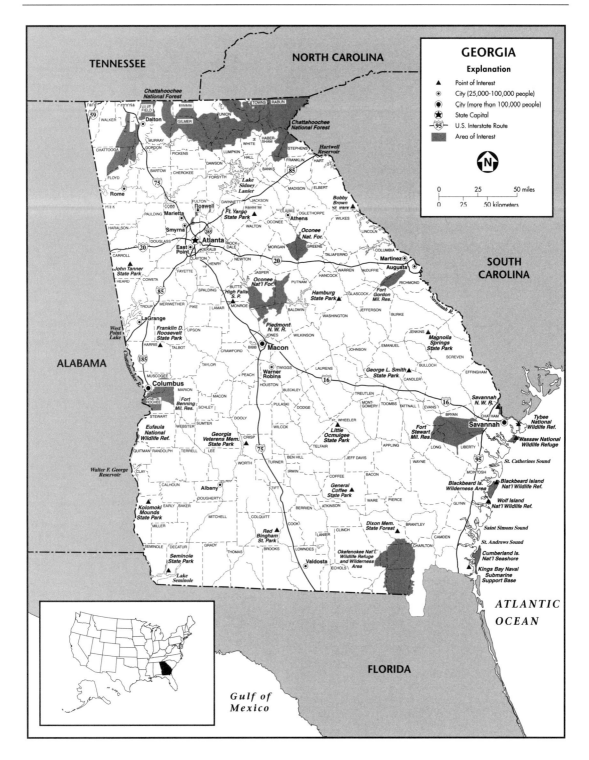

Photo credit: Georgia Department of Industry, Trade, and Tourism.

An inhabitant of Okefenokee Swamp.

4 PLANTS AND ANIMALS

Georgia has some 250 species of trees, 90% of which are of commercial importance. White and scrub pines, and northern red oak cover the mountain zone, while loblolly, yellow pines and whiteback maple are found throughout the piedmont. Pecan trees grow densely in southern Georgia, and white oak and cypress are plentiful in the eastern part of the state. Trees found throughout the state include scaly-bark and white hickories, sassafras, and various dogwoods and magnolias. Common flowering shrubs include yellow jasmine, flowering quince, and mountain laurel. Spanish moss grows in the coastal regions, and kudzu vines, origi-nally from Asia, are plentiful. The state lists 58 protected plants, of which 22—including smooth coneflower, fringed campion, and small whorled pogonia—are endangered.

Prominent among Georgia animals is the white-tailed (Virginia) deer, found in some 50 counties. Other common mammals include the black bear, muskrat, mink, and three species of squirrel: fox, gray, and flying. No fewer than 160 bird species breed in Georgia, among them the mockingbird, brown thrasher (the state bird), and numerous sparrows. There are 79 species of reptile, including such poisonous snakes as the rattler and copperhead. The state's 63 amphibian species consist mainly of various salamanders, frogs, and toads. The most popular freshwater game fish are trout, bream, bass, and catfish. Dolphins, porpoises, shrimp, oysters, and blue crabs are found off the Georgia coast.

Thirty rare or threatened animals include the indigo snake and the bald eagle. The state protects 23 species of wildlife, among them the colonial and Sherman's pocket gophers, right and humpback whales, manatee, brown pelican, American alligator, three species of sea turtles, shortnose sturgeon, and southern cave fish.

5 ENVIRONMENTAL PROTECTION

Georgia's greatest environmental problems are an increasingly scarce water supply, water pollution, and hazardous waste sites. In 1972, at the prodding of Governor Jimmy Carter, the general assembly created the Environmental Protection Division (EPD), which administers 21 state environmental laws, most of them passed during the 1970s. The EPD's Emergency Response Team is on call 24 hours a day to assist in environmental emergencies and averages about 2,000 calls per year. In 1999, there were 16 hazardous waste sites in the state.

6 POPULATION

Georgia, surpassing North Carolina, ranked 10th among the 50 states in 2000 with a population of 8,186,453. The population density was 141.4 persons per square mile (54.6 persons per square kilometer) in 2000.

About 65% of all Georgians lived in urban areas in 1990, and 35% in rural areas. The state's four largest cities in 2000 were Atlanta, 416,474; Augusta-Richmond, 199,775; Columbus, 186,291; Savannah, 131,510; and Athens-Clarke, 101,489. Georgia's median age is about two years below the national average of 35.3.

7 ETHNIC GROUPS

Most Georgians are of English or Scotch-Irish descent. In 1997, the number of Georgians with Asian or Pacific Islands ancestry was estimated at 137,000, or 1.8% of the population. Black citizens composed 28.4% of the total population (5th highest) and numbered 2.1 million in 1997. There were only an estimated 17,500 Native Americans in Georgia in 1997.

8 LANGUAGES

Except for the South Midland speech of the extreme northern up-country, Georgia English is typically Southern. However, a highly unusual variety of regional differences makes a strong contrast between northern up-country and southern low-country speech. In such words as *care* and *stairs,* for example, many up-country speakers have a vowel like that in *cat,* while many low-country speakers have a vowel like that in *pane.*

A distinctive variety of black English, called Gullah, is spoken in the islands off the Georgia and South Carolina coast, to which Creole-speaking slaves escaped from the mainland during the 17th and

Georgia Population by Race

Census 2000 was the first national census in which the instructions to respondents said, "Mark one or more races." This table shows the number of people who are of one, two, or three or more races. For those claiming two races, the number of people belonging to the various categories is listed. The U.S. government conducts a census of the population every ten years.

	Number	Percent
Total population	8,186,453	100.0
One race	8,072,265	98.6
Two races	106,506	1.3
White *and* Black or African American	18,367	0.2
White *and* American Indian/Alaska Native	19,232	0.2
White *and* Asian	13,643	0.2
White *and* Native Hawaiian/Pacific Islander	1,030	—
White *and* some other race	26,324	0.3
Black or African American *and* American Indian/Alaska Native	5,567	0.1
Black or African American *and* Asian	3,591	—
Black or African American *and* Native Hawaiian/Pacific Islander	941	—
Black or African American *and* some other race	9,776	0.1
American Indian/Alaska Native *and* Asian	937	—
American Indian/Alaska Native *and* Native Hawaiian/Pacific Islander	69	—
American Indian/Alaska Native *and* some other race	1,342	—
Asian *and* Native Hawaiian/Pacific Islander	1,000	—
Asian *and* some other race	4,115	0.1
Native Hawaiian/Pacific Islander *and* some other race	572	—
Three or more races	7,682	0.1

Source: U.S. Census Bureau. *Census 2000: Redistricting Data.* Press release issued by the Redistricting Data Office. Washington, D.C., March, 2001. A dash (—) indicates that the percent is less than 0.1.

18th centuries. Many personal names stem directly from West African languages.

About 5.7 million Georgians speak only English at home. Other languages spoken at home, and the number of people who speak them, include Spanish (122,295); German (29,480); French (34,422); and Korean (13,433).

9 RELIGIONS

There are approximately 3,450,000 known Protestants in Georgia. The leading denominations are the Southern Baptist Convention, 1,582,000; United Methodist, 530,000; Presbyterian, 101,000; Church of God (Cleveland, Tenn.), 96,000; and Episcopal, 63,000. Georgia has 210,000 Roman Catholics and an estimated 75,000 Jews.

10 TRANSPORTATION

Due to competition from the trucking industry, Class I rail trackage declined to 4,602 rail miles (7,409 kilometers) in 1995, and CSX and Norfolk Southern were the only Class I railroads operating within the state. As of 1996, Amtrak operated five long-distance trains through the state. In 1979, Atlanta inaugurated the first heavy rail mass-transit system in the state, including the South's first subway.

Georgia's old intracoastal waterway carries about one million tons of shipping annually and is also used by pleasure craft and fishing vessels. Savannah's modern port facilities handled 17.7 million tons of cargo in 1998. The coastal cities of Brunswick and St. Marys also have deepwater docks.

In the 1920s, Georgia became the gateway to Florida for motorists. During the 1980s, Atlanta invested $1.4 billion in a major freeway expansion program. In 1997, Georgia had 111,828 miles (179,931 kilometers) of public roads and 6.24 million registered motor vehicles. Hartsfield International Airport (Atlanta) is the hub of air traffic in the Southeast; it topped Chicago's O'Hare Airport as the world's busiest in 2000.

11 HISTORY

The Native Americans of the Master Farmer culture that reached its height in about AD 800 left impressive mounds at Ocmulgee (near Macon), and at Etowah (north of Atlanta). During the colonial period, the most important tribes were the Creek and the Cherokee. By clever diplomacy, the Creek were able to maneuver between the English on the one hand and the French and Spanish on the other. With the ascendancy of the English and the achievement of statehood, however, the Creek lost their leverage and were expelled from Georgia in 1826.

In an effort to avoid expulsion or annihilation, the Cherokee sought to adopt the Europeans' ways. Thanks to their remarkable linguist Sequoyah, they learned to write their own language, later running

Photo credit: Metro Atlanta Chamber of Commerce.

Atlanta skyline.

their own newspaper, the *Cherokee Phoenix,* and their own schools. Some even owned slaves. Unfortunately for the Cherokee, gold was discovered on their lands and they were expelled from their territory between 1832 and 1838. Thousands died on the march to Indian Territory (Oklahoma), known ever since as the Trail of Tears.

Georgia's first European explorer was Hernando de Soto of Spain, who crossed the region in 1540. By 1586 Spanish captain Pedro Menéndez de Avilés had established the mission of Santa Catalina de

Georgia Governors: 1776–2001

1776	William Ewen	
1776–1777	Archibald Bulloch	
1777	Button Gwinnett	President
1777–1778	John Adam Treutlen	
1778–1779	John Houstoun	
1779	John Wereat	President
1779–1780	George Walton	
1779–1782	Sir James Wright	
1780	Richard Howley	
1780	Stephen Heard	President
1780–1781	Myrick Davies	
1781–1782	Nathan Brownson	
1782–1783	John Martin	
1783–1784	Lyman Hall	
1784–1785	John Houstoun	
1785–1786	Samuel Elbert	
1786–1787	Edward Telfair	
1787–1788	George Mathews	
1788–1789	George Handley	Dem-Rep
1789	George Walton	Dem-Rep
1789–1793	Edward Telfair	Dem-Rep
1793–1796	George Mathews	Dem-Rep
1796–1798	Jared Irwin	Dem-Rep
1798–1801	James Jackson	Dem-Rep
1801	David Emanuel	Dem-Rep
1801–1802	Josiah Tattnall, Jr.	Dem-Rep
1802–1806	John Milledge	Dem-Rep
1806–1809	Jared Irwin	Dem-Rep
1809–1813	David Byrdie Mitchell	Dem-Rep
1813–1815	Peter Early	Dem-Rep
1815–1817	David Brydie Mitchell	Dem-Rep
1817–1819	William Rabun	Dem-Rep
1819	Matthew Talbot	Dem-Rep
1819–1823	John Clark	Dem-Rep
1823–1827	George Michael Troup	Dem-Rep
1827–1829	John Forsyth	Dem-Rep
1829–1831	George Rockingham Gilmer	Whig
1831–1835	Wilson Lumpkin	Union-Dem
1835–1837	William Schley	Unionist
1837–1839	George Rockingham Gilmer	Whig
1839–1843	Charles James McDonald	Democrat
1843–1847	George Walker Crawford	Whig
1847–1851	George Washington Towns	Democrat
1851–1853	Howell Cobb	Union-Dem
1853–1857	Herschel Vespasian Johnson	Union
1857–1865	Joseph Emerson Brown	Democrat
1865	James Johnson	Dem-Prov
1865–1868	Charles Jones Jenkins	Democrat
1868	Gen. Thomas Howard Ruger	Military
1868	Rufus Brown Bullock	Rep-Prov
1868–1871	Rufus Brown Bullock	Reconstructionist
1871–1872	Benjamin Conley	Reconstructionist
1872–1877	James Milton Smith	Democrat
1877–1882	Alfred Holt Colquitt	Democrat
1882–1883	Alexander Hamilton Stephens	Democrat
1883	James Stoddard Boynton	Democrat
1883–1886	Henry Dickerson McDaniel	Democrat
1886–1890	John Brown Gordon	Democrat
1890–1894	William Jonathan Northen	Democrat
1894–1898	William Yates Atkinson	Democrat
1898–1902	Allen Daniel Candler	Democrat
1902–1907	Joseph Meriwether Terrell	Democrat
1907–1909	Hoke Smith	Democrat
1909–1911	Joseph Mackey Brown	Democrat
1911	Hoke Smith	Democrat
1911–1912	John Marshall Slaton	Democrat
1912–1913	Joseph Mackey Brown	Democrat
1913–1915	John Marshall Slaton	Democrat
1915–1917	Nathaniel Edwin Harris	Democrat
1917–1921	Hugh Manson Dorsey	Democrat
1921–1923	Thomas William Hardwick	Democrat
1923–1927	Clifford Mitchell Walker	Democrat
1927–1931	Lamartine Griffin Hardman	Democrat
1931–1933	Richard Brevard Russell, Jr.	Democrat
1933–1937	Eugene Talmadge	Democrat
1937–1941	Eurith Dickinson Rivers	Democrat
1941–1943	Eugene Talmadge	Democrat
1943–1947	Ellis Gibbs Arnall	Democrat
1947	Herman Eugene Talmadge	Democrat
1947–1948	Melvin Ernest Thompson	Democrat
1948–1955	Herman Eugene Talmadge	Democrat
1955–1959	Samuel Marvin Griffin	Democrat
1959–1963	Samuel Ernest Vandiver, Jr.	Democrat
1963–1967	Carl Edward Sanders	Democrat
1967–1971	Lester Garfield Maddox	Democrat
1971–1875	James Earl Carter	Democrat
1975–1983	George Dekle Busbee	Democrat
1983–1991	Joe Frank Harris	Democrat
1991–1999	Zell Miller	Democrat
1999–	Roy E. Barnes	Democrat

Democrat Provisional – Dem-Prov
Democratic Republican – Dem-Rep
Republican Provisional – Rep-Prov
Union Democrat – Union-Dem

Gaule on St. Catherines Island. By 1700, Jesuit and Franciscan missionaries had established an entire chain of missions along the Sea Islands and on the lower Chattahoochee.

By 1702, however, the English had forced the Spaniards back to St. Augustine, Florida. In 1732, desiring a buffer between the valuable rice-growing colony of Carolina and Native American-held lands to the south and west, King George II granted a charter to a group who wanted to establish a colony in present-day Georgia. The first settlers, led by James Edward Oglethorpe, landed at Yamacraw Bluff on 12 February 1733. By 1742 Oglethorpe had fought off Spanish threats to the British colony.

Statehood

In 1752, Georgia became a royal colony. Its society, like that of Carolina, was shaped by the planting of rice, indigo, and cotton. After the French and Indian War, settlers began to pour into the Georgia backcountry above Augusta. Following the War of Independence, a period of rapid expansion began. Georgia ratified the US Constitution on 2 January 1788, becoming the fourth state of the Union. The invention of the cotton gin by Eli Whitney in 1793 made cotton cultivation profitable in the lands east of the Oconee River. The settlement of the cotton lands brought prosperity to Georgia.

Photo credit: Courtesy, Jimmy Carter Library.

Jimmy Carter, who was elected president of the United States in 1976, was born in Plains, Georgia. He was governor of Georgia from 1971 to 1975.

After South Carolina seceded from the Union in 1860, Georgia also withdrew and joined the Confederate States of America. In 1864, troops under General William Tecumseh Sherman moved relentlessly upon Atlanta, capturing it in September. In November, Sherman began his famous "march to the sea," and he presented Savannah as a Christmas present to President Abraham Lincoln.

After ratifying the 14th and 15th amendments, Georgia was readmitted to the Union on 15 July 1870. After the Democrats recovered control of the state in 1871, business interests dominated politics. Former Democratic Representative Thomas E. Watson, who declared himself a Populist during the early 1890s, incited anti-Black, anti-Jewish, and anti-Catholic sentiment in order to control a bloc of rural votes with which he dominated state politics for ten years.

Franklin D. Roosevelt's efforts to introduce the New Deal to Georgia after he became president in 1933 were blocked by Governor Eugene Talmadge. It was not until the administration of Governor Eurith D. Rivers (1937–41) that progressive social legislation was enacted. The Supreme Court order to desegregate public schools in 1954 provided Georgia politicians with an emotional issue they exploited to the maximum.

1960s–1990s

During the 1960s, Atlanta was the home base for the civil-rights efforts of Martin Luther King, Jr., though his campaign to end racial discrimination in Georgia focused mostly on the town of Albany. Federal civil-rights legislation in 1964 and 1965 changed the state's political climate by guaranteeing the vote to black citizens. A black man, Julian Bond, was elected to the state legislature in 1965. In 1973, Maynard Jackson was elected mayor of Atlanta, thus becoming the first black mayor of a large southern city. Governor Jimmy Carter's resolute renunciation of racism in his inaugural speech in 1971 marked a turning point in Georgia politics and was a key factor in his election to the presidency in 1976.

The prosperity of Atlanta in the 1970s and 1980s stemmed largely from its service-based economy. The decline of service industries in the early 1990s, however, pulled Atlanta and the state of Georgia as a whole into a recession. That decline was exemplified by the collapse in 1991 of one of the two airlines that used Atlanta as its hub, Eastern Airlines, which cost Atlanta 10,000 jobs. Nevertheless, the 1990s wintessed continued growth of the Atlanta metropolitan area. In early 1999, newly elected goverernor, Roy Barnes, spoke of creating a new regional transportation authority to alleviate the transportation logjam between the city and its ever-growing suburbs.

Georgia Presidential Vote by Political Parties, 1948–2000

Year	Georgia Winner	Democrat	Republican	States' Rights Democrat	Progressive
1948	*Truman (D)	254,646	76,691	85,136	1,636
1952	Stevenson (D)	456,823	198,961		
1956	Stevenson (D)	444,6878	222,778		
1960	*Kennedy (D)	458,638	274,472		
1964	Goldwater (R)	522,163	616,584		
1968	Wallace (AI)	334,440	380,111	535,550	
1972	*Nixon (R)	289,529	881,490		
1976	*Carter (D)	979,409	483,743	**1,071	1,1681
				Libertarian	
1980	Carter (D)	890,955	654,168	15,627	
1984	*Reagan (R)	706,628	1,068,722	1521	
					New All.
1988	*Bush (R)	714,792	1,081,331	8,435	5,099
					Ind. (Perot)
1992	*Clinton (D)	1,008,966	995,252	7,110	309,657
1996	Dole (R)	1,053,849	1,080,843	17,870	146,337
				Libertarian	
2000	*Bush (R)	1,116,230	1,419,720	36,332	13,273

* Won US presidential election.
** Write-in votes.

12 STATE GOVERNMENT

The legislature, called the general assembly, consists of a 56-seat senate and a 180-seat house of representatives. All the legislators serve two-year terms. Elected executives include the governor, lieutenant governor, secretary of state, attorney general, and state school superintendent.

To become law, a bill must be passed by both houses of the legislature and approved by the governor, or passed over the executive veto by a two-thirds vote in both houses. All revenue measures originate in the house, but the senate can propose, or concur in, amendments to these bills. Amendments to the constitution may be proposed by two-thirds votes of the elected members of each chamber and must then be ratified by popular vote.

13 POLITICAL PARTIES

Georgia voted solidly Democratic between 1870 and 1960, casting its electoral votes for the Democratic presidential candidate in every election until 1964, when Republican Barry Goldwater won the state. The state's 12 electoral votes went to independent candidate George C. Wallace in 1968 and Republican Richard Nixon in 1972. In 1976, Georgia's native son Jimmy Carter returned the state to the Democratic camp in presidential balloting.

Republican George W. Bush won 55% of the vote, and Democrat Al Gore won 43% in the 2000 presidential election. Roy Barnes, a Democrat, won the gubernatorial race in 1998. Georgia Senator Paul Coverdell, first elected in 1992 and reelected in 1998, passed away in 2000.

Photo credit: Metro Atlanta Chamber of Commerce.

Georgia's capitol in Atlanta.

Former Governor Zell Miller was chosen to finish out his term, and was then elected in 2000 to continue serving as Senator. Georgia's US House delegation consists of three Democrats and eight Republicans.

Congressman Newt Gingrich was instrumental in guiding the Republicans to control of both the House and the Senate in the 1994 elections. Following the election, Gingrich became the first Republican Speaker of the House in 40 years. However, after Republican losses in the November 1998 midterm elections, Gingrich stepped down as Speaker and announced he would resign his House seat in 1999.

14 LOCAL GOVERNMENT

Georgia has 156 counties, 534 municipal governments, and 473 special districts. In 1965, the legislature passed a home-rule law permitting local governments to amend their own charters. The traditional and most common form of municipal government is the mayor-council form. But city managers are employed by some communities, and a few make use of the commission system.

15 JUDICIAL SYSTEM

Georgia's highest court is the supreme court, consisting of a chief justice, presiding justice, and five associate justices. Georgia's general trial courts are the superior courts, which have exclusive jurisdiction in cases of divorce and land title, and in major criminal cases. Cases from local courts can be sent to the court of appeals. Each county has a probate court and separate juvenile courts. The prison population in Georgia numbered 41,665 in 1999. Georgia is second after Texas in number of executions. According to the FBI Crime Index, the crime rate per 100,000 inhabitants for 1998 was 5,463.

16 MIGRATION

The greatest population shifts during the 20th century have been from country to town and, after World War I, of black Georgians to northern cities. From 1985 to 1990, Georgia's net gain through migration was greater than that of any other state except California and Florida.

Georgia had a net gain of 598,000 from interstate migration during 1990–98, and a further gain of 90,000 from international migration. From 1980 to 1990, the proportion of native-born residents in Georgia fell from 71% to 64.5%.

17 ECONOMY

Georgia's economy underwent drastic changes as a result of World War II. The raising of poultry and livestock became more important than crop cultivation, and manufacturing replaced agriculture as the chief source of income. Georgia is a leader in the making of paper products, tufted textiles products, processed chickens, naval stores, lumber, and transportation equipment.

Textile manufacturing, Georgia's oldest industry, remains its most important source of income. However, that area has grown slowly in recent years, while most durable-goods industries, such as electrical machinery and appliances, have grown rapidly. The state economy suffered in the national recession of the early 1980s but performed better during the expansion of the latter part of the decade than the nation as a whole. Service industries grew dramatically, particularly health and business as well as finance, insurance, and real estate. In 1997, the state's gross product was tenth in the nation at $229 billion.

18 INCOME

The per capita (per person) income of Georgians has been low historically, at least since the Civil War. Georgia's per capita income rose to $25,839 in 1998, boosting the state's national rank to 26th. In 1998,

A container ship enters the Port of Savannah.

about 14.3% of all state residents were living below the poverty level.

19 INDUSTRY

Georgia had 9,804 manufacturing firms in 1997. The transport equipment, chemical, food-processing, apparel, and forest-products industries today rival textile industries in economic importance. The state's most famous product was created in 1886, when druggist John S. Pemberton developed the formula for what became Coca-Cola, the world's most widely known commercial product. In 1997, 13 of the nations' 500 largest industrial corpora-tions listed by *Fortune* magazine had headquarters in Georgia.

20 LABOR

Georgia's civilian labor force was estimated at 4 million in mid-1998. Of this total, 4.2% were unemployed. The most remarkable change in the labor force since World War II has been the rising proportion of women, whose share increased from less than 28% in 1940 to an estimated 60.4% in 1998.

The trend during the 1970s and early 1980s was toward increased employment in service industries and toward multiple job-holding. Employment in agriculture, the leading industry prior to World War II, continued its long-term decline. The mining, construction, and manufacturing industries registered employment increases but declined in importance relative to such sectors as trade and government.

Georgia is not considered to be a highly unionized state. In 1998, 7.4% of all workers were union members, numbering about 256,800.

21 AGRICULTURE

In 1999, Georgia's farm marketings totaled $5.2 billion (12th in the US). Georgia ranked first in the production of peanuts (40% of the national total) and pecans (26% of the national total).

Cotton was the mainstay of Georgia's economy through the early 20th century, and the state's plantations also grew corn, rice, tobacco, wheat, and sweet potatoes. World War I stimulated the cultivation of peanuts along with other crops. By the 1930s, tobacco and peanuts were challenging cotton for agricultural supremacy, and Georgia had also become an important producer of peaches, a product for which the "peach state" is still widely known.

Georgia's farmland area of 11.3 million acres (4.6 million hectares) represents 30% of its land area. There were 50,000 farms in 1998, with an average size of 226 acres (91 hectares).

The following table shows production and value for leading crops in 1998:

CROP	PRODUCTION	VALUE
Peanuts	1.5 million pounds	$408.8 million
Cotton	1.5million bales*	$501.4 million
Tobacco	.9 million pounds	NA
Corn	2.25 million bushels	$54 million
Pecans	40 million pounds	$48.8 million
Soybeans	4.6 million bushels	$24.7 million
Peaches	70 million pounds	$24.1 million
Wheat	10.3 million bushels	$26.8 million

*One bale weighs about 480 pounds.

22 DOMESTICATED ANIMALS

Georgia's cash receipts from livestock and livestock products account for more than half of the total farm income. Georgia ranks second only to Arkansas in total cash receipts from chickens and broilers, and second to California in receipts from eggs.

In 1999, Georgia had 1.3 million cattle and calves, valued at $676 million, and an estimated 430,000 hogs and pigs valued at $18.1 million in 1998. Cows kept for milk production numbered 97,000 in 1997. Poultry farmers sold some $2.28 billion of broilers in 1997.

23 FISHING

Georgia's total commercial catch of fish and shellfish in 1998 was 13 million pounds, valued at $23.7 million. Commercial fishing in Georgia involves more shellfish—mainly shrimp and crabs—than finfish, the most important of which are caught in the nets of shrimp trawlers. Leading finfish are snappers, groupers, tilefish, and porgy. Sport fishers catch bass, catfish, jackfish, bluegill, crappie, perch, and trout. Georgia issued 622,027 sport fishing licenses in 1998.

Photo credit: © A Stephenson/Woodfin Camp.

A young man harvests peanuts on a farm in Georgia.

24 FORESTRY

Georgia's forest area totals 24.4 million acres (9.8 million hectares). Forests cover 66% of the state's land area. The chief products of Georgia's timber industry are pine lumber and pine plywood for the building industry, hardwood lumber for the furniture industry, and pulp for the paper and box industry. In 1998, Georgia produced approximately 3.16 billion board feet of lumber, of which 88% was softwood (pine).

The two chief recreational forest areas are Chattahoochee National Forest, in the northern part of the state, and Oconee National Forest, in the central region. The state of Georgia has 864,583 acres (349,897 hectares) of National Forest System lands, 99% of which are within the boundaries of the two national forests. The Georgia State Forest Commission annually produces some 50 million seedlings in state nurseries; 83,000 acres (33,600 hectares) were reforested in 1996.

25 MINING

The estimated value of nonfuel minerals produced in Georgia in 1998 was $1.79 billion. Kaolin (a type of clay), valued at over $1 billion, accounted for 58% of the total estimated value of minerals produced in Georgia. Fuller's earth, common clay, and shale were also mined. In 1998 the state was once again the national leader in quantity and value of both kaolin and fuller's earth.

Georgia also ranked third in value of iron oxide pigments and was fifth in quantity of dimension stone. The state also ranked second nationally in the quantity and value of barite, which is used by the chemical and the industrial filler and pigments industries.

26 ENERGY AND POWER

Georgia is an energy-dependent state which produces only a small proportion of its energy needs, most of it through hydroelectric power. There are no commercially recoverable petroleum or natural-gas reserves, and the state's coal deposits are not of great importance. Georgia does have large amounts of timberland, however, and it has been estimated that 20–40% of the state's energy demands could be met by using wood that is currently wasted.

In 1996, Georgia's energy consumption per capita (per person) was 359.2 million Btu (84.6 million kilocalories), slightly more than the national average of 352 (85.6). In 1998, Georgia produced 108.7 billion kilowatt hours of electricity. In 1995, Georgia's four nuclear power plants accounted for 16% of the total electric capacity. Petroleum accounted for 39% of all fuel used in Georgia in 1994, coal for 29%, and natural gas for 15%.

27 COMMERCE

Georgia's wholesale trade in 1997 had total sales of $170 billion. The state ranked 10th in retail trade in 1992, with sales totaling $49.9 billion. Retail sales in the Atlanta area accounted for 53% of the total. Georgia exported goods worth $13 billion in 1998. Savannah is Georgia's most important export center.

28 PUBLIC FINANCE

Since the Georgia constitution forbids the state to spend more than it takes in from all sources, the governor attempts to reconcile the budget requests of the state department heads with the revenue predicted by economists for the coming fiscal year.

The total state revenues and expenditures for 1997 were: revenues, $24.03 billion; expenditures, $21.98 billion.

Georgia's state debt totaled more than $6.18 billion in 1997. Total state indebtedness in 1997 amounted to $826 per person.

29 TAXATION

Georgia was the last of the 13 original colonies to tax its citizens, but today its state tax structure is among the broadest in the US. It includes property and income taxes, as well as taxes on gasoline and tobacco. At 7.5¢ per gallon, Georgia's state tax on motor fuel was the lowest in the country in 1996. In 1951, Georgia enacted what at that time was the most all-inclusive sales tax in the US. This 4% tax is now the state's second-largest source of revenue. Georgia's state taxes in 1997 totaled $10.9

billion, or about $1,456 per person (37th lowest among the states).

30 HEALTH

Heart disease, cancer, and cerebrovascular disease are the leading causes of death in Georgia. In 1998, there were 156 community hospitals in Georgia with 25,236 beds. The average expense of general hospitals in 1998 was $903.80 per inpatient day and $6,042 per stay. In 1995, Georgia had 12,801 practicing nonfederal doctors and 48,400 registered nurses. Atlanta has been the site of the federal Centers for Disease Control since 1973. About 17.5% of the adult population in 1998 had no health insurance.

31 HOUSING

Post–World War II housing developments provided Georgia families with modern, affordable dwellings. The home-loan guarantee programs of the Federal Housing Administration and the Veterans Administration made modest down payments, low interest rates, and long-term financing the norm in Georgia.

Between 1940 and 1970, the number of housing units in the state doubled to 1.5 million. In 1999, there were an estimated 3.1 million housing units in Georgia. The median cost for housing to owners with a mortgage was $737 per month in 1990, and $182 per month for those without a mortgage. The median monthly rent of renter-occupied housing was $433.

32 EDUCATION

In 1998, 80% of the population age 25 or older had a high school diploma. The state offers full-day kindergarten statewide, and preschool for disadvantaged four-year-olds. In 1997, Georgia public schools enrolled 1.4 million students, of whom 365,429 attended high school. Expenditures for public elementary and secondary schools amounted to $5,349 per student in 1995/96 (28th among the states).

Georgia had 120 institutions of higher learning, 73 public and 47 private, with a total 308,600 students in 1994. Thirty-two public colleges are components of the University System of Georgia. The largest of these is the University of Georgia (Athens), with a 1996 enrollment of 29,404. The largest private university is Emory University (Atlanta), with 10,367 students in 1992/93.

33 ARTS

During the 20th century, Atlanta has replaced Savannah as the major art center of Georgia, while Athens, the seat of the University of Georgia, has continued to share in the cultural life of the university. The state has eight major art museums, as well as numerous private galleries. The Atlanta Art Association exhibits the work of contemporary Georgia artists. Georgia's Art Bus Program delivers art exhibits to Georgia communities, mostly in rural areas, for three-week periods.

The theater has enjoyed popular support since the first professional resident theater troupe began performing in Augusta in 1790. Atlanta has a resident theater, and there are community theaters in some 30 cities and counties.

The Georgia Dome in Atlanta.

Georgia has at least 11 symphony orchestras, ranging from the Atlanta Symphony to community and college ensembles throughout the state. Atlanta and Augusta have professional ballet touring companies, and Augusta has a professional opera company. Macon and Atlanta have become major recording centers, especially for popular music. The north Georgia mountain communities retain their traditional folk music.

34 LIBRARIES AND MUSEUMS

In 1998, the Georgia public library system included 33 regional and 24 county systems, each operating under its own board. The holdings of all public libraries totaled 15.3 million volumes in 19968 and the combined circulation was 34 million volumes. The University of Georgia had by far the largest academic collection, including over 3 million books.

Georgia has 179 museums, including the Telfair Academy of Arts and Sciences in Savannah, the Georgia State Museum of Science and Industry in Atlanta, and the Columbus Museum of Arts and Sciences. Atlanta's Cyclorama depicts the 1864 Battle of Atlanta.

Georgia abounds in historic sites. Sites administered by the National Park Service include the Chickamauga battlefield, Kennesaw Mountain battlefield, Fort Pulaski

National Monument, and Andersonville prison camp near Americus, all associated with the Civil War, as well as the Fort Frederica National Monument, an 18th-century English barracks on St. Simons Island. The Martin Luther King, Jr., National Historic Site was established in Atlanta in 1980. Also in Atlanta is former President Jimmy Carter's library, museum, and conference center complex.

35 COMMUNICATIONS

As of 1999, 92.1% of Georgian households had telephones. In 2000, Georgia had 416 radio stations, 183 AM and 233 FM. There were 51 television stations in that same year, and 1.7 million television-owning households. On 1 June, 1980, Atlanta businessman Ted Turner inaugurated the independent Cable News Network, (CNN). By the late 1980s, CNN had become well-known worldwide.

36 PRESS

In 1817, the *Savannah Gazette* became the state's first daily. After the Native American linguist Sequoyah gave the Cherokee a written language, Elias Boudinot gave them a newspaper, the *Cherokee Phoenix,* in 1828. Georgia authorities suppressed the paper in 1835, and Boudinot joined his tribe's tragic migration westward.

As of 1998, Georgia had 23 morning dailies, 11 evening dailies, and 27 Sunday newspapers. Leading newspapers with their 1998 daily circulations are: the *Atlanta Journal* and the *Atlanta Constitution* (303,698); the *Augusta Chronicle* (71,639); and the *Macon Telegraph* (68,996).

Periodicals published in Georgia include *Golf World, Atlanta Weekly, Robotics World,* and *Southern Accents.* Among the nation's better-known scholarly presses is the University of Georgia Press (Athens), which publishes the *Georgia Review.*

37 TOURISM, TRAVEL, AND RECREATION

Besides national forests and parks, major tourist attractions include the Okefenokee Swamp in southern Georgia; Stone Mountain near Atlanta; former President Jimmy Carter's home in Plains; the birthplace, church, and gravesite of Martin Luther King, Jr., in Atlanta; and the historic squares and riverfront of Savannah. The varied attractions of the Golden Isles include fashionable Sea Island. Georgia has long been a hunters' paradise. Waynesboro calls itself the "bird dog capital of the world," and Thomasville in South Georgia is a mecca for quail hunters.

38 SPORTS

There are four major league professional sports teams in Georgia, all in Atlanta: Major League Baseball's Atlanta Braves, the Atlanta Falcons of the National Football League, the Atlanta Hawks of the National Basketball Association, and the Atlanta Thrashers of the National Hockey League. Atlanta also hosted the 1996 Summer Olympic Games. The Atlanta 500 is one of the Winston Cup Grand National auto races. The Masters Golf Tournament has been played at the Augusta National Golf Club since 1934.

Photo credit: EPD Photos/National Archives

Civil rights leader Martin Luthor King, Jr. (1929–68) was born in Atlanta. King was the leader of the March on Washington in 1963, and winner of the Nobel Peace Prize in 1964.

Football and basketball dominate college sports. The University of Georgia Bulldogs play in the Southeastern Conference, and Georgia Tech's Yellow Jackets compete in the Atlantic Coast Conference. The Peach Bowl has been an annual post-season college football game in Atlanta since 1968. Professional fishing is one of the fastest-growing sports in the state. A popular summer pastime is rafting.

39 FAMOUS GEORGIANS

James Earl "Jimmy" Carter (b.1924), born in Plains, was the first Georgian to serve as president of the US. He was governor of the state (1971–75) before being elected to the White House in 1976. Clarence Thomas (b.1948) was appointed as a Supreme Court Justice in 1991. Dean Rusk (1909–94) was secretary of state in the Kennedy and Johnson administrations. Notable US senators in recent years were Herman Talmadge (b.1913), and Sam Nunn (b.1938). A Georgia member of Congress, Newt Gingrich (b. Pennsylvania 1943), served as Speaker of the US House of Representatives from 1994 until 1998.

Revolutionary War hero James Jackson (b.England, 1757–1806) organized the Democratic-Republican Party (today's Democratic Party) in Georgia. Confederate General Joseph Wheeler (1836–1906) became a major general in the US Army during the Spanish-American War. Other Civil War generals included W. H. T. Walker (1816–64), Thomas R. R. Cobb (1823–62), who also codified Georgia's laws, and John B. Gordon (1832–1904), later a US senator and governor of the state.

Among Georgia's notable Native Americans were Osceola (1800–38), who led the Seminoles into the Florida swamps rather than move west and rallied them during the Seminole War of 1835–42; Sequoyah (b.Tennessee, 1773–1843), who framed an alphabet for the Cherokee; and John Ross (Coowescoowe, b.Tennessee, 1790–1866), the first president of the Cherokee republic.

Distinguished black Georgians include civil-rights activists William Edward Burghardt (W.E.B.) DuBois (b.Massachusetts, 1868–1963). One of the best-known Georgians was Martin Luther King, Jr. (1929–68), born in Atlanta, leader of the March on Washington in 1963, and winner of the Nobel Peace Prize in 1964. Black Muslim leader Elijah Muhammad (Elijah Poole, 1897–1975) was also a Georgian. Other prominent black leaders include Atlanta Mayor and former UN Ambassador Andrew Young (b.Louisiana, 1932), former Atlanta Mayor Maynard Jackson (b.Texas, 1938), and Georgia Senator Julian Bond (b.Tennessee, 1940).

Famous Georgia authors include Joel Chandler Harris (1848–1908), Conrad Aiken (1889–1973), Erskine Caldwell (1903–87), Carson McCullers (1917–67), James Dickey (1923–97), and Flannery O'Connor (1925–64). Also notable is Margaret Mitchell (1900–49), whose Pulitzer Prize-winning *Gone With the Wind* (1936) typifies Georgia to many readers.

Entertainment celebrities include songwriter Johnny Mercer (1909–76); comedian Oliver Hardy (1877–1961); musicians Ray Charles (Ray Charles Robinson, b.1930), James Brown (b.1933), Little Richard (Richard Penniman, b.1935), Otis Redding (1941–67), Gladys Knight (b.1944), Brenda Lee (b.1944), and Amy Grant (b.1961); and actors Melvyn Douglas (1901–81), Joanne Woodward (b.1930), and Burt Reynolds (b.1936).

Major sports figures include baseball's "Georgia peach," Tyrus Raymond "Ty" Cobb (1886–1961); Jack Roosevelt "Jackie" Robinson (1919–72), the first black man to be inducted into the Baseball

Photo credit: EPD Photos/CSU Archives

Born in Narrows, Georgia in 1886, Ty Cobb was the first player selected for the Baseball Hall of Fame. One of the game's greatest hitters, he led the American League in batting 12 times and had a lifetime batting average of .367. He also batted over .400 three seasons, led the league in 12 offensive categories in 1911, and paced the Detroit Tigers to three American League pennants.

Hall of Fame; and Robert Tyre "Bobby" Jones (1902–71), winner of the "grand slam" of four major golf tournaments in 1930.

40 BIBLIOGRAPHY

Aylesworth, Thomas G. *The Southeast: Georgia, Kentucky, Tennessee.* New York: Chelsea House, 1996.

King, Coretta Scott. *My Life with Martin Luther King.* New York: Holt, Rinehart & Winston, 1970.

Lommel, Cookie. *James Oglethorpe.* Philadelphia: Chelsea House, 2000.

McAuliffe, Emily. *Georgia Facts and Symbols.* Mankato, Minn.: Hilltop Books, 1999.

Waters, Andrew, ed. *On Jordan's StormyBanks: Personal Accounts of Slavery in Georgia.* Winston-Salem, N.C.: John F. Blair, 2000.

Wills, Charles. *A Historical Album of Georgia.* Brookfield, Conn.: Millbrook Press, 1996.

Web sites

Georgia Industry, Trade & Tourism. Travel and Tourism. [Online] Available http://www.georgia.org/itt/tourism Accessed May 31, 2001.

State of Georgia. Georgia Government. [Online] Available http://www.state.ga.us/index/gagov.html Accessed May 31, 2001.

HAWAII

ORIGIN OF STATE NAME: Unknown. The name may stem from Hawaii Loa, traditional discoverer of the islands, or from Hawaiki, the traditional Polynesian homeland.

NICKNAME: The Aloha State.

CAPITAL: Honolulu.

ENTERED UNION: 21 August 1959 (50th).

SONG: "Hawaii Ponoi."

MOTTO: *Ua mau ke ea o ka aina i ka pono* (The life of the land is perpetuated in righteousness).

COAT OF ARMS: The heraldic shield of the Hawaiian kingdom is flanked by the figures of Kamehameha I, who united the islands, and Liberty, holding the Hawaiian flag. Below the shield is a phoenix surrounded by taro leaves, banana foliage, and sprays of maidenhair fern.

FLAG: Eight horizontal stripes, alternately white, red, and blue, represent the major islands, with the British Union Jack (reflecting the years that the islands were under British protection) in the upper left-hand corner.

OFFICIAL SEAL: Same as coat of arms, with the words "State of Hawaii 1959" above and the state motto below.

BIRD: Nene (Hawaiian goose).

FLOWER: Pua aloalo (hibiscus).

TREE: Kukui (candlenut).

ISLAND EMBLEMS: Each of the eight major islands has its own color and emblem.

> **HAWAII:** red; lehua (ohia blossom).
>
> **KALHOOLAWE:** gray; hinahina (beach heliotrope).
>
> **KAUAI:** purple; mokihana (fruit capsule of the *Pelea anisata*).
>
> **LANAI:** yellow; kaunaoa *(Cuscuta sandwichiana)*.
>
> **MAUI:** pink; lokelani (pink cottage rose).
>
> **MOLOKAI:** green; kukui (candlenut) blossom.
>
> **NIIHAU:** white; white pupa shell.
>
> **OAHU:** yellow; ilima *(Sida fallax)*.

TIME: 2 AM Hawaii-Aleutian Standard Time = noon GMT.

1 LOCATION AND SIZE

The State of Hawaii is an island group situated in the northern Pacific Ocean, about 2,400 miles (3,900 kilometers) west-southwest of San Francisco. The smallest of the five states on the Pacific Ocean, Hawaii ranks 47th in size among the 50 states. The 132 Hawaiian Islands have a total area of 6,470 square miles (16,758 square kilometers). The island chain extends over 1,576 miles (2,536 kilometers) north-south and 1,425 miles (2,293 kilometers) east-west. The collective coastline of the islands is 750 miles (1,207 kilometers).

2 TOPOGRAPHY

The 8 major and 124 minor islands that make up the State of Hawaii were formed by volcanic eruptions. Mauna Loa, on the island of Hawaii, is the world's largest active volcano, at a height of 13,675 feet (4,168 meters). The largest natural lake in the state is Halulu (182 acres—74 hectares) on Niihau. The longest rivers are Kaukonahua Stream (33 miles—53 kilometers) on Oahu, and Wailuku River (32 miles—51 kilometers) on Hawaii.

3 CLIMATE

Hawaii has a tropical climate cooled by trade winds. Normal daily temperatures in Honolulu average 72°F (22°C) in February and 78°F (26°C) in August. The record high for the state is 100°F (38°C), and the record low is 12°F (–11°C). Rainfall is extremely variable. Mt. Waialeale, on Kauai, said to be the rainiest place on earth, has a mean annual total of 496 inches (1,234 centimeters), while the driest areas average under 10 inches (25 centimeters). The highest tidal wave (tsunami) in the state's history reached 56 feet (17 meters).

4 PLANTS AND ANIMALS

Of 2,200 species and subspecies of plants, more than half are endangered, threatened, or extinct. The only land mammal native to the islands is the Hawaiian hoary bat, now endangered. Listed as threatened are the leatherback and green sea turtles.

Hawaii Population Profile

Total population in 2000:	1,211,537
Population change, 1990–2000:	9.3%
Hispanic or Latino†:	7.2%
Population by race	
One race:	78.6%
White:	24.3%
Black or African American:	1.8%
American Indian/Alaska Native:	0.3%
Asian:	41.6%
Native Hawaiian/Pacific Islander:	9.4%
Some other race:	1.3%
Two or more races:	21.4%

Population by Age Group

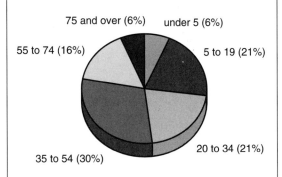

75 and over (6%) under 5 (6%)
55 to 74 (16%)
5 to 19 (21%)
35 to 54 (30%)
20 to 34 (21%)

Top Cities by Population

City	Population	% change 1990–2000
Honolulu	371,657	1.7
Hilo	40,759	7.8
Kailua	36,513	–0.8
Kaneohe	34,970	–1.3
Waipahu	33,108	5.3
Pearl	30,976	–0.1
Waimalu	29,371	–2.0
Mililani	28,608	–2.6
Kahului	20,146	19.3
Kihei	16,749	50.8

Notes: †A person of Hispanic or Latino origin may be of any race. NA indicates that data are not available.
Sources: U.S. Census Bureau. Public Information Office. *Demographic Profiles.* [Online] Available http://www.census.gov/Press-Release/www/2001/demoprofile.html. Accessed June 1, 2001. U.S. Census Bureau. *Census 2000: Redistricting Data.* Press release issued by the Redistricting Data Office. Washington, D.C., March, 2001.

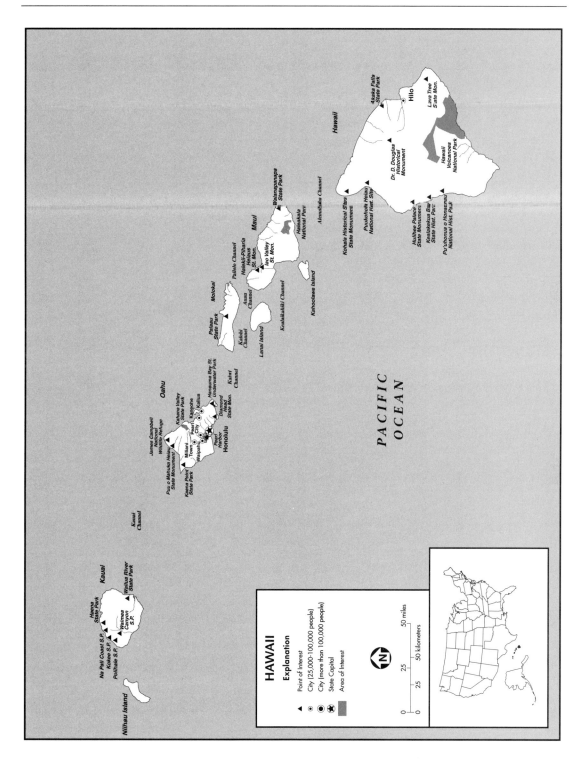

HAWAII

Explanation

▲ Point of Interest

⊙ City (25,000-100,000 people)

◉ City (more than 100,000 people)

✪ State Capital

▒ Area of Interest

50 miles

50 kilometers

PACIFIC OCEAN

Kauai

Niihau Island

Oahu

Molokai

Maui

Lanai Island

Kahoolawe Island

Hawaii

Hilo

Honolulu

Photo credit: Corel Corporation.

An area of devastation near the Kiluaea Crater. Although destructive at times, Hawaii's volcanoes are also beneficial. Not only do they add new land to the island chain, but they also form a soil that is high in nutrients.

The nene (the state bird), once close to extinction, now numbers in the hundreds and is on the increase.

5 ENVIRONMENTAL PROTECTION

Noise pollution requirements in Honolulu are among the strictest in the US, and air and water purity levels are well within federal standards. In 1998, there were four hazardous waste sites.

6 POPULATION

According to the 2000 census, Hawaii had a population of 1,211,537, falling behind states such as Maine and New Hampshire to rank 42nd among the 50 states. The Census Bureau projects a population of 1.34 million in 2005. Almost four-fifths of the population lives on Oahu. The state had a population density of about 188.6 persons per square mile (72.8 persons per square kilometer) in 2000. One-fifth of the population was 55 or older in 2000. Honolulu, by far the largest city, had a 2000 population of 371,657.

7 ETHNIC GROUPS

Of the state's nearly 1.2 million residents in 1997, 748,700 are Asian or Pacific Islanders; 395,800 are white; 35,400 are black; and 6,600 are Native American, Eskimo, or Aleut. At 63.1% in 1997, Hawaii's proportion of Asians and Pacific

Hawaii Population by Race

Census 2000 was the first national census in which the instructions to respondents said, "Mark one or more races." This table shows the number of people who are of one, two, or three or more races. For those claiming two races, the number of people belonging to the various categories is listed. The U.S. government conducts a census of the population every ten years.

	Number	Percent
Total population	1,211,537	100.0
One race	952,194	78.6
Two races	175,252	14.5
White *and* Black or African American	2,289	0.2
White *and* American Indian/Alaska Native	5,953	0.5
White *and* Asian	55,028	4.5
White *and* Native Hawaiian/Pacific Islander	31,485	2.6
White *and* some other race	7,728	0.6
Black or African American *and* American Indian/Alaska Native	645	0.1
Black or African American *and* Asian	1,936	0.2
Black or African American *and* Native Hawaiian/Pacific Islander	1,330	0.1
Black or African American *and* some other race	532	—
American Indian/Alaska Native *and* Asian	1,473	0.1
American Indian/Alaska Native *and* Native Hawaiian/Pacific Islander	1,259	0.1
American Indian/Alaska Native *and* some other race	225	—
Asian *and* Native Hawaiian/Pacific Islander	57,647	4.8
Asian *and* some other race	5,671	0.5
Native Hawaiian/Pacific Islander *and* some other race	2,051	0.2
Three or more races	84,091	6.9

Source: U.S. Census Bureau. *Census 2000: Redistricting Data.* Press release issued by the Redistricting Data Office. Washington, D.C., March, 2001. A dash (—) indicates that the percent is less than 0.1.

Islanders was the highest in the country, making Hawaii the only state with an Asian and Pacific Islander majority. About 8% of Hawaiians that year were Hispanic. Ethnic Hawaiians have been increasingly intent on preserving their cultural identity.

8 LANGUAGES

The Hawaiian legacy is apparent in the state's English. Newcomers soon add to their vocabulary *aloha* (love, good-bye), *haole* (white foreigner), *malihini* (newcomer), *mahimahi* (dolphinfish), *ukulele, muumuu,* and other common native words. Most native-born residents of Hawaiian ancestry speak one of several varieties of Hawaiian pidgin, a common language with elements of Hawaiian, English, and other Asian and Pacific languages. Approximately 75% of Hawaiians speak only English at home. Other languages spoken at home, and the number of speakers, include Japanese (69,587); Tagalog (55,341); and Chinese (26,366).

9 RELIGIONS

An estimated 232,700 Hawaiians consider themselves Roman Catholics, and 158,047 view themselves as Protestants. Mormons (Church of Jesus Christ of Latter-day Saints) number about 38,000.

10 TRANSPORTATION

Hawaii has only two railroads: the non-profit Hawaiian Railway Society, with 6.5 miles (10.5 kilometers) of track on Oahu, and the commercial-recreational Lahaina, Kaanapali & Pacific on Maui, with 6 miles (10 kilometers) of track. The islands of Oahu, Hawaii, Maui, and Kauai have public bus systems. In 1997, Hawaii had 4,165 miles (6,701 kilometers) of roads and streets. There were 442,889 passenger cars registered in 1997, along with 245,956 trucks and 3,959 buses.

All scheduled inter-island passenger traffic and most trans-Pacific travel is by air. In 1996, the state had 46 aircraft facilities—30 airports and 16 heliports. The busiest air terminal, Honolulu International Airport, accounts for about 64% of the state's boarded passengers and was 23d in the nation in 1996 at 9.1 million.

11 HISTORY

The Western world learned of the Hawaiian islands in 1778, when an English navigator, Captain James Cook, sighted Oahu. At that time, each island was ruled by a hereditary chief under a caste system called *kapu*. Contact with European sailors and traders exposed the Polynesians to smallpox, venereal disease, liquor, firearms, and Western technology—and fatally weakened the *kapu* system. Within 40 years of Cook's arrival, one of the island chiefs, Kamehameha (r.1810–19), had conquered Maui and Oahu and established a royal dynasty in what became known as the Kingdom of Hawaii. His son, Liholiho, was proclaimed Kamehameha II in 1819.

After the death of Kamehameha II in 1824, his brother, Kauikeaouli, was proclaimed King Kamehameha III. His reign saw the establishment of public schools, the first sugar plantation, and a two-chamber legislature. Hawaii's first written constitution was adopted in 1840, and in 1848, a land reform called the Great Mahele abolished the feudal land system, fostering the expansion of sugar plantations. The 1840s and 1850s saw recognition of the kingdom from the US, Britain, and France. The following decades witnessed the arrival of Chinese contract laborers and the increasing influence of American sugar planters.

In 1893, the reigning monarch, Queen Liliuokalani, was overthrown in an American-led revolution that produced a provisional government under the leadership of Sanford B. Dole. After unsuccessfully requesting annexation by the US, Hawaii's government drafted a new constitution and on 4 July 1894 proclaimed the Republic of Hawaii. After the Spanish-American War, which fueled expansionist feelings in the US and pointed up the nation's strategic interests in the Pacific, the US annexed Hawaii, effective June 1900.

Notable in the territorial period were a steady US military buildup; the creation of a pineapple-canning industry; the growth of tourism (spurred in 1936 by the inauguration of commercial air service); and a rising desire for statehood. The Japanese attack on Pearl Harbor on 7 December 1941, crippling the US Pacific fleet and causing some 4,000 casualties, quickly turned Hawaii into an armed camp under martial law.

Hawaiians pressed for statehood after World War II, but Congress was reluctant, partly because of racial hostility and partly because of fears that Hawaii's powerful International Longshoremen's and Warehousemen's Union was Communist-controlled. Not until 21 August 1959, after Alaska became the 49th state, did Hawaii become the 50th. Since then, defense and tourism have been the mainstays of Hawaii's economy, with the state playing an increasingly important role as an economic, educational, and cultural bridge between the US and the nations of Asia and the Pacific.

12 STATE GOVERNMENT

Hawaii has a two-chamber legislature of 25 senators and 51 representatives. The governor and lieutenant governor are elected for four-year terms and must be of the same political party. They are the only elected officers of the executive branch, except for members of the Board of Education. There are 17 executive departments, each under the supervision of the governor and headed by a single appointed executive.

Hawaii Governors: 1959–2001

1959–1962	William Francis Quinn	Republican
1962–1974	John Anthony Burns	Democrat
1974–1986	George Ryoichi Ariyoshi	Democrat
1986–1994	John Waihee III	Democrat
1994–	Benjamin J. Cayetano	Democrat

13 POLITICAL PARTIES

Before statehood, the Republican Party dominated the political scene. Since the 1960s, however, Hawaii has been solidly Democratic. As of 2001, Hawaii's governor, the majorities of both houses of the state legislature, its senators, and its two US Representatives were all Democrats. Democrats held 22 of the seats in the Senate while Republicans held just 3. In the House, Democrats held 32 seats to the Republicans 19. Democrat Al Gore won with 56% of the vote in the presidential election in 2000, while Republican George W. Bush garnered 37%. As of 2001, 19 women served in the state legislature.

Hawaii Presidential Vote by Major Political Parties, 1960–2000

YEAR	HAWAII WINNER	DEMOCRAT	REPUBLICAN
1960	*Kennedy (D)	92,410	92,295
1964	*Johnson (D)	163,249	44,022
1968	Humphrey (D)	141,324	91,425
1972	*Nixon (R)	101,433	168,933
1976	*Carter (D)	147,375	140,003
1980	Carter (D)	135,879	130,112
1984	*Reagan (R)	147,154	185,050
1988	Dukakis (D)	192,364	158,625
1992**	*Clinton (D)	179,310	136,822
1996**	*Clinton (D)	205,012	113,943
2000	Gore (D)	205,286	137,845

* Won US presidential election.
**Independent candidate Ross Perot received 53,003 votes in 1992 and 27,358 votes in 1996.

14 LOCAL GOVERNMENT

The state is divided into four principal counties—Hawaii, Maui, Honolulu (coextensive with the city of Honolulu and covering all of Oahu), and Kauai—and a fifth county of Kalawao (administered by the state Department of Health), consisting of that part of Molokai more commonly known as the Kalaupapa Settlement, primarily for the care and treatment of persons suffering from leprosy. Since there are no further subdivisions, the counties provide some services traditionally performed in other states by cities, towns, and villages. On the other hand, the state government provides many functions normally performed by counties on the mainland. Each of the four principal counties has an elected council and a mayor.

15 JUDICIAL SYSTEM

The supreme court, the highest in the state, consists of a chief justice and four associate justices. The state is divided into four judicial circuits with 22 circuit court judges and 4 intermediate appeals court judges. Circuit courts are the main trial courts, having jurisdiction in most civil and criminal cases. District courts function as inferior courts within each judicial circuit; district court judges may also preside over family court proceedings. Hawaii also has a land court and a tax appeal court. Hawaii's crime rate in 1998 per 100,000 was 5,330. There were 4,943 persons in the state's jails and prisons in 1999.

16 MIGRATION

Since the early 1970s, about 40,000 mainland Americans have come each year to live in Hawaii. More than half are military personnel and their dependents, on temporary residence during their term of military service. During 1990–98, interstate migration resulted in a net loss of 80,300, partially offset by a net gain from international migration of 51,500. Residents born within Hawaii made up 56.1% of the population in 1990.

17 ECONOMY

Tourism remains Hawaii's leading employer, revenue producer, and growth area. However, agricultural diversification—including the cultivation of flowers and nursery products, papaya, and macadamia nuts—fish farming, manganese nodule mining, and film and television production have broadened the state's economic base.

18 INCOME

Average per capita (per person) income in Hawaii in 1998 was $26,759 (21st in the US). In the same year, 12.3% of all Hawaii residents were below the federal poverty level.

19 INDUSTRIES

Food and food products account for about one-third of the total annual value of shipments by manufacturers. Other major industries are clothing; stone, clay, and glass products; fabricated metals; and shipbuilding.

20 LABOR

The civilian labor force in mid-1998 was 596,200, and there was an unemployment rate of 6.2%. Some 26.5% of all workers were union members in 1998, the second highest rate among the states.

21 AGRICULTURE

Export crops—especially sugarcane and pineapple—dominate Hawaiian agriculture, which had farm receipts exceeding $527 million in 1999. Sugar and pineapple sales accounted for 26% and 18%, respectively, of total farm receipts in 1995. Crop production for 1995 included sugarcane, 4 million tons; pineapples, 345,000 tons; and macadamia nuts, 25,000 tons. In 1995, sugarcane acreage amounted to 48,500 acres (19,600 hectares), down from 226,580 acres (91,700 hectares) in 1973. The islands of Hawaii (Maui, Molokai, Oahu, and Kauai) are the only place in the US where coffee is grown commercially; production totaled 9 million pounds in 1998/99.

22 DOMESTICATED ANIMALS

Livestock products account for 15% of Hawaii's farm income. In 1999, Hawaii had 173,000 cattle, valued at $85 million. There were also 29,000 hogs worth $3.8 million. Poultry farms produced 172 million eggs in 1997. Eggs are one of the few farm commodities in which Hawaii is close to self-sufficient.

23 FISHING

Although expanding, Hawaii's commercial catch remains surprisingly small: 36.4 million pounds (16.3 million kilograms), worth $62 million, in 1998. The most valuable commercial species caught are swordfish and bigeye tuna. Sport fishing is extremely popular, with bass, bluegill, tuna, and marlin among the most sought-after varieties.

24 FORESTRY

As of 1997, Hawaii had 1.74 million acres (707,940 hectares) of forestland and water reserves. Production of lumber and plywood falls far short of local demand. Most locally grown wood is used to make furniture, flooring, and craft items.

Photo credit: Corel Corporation.

Hawaii's famous Waikiki Beach on the island of Oahu. Income generated from tourism is important to Hawaii's economy.

25 MINING

The value of Hawaii's nonfuel mineral production in 1998 was estimated at $93.7 million. Crushed stone, construction sand and gravel, and portland cement were the principal mineral commodities produced. Modest masonry cement and gemstone production was also reported. Mineral production in Hawaii is mainly for the local construction industry.

26 ENERGY AND POWER

Lacking native fossil fuels and nuclear installations, Hawaii depends on imported petroleum for 91% of its energy needs. Only a tiny fraction of Hawaii's electric production comes from alternative energy sources. In 1995, electric power production totaled 10.6 billion kilowatt hours.

27 COMMERCE

In 1997, sales from wholesale trade amounted to $7.7 billion. Retail sales amounted to $13 billion. Foreign imports to Hawaii totaled $3.2 billion in 1994, while exports exceeded $980 million.

28 PUBLIC FINANCE

Hawaii's biennial budget is the responsibility of the Department of Budget and Finance. The revenues for the 1997 fiscal year were $6.7 billion, and the expenditures were $6.09 million. The debt of the Hawaii state government at the end of fiscal 1997 was $5.25 billion, or $4,425 per capita (per person).

29 TAXATION

Hawaii's state tax burden in 1997 was $2,602 per person—only Alaska's was higher. There are personal income taxes, a capital gains tax, a business income tax, a broad-based general excise tax, and a 4% tax on retail sales of goods and services. Taxes on estates, fuel, liquor, and tobacco are also imposed, and the property tax is a major source of county income. Hawaii's total federal tax burden in 1995 was $6.4 billion, or $5,400 per person.

30 HEALTH

Death rates from heart diseases, cancer, cerebrovascular diseases, accidents, and

Photo credit: Corel Corporation.

A surfer rides the wave at Sunset Beach.

suicide are all below national rates. However, Hawaii ranks second among the states in the frequency of smoking-attributed deaths. In 1998, Hawaii had 20 community hospitals, with 2,791 beds. As of 1996 there were 3,309 nonfederal physicians and surgeons in Hawaii. Average hospital expense in 1998 was $1,054 per inpatient day.

31 HOUSING

In 1999 there were an estimated 440,000 housing units. Hawaii has a greater proportion of condominiums (21%) than any other state. In 1996, 3,927 new housing units were authorized (69% single family dwellings), with a value of $486 million.

Renters throughout Hawaii had a median monthly cost of $650, higher than in any other state.

32 EDUCATION

Education has developed rapidly in Hawaii: 84.6% of all state residents 25 years of age or older had completed high school in 1998. Hawaii is the only state with a single, unified public school system. In 1996/97 there were 248 public schools with 11,668 teachers and 188,485 students. Expenditures for public elementary and secondary schools amounted to $5,831 per student in 1995/96 (18th among the states). In addition, 121 private schools had 30,537 pupils in 1993. The University of Hawaii's Manoa campus is by far the largest, with 20,010 students in 1994. Smaller campuses are located at Hilo and West Oahu. Hawaii's six community colleges enrolled 27,905 in 1994.

33 ARTS

Performance facilities in Honolulu include the Neal Blaisdell Center, the John F. Kennedy Theater at the University of Hawaii, and the Waikiki Shell for outdoor concerts. Oahu cultural institutions include the Honolulu Symphony Orchestra, the Honolulu Community Theater, Windward Theater Guild, and the Polynesian Cultural Center.

34 LIBRARIES AND MUSEUMS

The Hawaii state library system had 49 facilities in 1996, with a combined book stock of 3.5 million. During the same year, the University of Hawaii library system had 3 million volumes. Hawaii has 42 major museums and cultural attractions. Among the most popular sites are the USS *Arizona* Memorial at Pearl Harbor; Polynesian Cultural Center; Sea Life Park; and the Honolulu Academy of Arts.

35 COMMUNICATIONS

In 1999, 96.3% of Hawaii's occupied housing units had telephones. Hawaii had 29 AM radio stations and 46 FM stations as of 2000, as well as 28 television stations. A total of 27,025 domain names were registered in 2000.

36 PRESS

In 1998, Hawaii had six English daily newspapers: the *Honolulu Advertiser, Honolulu Star-Bulletin, Hawaii Tribune-Herald, Maui News, West Hawaii Today,* and *The Garden Island*. The combined average circulation of the daily papers in 1997 was 40,797 Monday through Saturday, and 52,780 on Sunday.

37 TOURISM, TRAVEL, AND RECREATION

Jet air service has fueled the Hawaii travel boom in recent decades. Over 2.7 million visitors come annually from foreign countries. Visitors come for scuba diving, snorkeling, swimming, and sailing; for the hula, luau, lei, and other distinctive island pleasures; for the tropical climate and magnificent scenic beauty; and for a remarkable variety of recreational facilities, including 7 national parks and historic sites, 74 state parks, 626 county parks, 17 public golf courses, and 1,600 recognized surfing sites.

38 SPORTS

Hawaii has no major league professional sports team. The Pro Bowl (the National Football League's all-star game) is played in Honolulu on the weekend following the Super Bowl. The Aloha Bowl, a major college football post-season game since 1982, is annually played on Christmas Day in Honolulu. Hawaii is also the site of the annual Duke Kahanamoku and Makaha surfing meets and the world-famous Ironman Triathlon competition.

39 FAMOUS HAWAIIANS

Hawaii's best-known federal officeholder is Daniel K. Inouye (b.1924), a US senator since 1962 and the first person of Japanese ancestry ever elected to Congress. George R. Ariyoshi (b.1926), who was elected governor of Hawaii in 1974, was the first Japanese-American to serve as chief executive of a state. Commanding figures in Hawaiian history are King Kamehameha I (1758?–1819), who unified the islands through conquest, and Kamehameha III (Kauikeaouli, 1813–54), who transformed Hawaii into a constitutional monarchy. Sanford B. Dole (1844–1926) led a revolutionary movement that overthrew Queen Liliuokalani (1838–1917) and ultimately secured annexation by the US. Duke Kahanamoku (1889–1968) held the Olympic 100-meter free-style swimming record for almost 20 years.

40 BIBLIOGRAPHY

Goldberg, Jake. *Hawaii.* New York: Benchmark Books, 1998.

Grabowski, John F. *The Pacific: California, Hawaii.* New York: Chelsea House Publishers, 1992.

Hintz, Martin. *Hawai'i.* New York: Children's Press, 1999.

Photo credit: EPD Photos.

Daniel K. Inouye, a US senator since 1962, is the first person of Japanese ancestry ever elected to Congress.

Johnston, Joyce. *Hawaii.* Minneapolis: Lerner, 1995.

Kummer, Patricia K. *Hawaii.* Mankato, Minn.: Capstone Press, 1998.

McAuliffe, Emily. *Hawaii Facts and Symbols.* Mankato, Minn.: Hilltop Books, 2000.

Web sites

Hawaii Information for School Reports. [Online] Available http://www.gohawaii.com/hokeo/school/report.html Accessed May 31, 2001.

Hawaii Visitors & Convention Bureau. [Online] Available http://www.visit.hawaii.org/ Accessed May 31, 2001.

State of Hawaii. Information about the State of Hawaii Government. [Online] Available http://www.ehawaiigov.org/government/html/index.html/ Accessed May 31, 2001.

IDAHO

State of Idaho

ORIGIN OF STATE NAME: Apparently coined by a lobbyist-politician, George M. Willing, who claimed the word came from an Indian term meaning "gem of the mountains."

NICKNAME: The Gem State.

CAPITAL: Boise.

ENTERED UNION: 3 July 1890 (43d).

SONG: "Here We Have Idaho."

MOTTO: *Esto perpetua* (May it endure forever).

FLAG: On a blue field with gilt fringe, the state seal appears in the center with the words "State of Idaho" on a red band below.

OFFICIAL SEAL: With cornucopias at their feet, a female figure (holding the scales of justice in one hand and a pike supporting a liberty cap in the other) and a miner (with pick and shovel) stand on either side of a shield depicting mountains, rivers, forests, and a farm; the shield rests on a sheaf of grain and is surmounted by the head of a stag above whose antlers is a scroll with the state motto. The words "Great Seal of the State of Idaho" surround the whole.

BIRD: Mountain bluebird.

FLOWER: Syringa.

TREE: Western white pine.

GEM: Star garnet.

HORSE: Appaloosa.

TIME: 5 AM MST = noon GMT; 4 AM PST = noon GMT.

1 LOCATION AND SIZE

Idaho is the smallest of the eight Rocky Mountain states and 13th in size among the 50 states. The total area of Idaho is 83,564 square miles (216,431 square kilometers). Idaho extends a maximum of 305 miles (491 kilometers) east-west and 479 miles (771 kilometers) north-south. Its total boundary length is 1,787 miles (2,876 kilometers).

2 TOPOGRAPHY

Idaho is extremely mountainous. Its northern two-thirds consists of a mountain massif (a single block of the earth's crust) broken only by valleys and by the Big Camas and Palouse Country prairies. The Snake River Plain extends east–west across Idaho from Yellowstone National Park to the Boise area, curving around the southern end of the mountain mass. A forested high-mountain area juts into the southeastern corner; the rest of Idaho's southern edge consists mostly of low, dry mountains. More than 150 peaks rise above 10,000 feet (3,000 meters), of which the highest is Mt. Borah, at 12,662 feet (3,859 meters).

The largest lakes are Pend Oreille (180 square miles—466 square kilometers), Coeur d'Alene, and Priest in the panhandle, and Bear on the Utah border. The Snake River that dominates southern Idaho is one of the longest in the US, extending 1,038 miles (1,671 kilometers) across Wyoming, Idaho, and Washington. The Salmon, Clearwater, Kootenai, Bear, Boise, and Payette are other major rivers.

3 CLIMATE

The four seasons are distinct in Idaho but do not occur at the same time in all parts of the state. Mean temperatures in Boise range from 30°F (–1°C) in January to 75°F (24°C) in July. The record low temperature is –60°F (–51°C); the record high, 118°F (48°C). Precipitation in southern Idaho averages 13 inches (33 centimeters) per year; in the north, over 30 inches (76 centimeters).

4 PLANTS AND ANIMALS

Idaho has some 3,000 native plants. Evergreens include Douglas fir and western white pine (the state tree). Oak/mountain mahogany and ponderosa pine are among the other main forest types. Syringa is the state flower. Game mammals include the elk, mountain sheep, antelope, black bear, moose, mule deer and white-tailed deer. Pheasant, partridge, quail, and forest grouse are the main game birds, and there are trout, salmon, and bass in Idaho's lakes and streams. The grizzly bear is listed as threatened, while the woodland caribou, bald eagle, Arctic and American and peregrine falcons are endangered.

Idaho
Population Profile

Total population in 2000:	1,293,953
Population change, 1990–2000:	28.5%
Hispanic or Latino†:	7.9%
Population by race	
One race:	98.0%
White:	91.0%
Black or African American:	0.4%
American Indian/Alaska Native:	1.4%
Asian:	0.9%
Native Hawaiian/Pacific Islander:	0.1%
Some other race:	4.2%
Two or more races:	2.0%

Population by Age Group

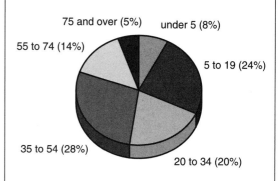

75 and over (5%)   under 5 (8%)
55 to 74 (14%)
5 to 19 (24%)
35 to 54 (28%)
20 to 34 (20%)

Top Cities by Population

City	Population	% change 1990–2000
Boise City	185,787	47.8
Nampa	51,867	82.9
Pocatello	51,466	11.7
Idaho Falls	50,730	15.5
Meridian	34,919	263.9
Couer d'Alene	34,514	40.5
Twin Falls	34,469	24.9
Lewiston	30,904	10.0
Caldwell	25,967	41.1
Moscow	21,291	15.0

Notes: †A person of Hispanic or Latino origin may be of any race. NA indicates that data are not available.
Sources: U.S. Census Bureau. Public Information Office. *Demographic Profiles.* [Online] Available http://www.census.gov/Press-Release/www/2001/demoprofile.html. Accessed June 1, 2001. U.S. Census Bureau. *Census 2000: Redistricting Data.* Press release issued by the Redistricting Data Office. Washington, D.C., March, 2001.

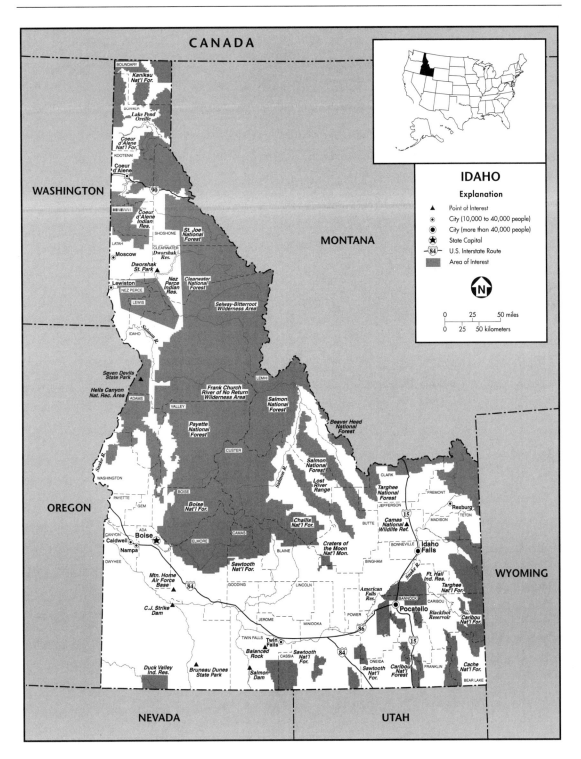

CANADA

WASHINGTON

MONTANA

OREGON

WYOMING

NEVADA

UTAH

BOUNDARY
Kaniksu
Nat'l For.

BONNER

Lake Pend
Oreille

Coeur
d'Alene
Nat'l For.

KOOTENAI

Coeur
d'Alene

90

Coeur
d'Alene
Indian
Res.

SHOSHONE

St. Joe
National
Forest

CLEARWATER

LATAH

Moscow

Dworshak
Res.

Dworshak
St. Park

Nez
Perce
Indian
Res.

Clearwater
National
Forest

Lewiston

NEZ PERCE

LEWIS

Selway-Bitterroot
Wilderness Area

Salmon R.

IDAHO

Seven Devils
State Park

LEMHI

Hells Canyon
Nat. Rec. Area

ADAMS

Frank Church
River of No Return
Wilderness Area

VALLEY

Salmon
National
Forest

Beaver Head
National
Forest

Payette
National
Forest

CUSTER

Salmon R.

Salmon
National
Forest

CLARK

Targhee
National
Forest

FREMONT

JEFFERSON

Lost
River
Range

BOISE

Boise
Nat'l For.

Rexburg

MADISON

TETON

Camas
National
Wildlife Ref.

Challis
Nat'l For.

BUTTE

BONNEVILLE

Idaho
Falls

ADA

CANYON

Caldwell

Boise

Nampa

ELMORE

CAMAS

BLAINE

Craters of
the Moon
Nat'l Mon.

BINGHAM

Ft. Hall
Ind. Res.

Targhee
Nat'l For.

OWYHEE

Mtn. Home
Air Force
Base

84

Sawtooth
Nat'l For.

GOODING

LINCOLN

American
Falls
Res.

BANNOCK

Pocatello

CARIBOU

Blackfoot
Reservoir

Caribou
Nat'l For.

C.J. Strike
Dam

JEROME

MINIDOKA

POWER

86

15

Duck Valley
Ind. Res.

Bruneau Dunes
State Park

Balanced
Rock

TWIN FALLS

Twin
Falls

CASSIA

Sawtooth
Nat'l
For.

ONEIDA

84

Sawtooth
Nat'l
For.

Caribou
Nat'l
Forest

FRANKLIN

Cache
Nat'l For.

Salmon
Dam

BEAR LAKE

Snake R.

Snake R.

WASHINGTON

PAYETTE

GEM

Snake R.

IDAHO

Explanation

▲ Point of Interest
◉ City (10,000 to 40,000 people)
● City (more than 40,000 people)
★ State Capital
84 U.S. Interstate Route
Area of Interest

N

0   25   50 miles
0   25   50 kilometers

Mt. Borah, Idaho's highest peak.

5 ENVIRONMENTAL PROTECTION

Air quality has improved greatly since the late 1970s. Emissions have dropped to the point that no carbon monoxide violations have occurred for several years. Water quality is generally good. Most of the existing problems stem from runoff from agricultural lands. Since 1953, nuclear waste has been buried at the Idaho National Engineering Laboratory west of Idaho Falls or discharged in liquid form into the underground aquifer. As of 1995, Idaho had ten hazardous waste sites.

6 POPULATION

Idaho's population at the 2000 census was 1,293,953—surpassing states such as Maine and New Hampshire to rank 39th among the 50 states. The population projection for 2005 is nearly 1.5 million. Boise's 2000 population was 185,787; Nampa was next with 51,867; and Pocatello with 51,466. The state's population density was 15.6 persons per square mile (6 per square kilometer) in 2000, far below the national average of 79.6 persons per square mile (30.7 per square kilometer). Idaho ranked fifth in the percentage growth rate of population between 1990 and 2000, which stood at 28.5% in 2000.

7 ETHNIC GROUPS

At an estimated 97% in 1997, Idaho had the 4th highest ratio of white population

---

Idaho Population by Race

Census 2000 was the first national census in which the instructions to respondents said, "Mark one or more races." This table shows the number of people who are of one, two, or three or more races. For those claiming two races, the number of people belonging to the various categories is listed. The U.S. government conducts a census of the population every ten years.

	Number	Percent
Total population	1,293,953	100.0
One race.	1,268,344	98.0
Two races.	24,265	1.9
White *and* Black or African American	1,725	0.1
White *and* American Indian/Alaska Native	8,112	0.6
White *and* Asian.	3,929	0.3
White *and* Native Hawaiian/Pacific Islander	673	0.1
White *and* some other race.	8,094	0.6
Black or African American *and* American Indian/Alaska Native	158	—
Black or African American *and* Asian.	79	—
Black or African American *and* Native Hawaiian/Pacific Islander	12	—
Black or African American *and* some other race.	222	—
American Indian/Alaska Native *and* Asian	143	—
American Indian/Alaska Native *and* Native Hawaiian/Pacific Islander	42	—
American Indian/Alaska Native *and* some other race	425	—
Asian *and* Native Hawaiian/Pacific Islander.	254	—
Asian *and* some other race	320	—
Native Hawaiian/Pacific Islander *and* some other race.	77	—
Three or more races	1,344	0.1

Source: U.S. Census Bureau. *Census 2000: Redistricting Data.* Press release issued by the Redistricting Data Office. Washington, D.C., March, 2001. A dash (—) indicates that the percent is less than 0.1.

---

among the states. The 1997 federal estimate also included 16,300 Native Americans (1.3%). There is a very small population of African Americans (about 6,600 in 1997, or 0.5%) and a somewhat larger number (13,200, or 1.1%) of Asian-Pacific peoples, primarily Japanese. There were 86,000 persons of Hispanic origin in Idaho, and a very visible Basque community in the Boise area.

8 LANGUAGES

In Idaho, English is a merger of Northern and North Midland features, with certain Northern pronunciations marking the panhandle. More than 93% of the people spoke only English at home in 1990. Spanish speakers numbered 37,081.

9 RELIGIONS

The Church of Jesus Christ of Latter-day Saints (Mormon) has been the leading religion in Idaho since 1860; with about a quarter of the population, the number of Mormons in Idaho is second only to that in Utah. Catholicism predominates north of Boise. According to 1990 estimates, Idaho has about 268,060 Mormons, 13,303 members of various Lutheran denominations, and 20,979 United Methodists. In 1990 there were 232,780 Roman Catholics and an estimated 320 Jews.

Skyline view of Boise, Idaho's state capital.

10 TRANSPORTATION

In 1997, Idaho had 60,440 miles (97,248 kilometers) of public roads, 94% of them rural. There were nearly 1.1 million registered vehicles in that same year. There were 1,832 rail miles (2,948 kilometers) used by the seven railroads operating within the state in 1997. Amtrak provides limited passenger service to several cities; the number of Idaho riders in 1995/96 was 14,497. Boise's modern airport boarded 1.2 million passengers during 1996. The Lewiston Port on the Snake River links Idaho with the Pacific via navigable waterways in Washington State.

11 HISTORY

The Shoshone, Northern Paiute, Salishan, and Shapwailutan tribal families were living in the area now known as Idaho when fur trappers and missionaries arrived in the early 1800s. The Oregon Trail opened in 1842, but for two decades people used it only to cross Idaho, not to settle there. In 1860 Mormons from Utah established Franklin, Idaho's first permanent settlement, and began farming. Gold was discovered that summer in northern Idaho. A gold rush, lasting several years, led directly to the organizing of the Idaho Territory on 10 July 1863.

Idaho's population nearly doubled between 1870 and 1880. The threat to Native American hunting and fishing grounds posed by growing white settlement touched off a series of wars in the late 1870s, the most famous being the Nez Percé War. With a population of 88,548 in 1890, Idaho was eligible to enter the Union, becoming the 43d state on 3 July.

From 1895 onward, federal land and irrigation projects fostered rapid economic growth. The modern timber industry began in 1906 with the completion of one of the nation's largest sawmills at Potlatch. By World War I, agriculture was a leading enterprise. Between the wars, Idaho suffered first from a farm depression in the 1920s, then from the nationwide Great Depression of the 1930s. After the war, an agri-industrial base was created, with fertilizers and potato-processing leading the way. In recent decades, population expansion and the push for economic growth have collided with a new interest in the environment, creating controversies over land-use planning, mineral development, and water supply and dam construction.

12 STATE GOVERNMENT

The legislature, consisting of a 35-seat senate and a 70-member house of representatives, meets regularly for 60–90 days a year. The executive branch is headed by the governor, lieutenant governor, and five other elected officials. The governor can sign or veto a bill or let it become law without his signature. Vetoes may be overridden by a two-thirds vote of each legislative house.

Idaho Governors: 1890–2001

1890–1891	George Laird Shoup	Republican
1891–1893	Norman Bushnell Willey	Republican
1893–1897	William John McConnell	Republican
1897–1901	Frank Steunenberg	Popularist Democrat
1901–1903	Frank Williams Hunt	Democrat
1903–1905	John Tracey Morrison	Republican
1905–1909	Frank Robert Gooding	Republican
1909–1911	James Henry Brady	Republican
1911–1913	James Henry Hawley	Democrat
1913–1915	John Michiner Haines	Republican
1915–1919	Moses Alexander	Democrat
1919–1923	David William Davis	Republican
1923–1927	Charles Calvin Moore	Republican
1927–1931	H. Clarence Baldridge	Republican
1931–1937	C. Ben Ross	Democrat
1937–1939	Barzilla Worth Clark	Democrat
1939–1941	Clarence Alfred Bottolfsen	Republican
1941–1943	Chase Addison Clark	Democrat
1943–1945	Clarence Alfred Bottolfsen	Republican
1945	Charles Clinton Gossett	Democrat
1945–1947	Arnold Williams	Democrat
1947–1951	Charles Armington Robins	Republican
1951–1955	Leonard Beck Jordan	Republican
1955–1967	Robert Eben Smylie	Republican
1967–1971	Don William Samuelson	Republican
1971–1977	Cecil Dale Andrus	Democrat
1977–1987	John Victor Evans	Democrat
1987–1995	Cecil Dale Andrus	Democrat
1995–1999	Philip E. Batt	Republican
1999–	Dirk Kempthorne	Republican

13 POLITICAL PARTIES

Idahoans usually vote Republican in presidential elections. In 2000 Republican George W. Bush received 69% of the vote while Democrat Al Gore won 28% of the vote. However, while the state has become increasingly conservative politically since the early 1960s, Democrats were elected governor during 1970–92.

In November 1998, Republican US Senator Dirk Kempthorne won election as governor, and was reelected in 2000. Following the November 2000 elections, the state legislature had 32 Republicans and 3 Democrats in the state senate and 61 Republicans and 9 Democrats in the state house. Idaho's US Representatives in

1999, Helen Chenoweth and Mike Simpson, were both Republican.

Idaho Presidential Vote by Major Political Parties, 1948–2000

YEAR	IDAHO WINNER	DEMOCRAT	REPUBLICAN
1948	*Truman (D)	107,370	101,514
1952	*Eisenhower (R)	395,081	180,707
1956	*Eisenhower (R)	105,868	166,979
1960	Nixon (R)	138,853	161,597
1964	*Johnson (D)	148,920	143,557
1968	*Nixon (R)	389,273	165,369
1972	*Nixon (R)	380,826	199,384
1976	Ford (R)	126,549	204,151
1980	*Reagan (R)	110,192	290,699
1984	*Reagan (R)	108,510	297,523
1988	*Bush (R)	147,272	253,881
1992**	Bush (R)	137,013	202,645
1996**	Dole (R)	165,443	256,595
2000	*Bush (R)	138,637	336,937

* Won US presidential election.
** Independent candidate Ross Perot received 130,395 votes in 1992 and 62,518 votes in 1996.

14 LOCAL GOVERNMENT

As of 1997, Idaho had 44 counties, 199 municipal governments, 113 school districts, and 784 special districts. Most counties elect three commissioners and other officers. Nearly all cities have an elected mayor and a council of four to six members.

15 JUDICIAL SYSTEM

Idaho's highest court, the supreme court, consists of five justices. There is a three-member court of appeals. The district court is the main trial court in civil and criminal matters, while magistrates' courts handle traffic, misdemeanor, and minor civil cases and preliminary hearings in felony cases. Idaho's crime rates are low in almost every category. The total rate in 1998 was 3,714.6 per 100,000. In 1997 there were 4,397 inmates in state and federal prisons.

16 MIGRATION

Since 1960, immigrants have come largely from California. Idaho suffered a net loss from migration of 109,000 persons between 1940 and 1970, but had a net gain of 110,000 persons in the 1970s. During the 1980s, Idaho had a net loss of 28,000 persons from migration, but this trend was offset by interstate migration gains of 128,500 during 1990–98.

17 ECONOMY

Currently, agriculture, mining, forest products, and food processing comprise Idaho's largest industries. The early 1980s brought a national recession to Idaho. Recovery, which required a restructuring of Idaho's mining, forest products, and agricultural industries, has come slowly. In some areas of the economy, the labor force has shrunk permanently. Modernization in lumber and wood products eliminated hundreds of jobs. Employment in chemical manufacturing, the paper industry, electronics, and tourism increased. Disputes with the federal government over the management of federal lands—60% of Idaho's public land—remain central to discussion of Idaho's economic policy.

18 INCOME

Per capita (per person) income in Idaho in 1998 was $22,079, 44th in the US. Total personal income was $27.18 billion in the same year. Some 13.2% of all state residents were living below the federal poverty level in 1998.

Photo credit: James W. Davis.

Thousands of acres of irrigated Idaho potatoes are grown on the Snake River Plain.

19 INDUSTRY

Resource industries—food processing, chemical manufacturing, and lumber production—form the backbone of manufacturing in Idaho. Some northern California computer companies, including Hewlett Packard, have opened or expanded plants in Idaho. Electronics manufacturers headquartered in Idaho include Advanced Input Devices and Micron Technology.

20 LABOR

Idaho's civilian labor force was 653,000 in mid-1998, with an unemployment rate of 5%. Nonagricultural employment in mid-1998 amounted to 519,400, of which mining accounted for 3,200; manufacturing, 75,700; construction, 32,200; transportation and utilities, 24,300; trade, 130,600; finance, insurance, and real estate, 26,900; services, 124,100; and government, 102,400. Some 7.8% of all workers were union members as of 1998.

21 AGRICULTURE

Farm marketings were about $3.2 billion in 1999 (22d in the US), when Idaho led the US in potato production. In 1998, the state produced about 14 billion pounds of potatoes (28% of the national total). About three-fourths of the crop is processed into frozen french fries, instant mashed potatoes, and other products. Other leading crops were hay, 5.5 million tons; wheat, 102 million bushels; and barley, 59.2 million bushels.

22 DOMESTICATED ANIMALS

In 1999, there were 1.9 million cattle and calves in Idaho, worth $1.3 billion. The state had 27,000 hogs and pigs, valued at $1.2 million. In 1997, 272,000 dairy cows produced 5.15 billion pounds (1.8 billion kilograms) of milk. Cattle products make up about 22% of agricultural receipts, and dairy products account for 15%.

23 FISHING

Sport fishermen catch trout, salmon, steelhead, bass, and 32 other game-fish species. Idaho is a leading producer of farm-raised trout. Idaho hatcheries ship over seven million fish annually, mostly trout and salmon.

24 FORESTRY

Idaho forests cover 21.9 million acres (8.8 million hectares), or 41% of the land area. Idaho forests are used increasingly for skiing, hunting, and other recreation, as well as for timber and pulp. The total lumber production is nearly 2 billion board feet (0.17 billion cubic feet/4.7 million cubic meters) annually. Manufactured shipments of logs in 1997 were valued at $490.4 million.

25 MINING

The estimated value of nonfuel mineral production for Idaho in 1997 was $444 million. Phosphate rock, gold, construction sand and gravel, and molybdenum were the most valuable commodities. Idaho is the only state that produces antimony and vanadium ore, and is the leading producer of industrial garnet.

26 ENERGY AND POWER

In 1998, electric power production (entirely hydroelectric) totaled 12 billion kilowatt hours. About half of Idaho's irrigation depends on electric pumping, and electrical energy consumption regularly exceeds the state's supply. Idaho's large size, widespread and relatively rural population, and lack of public transportation foster reliance on motor vehicles and imported petroleum products. Hot water from thermal springs is used to heat a few buildings in Boise.

27 COMMERCE

In 1997 Idaho's wholesale establishments registered nearly $11 billion in sales. Retail sales exceeded $12 billion that year. Boise is the headquarters of the Albertson's supermarket chain, a large retailer with over $10 billion in sales annually. Exports of goods produced in Idaho totaled $1.5 billion in 1998.

28 PUBLIC FINANCE

Idaho's annual budget, prepared by the Division of Financial Management, is submitted by the governor to the legislature for amendment and approval. Revenues for 1997 were estimated at $4.29 billion and expenditures at $3.67 billion.

29 TAXATION

The state tax burden in 1997 amounted to $1,620 per person, 23d lowest among the states. As of 1996, the personal income tax ranged from 2% to 8.2%, the corporate income tax was 8%, and the general sales tax was 5%. The state also levies taxes on inheritances, alcoholic beverages, cigarettes and tobacco products, motor fuels, insurance premiums, hotel/motel rooms and campgrounds, ores mined and extracted, oil and gas produced, and electric utilities. Property taxes are the only major source of local revenue.

30 HEALTH

Death rates in Idaho from accidents and adverse effects, motor vehicle accidents, and suicide are above the respective national rates. Death rates for heart diseases, cancer, and cerebrovascular diseases, however, are below their corresponding national rates. High birth and low death rates are reflected in the state's younger–than–average population. In all, 42 community hospitals had 3,414 beds in 1998. The average expense for hospital care provided in 1998 was $832 per inpatient day, among the lowest in the US.

31 HOUSING

Single-family housing predominates in Idaho. In 1999 there were an estimated 503,000 housing units. The median monthly expense for owner-occupied housing by mortgage holders and median gross monthly rent were below the national averages. In 1998, 11,700 new private units worth $1.3 billion were authorized.

32 EDUCATION

Nearly 83% of Idahoans over 25 are high school graduates, well above the national average.

As of fall 1997, public educational institutions enrolled 244,403 students. Expenditures for public elementary and secondary schools amounted to $4,237 per student in 1995/96 (46th among the states). Idaho's 11 institutions of higher learning had 61,641 students in the fall of 1997. The leading public higher educational institutions are the University of Idaho at Moscow; Idaho State University (Pocatello); Boise State University; and Lewis-Clark State College in Lewiston. There are two public community colleges and five private institutions.

33 ARTS

The Boise Philharmonic is Idaho's leading professional orchestra. Other symphony orchestras are in Coeur d'Alene, Moscow, Pocatello, and Twin Falls. Boise and Moscow have seasonal theaters. The Idaho Commission on the Arts and Humanities, founded in 1966, offers grants to support both creative and performing artists.

34 LIBRARIES AND MUSEUMS

Idaho's 110 public libraries have a combined book stock of nearly 3.5 million volumes and a total circulation of more than 8 million. The largest public library system is the Boise Public Library and Information Center. The leading academic library is at the University of Idaho (Moscow). The state also has 31 museums, notably the Boise Art Museum, Idaho State Historical Museum (Boise), and the Idaho Museum of Natural History (Pocatello).

35 COMMUNICATIONS

As of 1999, 93.8% of Idaho's occupied housing units had telephones. As of 2000, the state had 114 operating radio stations (46 AM, 68 FM) and 18 television stations. A total of 21,563 domain names were registered in 2000.

36 PRESS

Idaho had 12 daily newspapers in 1998, and 8 Sunday papers. The most widely read newspaper was the (morning) *Idaho Statesman,* published in Boise, with a circulation of 65,874 daily and 87,401 on Sundays.

37 TOURISM, TRAVEL, AND RECREATION

Tourists come to Idaho primarily for outdoor recreation—river trips, skiing, camping, hunting, fishing, and hiking. There are 19 ski resorts, of which by far the most famous is Sun Valley. Tourist attractions include the Craters of the Moon National Monument, the Nez Percé National Historical Park, and two US parks.

38 SPORTS

Idaho has no major league professional team, although the Atlanta Braves have a farm team in Idaho Falls. In college sports, the Idaho State Bengals and the University of Idaho Vandals play Division I basketball in the Big Sky Conference. World chariot racing championships have been held at Pocatello, as are the National Circuit Rodeo Finals.

39 FAMOUS IDAHOANS

Leading federal officeholders born in Idaho include Ezra Taft Benson (1899–1994), US secretary of agriculture from 1953 to 1961, and Cecil D. Andrus (b.Oregon, 1931), governor of Idaho from 1971 to 1977 and secretary of the interior

from 1977 to 1981. Republican William E. Borah (b.Illinois, 1865–1940) served in the US Senate from 1907 until his death, chairing the foreign relations committee for 16 years. Senator Frank Church (1924–84) became chairman of the same committee in 1979; however, he was defeated in his bid for a fifth term in 1980. Important state officeholders were the nation's first Jewish governor, Moses Alexander (b.Germany, 1853–1932), and New Deal governor C. Ben Ross (1876–1946).

Idaho was the birthplace of poet Ezra Pound (1885–1972). Nobel Prize-winning novelist Ernest Hemingway (b.Illinois, 1899–1961) is buried at Ketchum. Gutzon Borglum (1871–1941), the sculptor who carved the Mt. Rushmore National Memorial in South Dakota, was an Idaho native. Baseball slugger Harmon Killebrew (b.1936) and football star Jerry Kramer (b.1936) are Idaho's leading sports personalities.

40 BIBLIOGRAPHY

Aylesworth, Thomas G. *The Northwest: Alaska, Idaho, Oregon, Washington.* New York: Chelsea House, 1996.
Kule, Elaine A. *Idaho Facts and Symbols.* Mankato, Minn.: Hilltop Books, 2000.
Kummer, Patricia K. *Idaho.* Mankato, Minn.: Capstone, 1999.
Stefoff, Rebecca. *Idaho.* New York: Benchmark Books, 2000.
Thompson, Kathleen. *Idaho.* Austin, Tex.: Raintree Steck-Vaughn, 1996.

Web sites
Idaho Travel and Tourism. Discover Idaho, The Official Idaho Travel Guide. [Online] Available http://www.visitid.org/ Accessed May 31, 2001.
State of Idaho. [Online] Available http://www.accessidaho.org/index.html Accessed May 31, 2001.

ILLINOIS

State of Illinois

ILLINOIS

ORIGIN OF STATE NAME: French derivative of *Iliniwek*, meaning "tribe of superior men," a Native American group formerly in the region.

NICKNAME: The Prairie State.

SLOGAN: Land of Lincoln.

CAPITAL: Springfield.

ENTERED UNION: 3 December 1818 (21st).

SONG: "Illinois."

MOTTO: State Sovereignty–National Union.

FLAG: The inner portion of the state seal and the word "Illinois" on a white field.

OFFICIAL SEAL: An American eagle perched on a boulder holds in its beak a banner bearing the state motto; below the eagle is a shield resting on an olive branch. Also depicted are the prairie, the sun rising over a distant eastern horizon, and, on the boulder, the dates 1818 and 1868, the years of the seal's introduction and revision, respectively. The words "Seal of the State of Illinois Aug. 26th 1818" surround the whole.

ANIMAL: White-tailed deer.

BIRD: Cardinal.

FISH: Bluegill.

FLOWER: Violet.

TREE: White oak.

MINERAL: Fluorite.

INSECT: Monarch butterfly.

TIME: 6 AM CST = noon GMT.

1 LOCATION AND SIZE

Illinois ranks 24th in size among the 50 states. Its area totals 56,345 square miles (145,934 square kilometers). Illinois extends 211 miles (340 kilometers) east-west; its maximum north-south extension is 381 miles (613 kilometers). Its boundaries total 1,297 miles (2,088 kilometers).

2 TOPOGRAPHY

Illinois is predominantly flat. Lying wholly within the Central Plains, the state's physical features are uniform, relieved mainly by rolling hills in the northwest and throughout the southern third of the state. The highest natural point, Charles Mound, is only 1,235 feet (376 meters) above sea level—far lower than Chicago's towering skyscrapers. The low point is 279 feet (85 meters) above sea level. Most of the state's 2,000 lakes of 6 acres (2.4 hectares) or more were created by dams. The most important rivers are the Illinois, the Wabash, the Ohio, and the Mississippi. Illinois has three man-made lakes. The artificial Lake Carlyle (41 square miles—106 square kilometers) is the largest body of inland water.

3 CLIMATE

Illinois has a temperate climate, with cold, snowy winters and hot, humid summers. The seasons are sharply differentiated by region: mean winter temperatures are 22°F (–6°C) in the north and 37°F (3°C) in the south. Mean summer temperatures are 70°F (21°C) in the north and 77°F (25°C) in the south. The record high, 117°F (47°C), was set at East St. Louis on 14 July 1954; the record low, –35°F (–37°C), was registered at Mt. Carroll on 22 January 1930. Average annual precipitation is 36 inches (91 centimeters). An annual snowfall of 37 inches (94 centimeters) is normal for northern Illinois, decreasing to 24 inches (61 centimeters) or less in the central and southern regions.

4 PLANTS AND ANIMALS

About 90% of the oak and hickory forests that once were common in the north have been cut down for fuel and lumber. In the forests that do remain, mostly in the south, typical trees are black oak, sugar maple, box elder, and slippery elm. Characteristic wildflowers are the Chase aster, lupine, and primrose violet. The small-whorled pogonia is endangered.

The bison, elk, bear, and wolves that once roamed freely have long since vanished. Deer are abundant and among the state's fur-bearing mammals are also opossum, raccoon, mink, and muskrat. More than 350 birds have been identified, with such game birds as ruffed grouse, wild tur-

Illinois Population Profile

Total population in 2000:	12,419,293
Population change, 1990–2000:	8.6%
Hispanic or Latino†:	12.3%
Population by race	
One race:	98.1%
White:	73.5%
Black or African American:	15.1%
American Indian/Alaska Native:	0.2%
Asian:	3.4%
Native Hawaiian/Pacific Islander:	—
Some other race:	5.8%
Two or more races:	1.9%

Population by Age Group

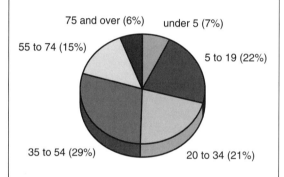

75 and over (6%) under 5 (7%)
55 to 74 (15%)
5 to 19 (22%)
35 to 54 (29%)
20 to 34 (21%)

Top Cities by Population

City	Population	% change 1990–2000
Chicago	2,896,016	4.0
Rockford	150,115	7.7
Aurora	142,990	43.6
Naperville	128,358	50.4
Peoria	112,936	–0.5
Springfield	111,454	5.9
Joliet	106,221	38.2
Elgin	94,487	22.7
Waukegan	87,901	26.7
Cicero	85,616	27.0

Notes: †A person of Hispanic or Latino origin may be of any race. NA indicates that data are not available.
Sources: U.S. Census Bureau. Public Information Office. *Demographic Profiles.* [Online] Available http://www.census.gov/Press-Release/www/2001/demoprofile.html. Accessed June 1, 2001. U.S. Census Bureau. *Census 2000: Redistricting Data.* Press release issued by the Redistricting Data Office. Washington, D.C., March, 2001.

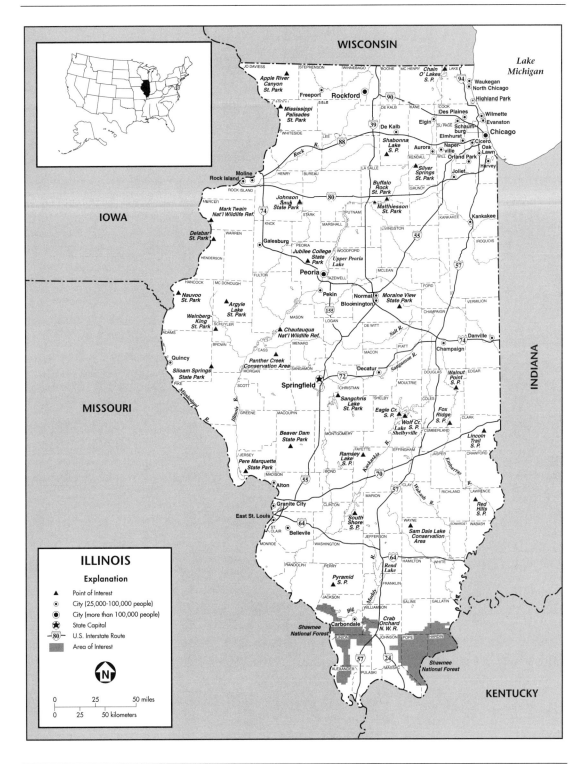

ILLINOIS

Explanation

▲ Point of Interest
◎ City (25,000-100,000 people)
◉ City (more than 100,000 people)
★ State Capital
─80─ U.S. Interstate Route
▨ Area of Interest

0   25   50 miles
0   25   50 kilometers

key, and bobwhite quail especially prized. Other native birds are the cardinal (the state bird), horned lark, and blue jay. Mallard and black ducks are common, and several subspecies of the Canada goose are also found. Coho salmon were introduced into Lake Michigan in the 1960s, thus reviving sport fishing. Endangered species include the gray and Indiana bats, Hine's emerald dragonfly, and the least tern.

5 ENVIRONMENTAL PROTECTION

The 1970s saw a noticeable improvement in environmental quality. Dirty air became less common—though clean-air requirements crippled the state's high-sulfur coal industry. The Illinois EPA maintains more than 200 air-monitoring stations and conducts about 3,000 facility inspections each year. Since Illinois formerly produced about six million tons of hazardous wastes annually (second only to New Jersey), the state agency has pinpointed and cleaned up some of its hazardous waste sites. A 1997 law regulates underground storage tanks in order to limit contamination from underground releases.

6 POPULATION

At the 2000 census, Illinois surpassed Pennsylvania and ranked fifth among the 50 states, with a population of 12,419,293, or 223.4 persons per square mile (86.3 persons square kilometer). The national density average is much less at 79.6 persons per square mile (30.7 per sqaure kilometer). The projected population for 2005 is 12.27 million. The age distribution of the state's population in 2000 closely mirrored the national pattern, with 29% under age 19 and 6% aged 75 or older.

By 1990, 83% of the population lived in metropolitan areas. With a population of nearly 2.9 million in 2000, the city of Chicago was the third-largest city in the nation. The state's other major cities, with their 2000 populations, were Rockford, 150,115; Aurora, 142,990; Naperville, 128,358; and Peoria, 112,936. The state's capital, Springfield, had a 2000 population of 111,454.

7 ETHNIC GROUPS

In 1997, Illinois had an estimated 26,600 Native Americans (0.2%) and 1.8 million blacks (15.3%). In 1997, the estimated number of Illinoisans of Hispanic origin was 1.18 million, chiefly in Chicago. There were 557,536 persons of Mexican origin, 121,871 Puerto Ricans, and 14,625 Cubans. Most of the remainder came from other Caribbean and Latin American countries. In 1990 there were 44,077 Chinese in Illinois, 26,579 Japanese, 66,984 Filipinos, 42,167 Koreans, and 8,550 Vietnamese.

Members of non-British European ethnic groups are prevalent in all the state's major cities and in many farming areas. In 1990, the most common European countries of origin were Poland (80,594), Germany (39,920), Italy (33,812), the former Yugoslavia (20,953), and the former Soviet Union (19,507). There were also significant numbers of Scandinavians, Irish, Lithuanians, Serbs, and East European Jews. Most ethnic groups in Illinois

---

Illinois Population by Race

Census 2000 was the first national census in which the instructions to respondents said, "Mark one or more races." This table shows the number of people who are of one, two, or three or more races. For those claiming two races, the number of people belonging to the various categories is listed. The U.S. government conducts a census of the population every ten years.

	Number	Percent
Total population	12,419,293	100.0
One race	12,184,277	98.1
Two races	223,969	1.8
White *and* Black or African American	32,903	0.3
White *and* American Indian/Alaska Native	24,787	0.2
White *and* Asian	30,451	0.2
White *and* Native Hawaiian/Pacific Islander	1,716	—
White *and* some other race	97,454	0.8
Black or African American *and* American Indian/Alaska Native	6,281	0.1
Black or African American *and* Asian	3,098	—
Black or African American *and* Native Hawaiian/Pacific Islander	526	—
Black or African American *and* some other race	10,140	0.1
American Indian/Alaska Native *and* Asian	1,830	—
American Indian/Alaska Native *and* Native Hawaiian/Pacific Islander	79	—
American Indian/Alaska Native *and* some other race	2,538	—
Asian *and* Native Hawaiian/Pacific Islander	2,084	—
Asian *and* some other race	8,661	0.1
Native Hawaiian/Pacific Islander *and* some other race	1,421	—
Three or more races	11,047	0.1

Source: U.S. Census Bureau. *Census 2000: Redistricting Data.* Press release issued by the Redistricting Data Office. Washington, D.C., March, 2001. A dash (—) indicates that the percent is less than 0.1.

---

maintain their own newspapers, clubs, festivals, and houses of worship.

8 LANGUAGES

A number of place-names—Illinois itself, Chicago, Peoria, Kankakee, and Ottawa—attest to the early presence of various Algonkian-speaking tribes. Excepting the Chicago metropolitan area and the extreme northwestern corner of Illinois, the northern quarter of the state is dominated by Northern speech, while settlement from Pennsylvania and Ohio led to a mix of Northern and North Midland speech in central Illinois. Migration from South Midland areas in Indiana and Kentucky affected basic speech in the southern third of Illinois, known as Egypt.

Metropolitan Chicago has experienced such complex immigration that, although it still has a basic Northern/North Midland mix, elements of almost all varieties of English appear somewhere. Educational policies were reassessed in the 1970s, when the state legislature mandated bilingual classes for immigrant children, especially Spanish speakers. In 1990, English was spoken at home by 85.8% of all state residents five years of age and older. Speakers of other languages included Spanish, 728,380; Polish, 143,480; German, 84,625; and Italian, 66,903.

Chicago River harbor locks and lighthouse.

9 RELIGIONS

Today, the largest Christian denomination is the Roman Catholic Church, with 3,611,000 members. The largest Protestant denomination is the United Methodist Church, with 440,000 members, followed by the Lutheran Church–Missouri Synod, 223,000; Southern Baptist Convention, 293,000; Presbyterian Church, 158,000; and United Church of Christ, 185,000. The Jewish population was estimated at over 268,000 in 1994.

10 TRANSPORTATION

The fact that Illinois is intersected by several long-distance transportation routes has been of central importance in the state's economic development. The state has access to the east by way of the major rivers and the Great Lakes system. Most of the nation's rail lines converge on Illinois. Chicago has been one of the main US railroad centers since the late 19th century. Interstate highways also cross the state, and Chicago's central location has made it a major transfer point for airline connections.

Chicago is the hub of Amtrak's passenger service, which operated approximately 20 train routes through Illinois in 1996. The total number of riders through the state's 35 stations amounted to over 2.5 million that year. There were 44 railroad companies operating 7,572 route miles (12,183 kilometers) of track within the state in 1998. In 1996, the state ranked first in rail carloads handled, total tons carried by rail, and total railroad employment.

Mass transit is of special importance to the Chicago metropolitan area. Buses and commuter railroads are essential to daily movement. Chicago's commuter railroads use a combination of underground and elevated tracks. However, the number of riders declines every year, as fewer people work in the central city and more choose the privacy and convenience of travel by automobile. Outside Chicago, bus service, Amtrak, and commuter flights are still available in many of the larger cities.

In 1997, 137,785 miles (221,696 kilometers) of public roadway served 8.4 million registered vehicles—including 5.85 million automobiles and 2.57 million

Photo credit: William Semple.

View under elevated transit line, Wabash St.

trucks. The Interstate Highway System totaled 2,163 miles (3,480 kilometers) in the state in 1996.

Barge traffic along the Mississippi, Ohio, and Illinois rivers remains important, especially for the shipment of grain. The Port of Chicago is the largest on the Great Lakes, handling 25.9 million tons of cargo in 1998, mostly grain and iron ore. Until 2000, Chicago's O'Hare International was the busiest airport in the country. With 680 airports and over 280 heliports, Illinois is also an important center for general aviation. There were 18,693 licensed pilots and 6,177 operating civilian aircraft in the state in 1997.

[11] HISTORY

When European explorers arrived in Illinois in the 17th century, the region was inhabited by Algonkian-speaking tribes, including the Kickapoo, Sauk, Potawatomi, Ojibwa, and Peoria. Constant warfare with tribes from neighboring areas, plus disease and alcohol introduced by European fur traders and settlers, combined to devastate the tribal population. Defeat of the tribes in the Black Hawk War (1832) led to a series of treaties that removed all of the Native Americans to lands across the Mississippi River.

The first permanent European settlement in Illinois was a mission built by French Catholic priests at Cahokia, near present-day St. Louis, in 1699. In 1765, under the Treaty of Paris that ended the French and Indian War, the British took control of the Illinois country but established no settlements of their own. During the American Revolution, troops from Virginia captured the small British forts at Cahokia and Kaskaskia in 1778, after which Virginia governed Illinois as its own territory. In 1787, Illinois became part of the newly organized Northwest Territory, and in 1800, it was included in the Indiana Territory.

Statehood

Nine years later the Illinois Territory, including the present state of Wisconsin, was created, and a territorial legislature was formed in 1812. During the War of 1812, British and Native American forces combined in a last attempt to push back American expansion into the Illinois country, and much fighting took place in the area. On 3 December 1818, Illinois was formally admitted to the Union as the 21st state. The capital was moved from Vandalia to Springfield in 1839.

The withdrawal of British influence after the War of 1812 and the final defeat of the Native American tribes in the Black Hawk War of 1832 opened the fertile prairies to white settlers from the south, especially Kentucky. Despite a heavy state debt resulting from the collapse of ambitious financial development schemes in the 1830s, the arrival after 1840 of energetic Yankee pioneers, attracted by the rich soil and excellent water routes, guaranteed rapid growth.

During the Civil War, Illinois sent half its young men to the battlefield and supplied the Union armies with huge amounts of food, feed, and horses. The wartime administration of Republican Governor Richard Yates guaranteed full support for the policies of Abraham Lincoln, who had been prominent in Illinois political life since the 1840s and had been nominated for the presidency in 1860 at a Republican convention held in Chicago.

Economic and population growth quickened after 1865, and Chicago became the principal city of the Midwest. Responding to opportunities presented by the coming of the railroads, hundreds of small towns and cities built banks, grain elevators, retail shops, small factories, stately courthouses, and schools, in an abundance of civic pride.

During the second half of the 19th century, Illinois was a center of the American labor movement. Workers joined the Knights of Labor in the 1870s and 1880s and fought for child-labor laws and the eight-hour day. Union organizing led to several spectacular incidents, including the Haymarket riot in 1886 and the violent Pullman strike in 1894. After the great fire of 1871 destroyed Chicago's downtown section, the city's wealthy elite dedicated itself to rebuilding Chicago and making it one of the great metropolises of the world. Immense steel mills, meat-packing plants, and factories sprang up, and growth was tremendous in the merchandising, banking, and transportation fields.

Twentieth Century

The first three decades of the 20th century witnessed almost unbroken prosperity in all sections except Egypt, the downstate region where poor soil and the decline of the coal industry produced widespread poverty. The slums of Chicago were poor, too, because most of the hundreds of thousands of new immigrants arrived nearly penniless. After 1920, however, large-scale immigration ended and the immigrants achieved steady upward mobility, based on hard work, savings, and education. During the Prohibition era, a vast organized crime empire rose to prominence, giving Chicago and Joliet a reputation for gangsterism, violence, and corruption.

The Great Depression of the 1930s affected the state unevenly, with agriculture hit first and recovering first. Industries began shutting down in 1930 and did not fully recover until massive military contracts during World War II restored full prosperity. The depression destroyed

Illinios Governors: 1818–2001

1818–1822	Shadrach Bond	Dem-Rep	1893–1897	John Peter Altgeld	Democrat
1822–1826	Edward Coles	Dem-Rep	1897–1905	John Riley Tanner	Republican
1826–1830	Ninian Edwards	Republican	1905–1909	Richard Yates	Republican
1830–1834	John Reynolds	Democrat	1909–1913	Charles Samuel Deneen	Republican
1834	William Lee Davidson Ewing	Democrat	1913–1917	Edward Fitzsimmons Dunne	Democrat
1834–1838	Joseph Duncan	Whig	1917–1925	Frank Orren Lowden	Republican
1838–1842	Thomas Carlin	Democrat	1925–1929	Lennington Small	Republican
1842–1849	Thomas Ford	Democrat	1929–1937	Louis Lincoln Emmerson	Republican
1849–1853	Augustus C. French	Democrat	1937–1940	Henry Horner	Democrat
1853–1857	Joel Aldrich Matteson	Democrat	1940–1945	John Henry Stelle	Democrat
1857–1860	William Harrison Bissell	Republican	1945–1949	Dwight Herbert Green	Republican
1860–1861	John Wood	Republican	1949–1957	Adlai Ewing Stevenson II	Democrat
1861–1865	Richard Yates	Republican	1957–1965	William Grant Stratton	Republican
1865–1869	Richard James Oglesby	Republican	1965–1968	Otto Kerner	Democrat
1869–1873	John McAuley Palmer	Republican	1968–1969	Samuel Harvey Shapiro	Democrat
1873	Richard James Oglesby	Republican	1969–1973	Richard Buell Ogilvie	Republican
1873–1881	John Lourie Beveridge	Republican	1973–1977	Daniel Walker	Democrat
1881–1883	Shelby Moore Cullom	Republican	1977–1991	James Robert Thompson	Republican
1883–1885	John Marshall Hamilton	Republican	1991–1999	James Edgar	Republican
1885–1889	Richard James Oglesby	Republican	1999–	George H. Ryan	Republican
1889–1893	Joseph Wilson Fifer	Republican			

Democratic Republican – Dem-Rep

the credibility of the pro-business Republican regime that had run the state since 1856, as blacks, white ethnics, and factory workers responded enthusiastically to Franklin Roosevelt's New Deal.

The goals of personal security and prosperity dominated Illinois life in the postwar period. However, events in the 1960s and 1970s—assassinations, the Viet Nam war, the race riots, and the violence that accompanied the 1968 Democratic National Convention in Chicago—coupled with a new awareness of such issues as poverty and environmental pollution, helped reshape attitudes in Illinois. This transformation was perhaps best shown in Chicago, where voters elected Jane Byrne the city's first woman mayor in 1979 and chose Harold Washington as its first black mayor in 1983.

The economy of Illinois, like other "rust belt" states, suffered a severe recession in the early 1980s. Hit hard by foreign competition, producers of steel, machine tools, and automobiles engaged in massive layoffs. By the end of the decade, the economy had begun to rebound, but many industrial jobs were permanently lost, as industries sought to improve their efficiency and productivity through automation. In 1990, the unemployment rate in Illinois was 7.2%, in contrast to the national average of 5.2%.

In 1992, the 60-mile maze of tunnels beneath downtown Chicago ruptured, filling basements with up to 30 feet of water, and forcing the temporary closure of the Chicago Board of Trade and City Hall. A year later, flooding of the Mississippi and Illinois rivers caused $1.5 billion of damage in the western part of the state and forced 12,800 people to evacuate their homes.

12 STATE GOVERNMENT

Under the 1970 constitution, as amended, the upper house of the general assembly consists of a senate of 59 members who are elected to four-year terms on a two-year cycle. In November 1980, Illinois voters chose to reduce the size of house membership from 177 to 118 (two representatives from each district). The executive officers elected statewide are the governor and lieutenant governor (who run jointly), secretary of state, treasurer, comptroller, and attorney general. Each serves a four-year term and is eligible for reelection.

Bills passed by both houses of the legislature become law if signed by the governor; if left unsigned for 60 days while the legislature is in session or 90 days after it adjourns; or if vetoed by the governor but passed again by three-fifths of the elected members of each house. Constitutional amendments require a three-fifths vote by the legislature for placement on the ballot. Either a simple majority of those voting in the election or three-fifths of those voting on the amendment is sufficient for ratification.

13 POLITICAL PARTIES

Politically, Illinois is a closely balanced state, with a slight Republican predominance from 1860 to 1930 giving way to a highly competitive situation statewide.

The party balance changed with the rise of the powerful Cook County Democratic organization in the 1930s. Built by Mayor Anton Cermak and continued from 1955 to 1976 by six-term Mayor Richard J. Daley, the Chicago "Democratic machine" totally controlled the city,

Illinois Presidential Vote by Political Parties, 1948–2000

YEAR	ILLINOIS WINNER	DEMOCRAT	REPUBLICAN	SOCIALIST LABOR	PROHIBITION	COMMUNIST
1948	*Truman (D)	1,994,715	1,961,103	3,118	11,959	—
1952	*Eisenhower (R)	2,013,920	2,457,327	9,363	—	—
1956	*Eisenhower (R)	1,775,682	2,623,327	8,342	—	—
1960	*Kennedy (D)	2,377,846	2,368,988	10,560	—	—
1964	*Johnson (D)	2,796,833	1,905,946	—	—	—
					AMERICAN IND.	
1968	*Nixon (R)	2,039,814	2,174,774	13,878	390,958	—
					AMERICAN	
1972	*Nixon (R)	1,913,472	2,788,179	12,344	2,471	4,541
					LIBERTARIAN	
1976	Ford (R)	2,271,295	2,364,269	2,422	8,057	9,250
				CITIZENS		
1980	*Reagan (R)	1,981,413	2,358,094	10,692	38,939	9,711
1984	*Reagan (R)	2,086,499	2,707,103	2,716	10,086	—
1988	*Bush (R)	2,215,940	2,310,939	10,276	14,944	—
				NEW ALLIANCE		IND. (Perot)
1992	*Clinton (D)	2,453,350	1,734,096	5,267	9,218	840,515
1996	*Clinton (D)	2,341,744	1,587,021	—	22,548	346,408
				PROGRESSIVE (Nader)	REFORM	LIBERTARIAN
2000	Gore (D)	2,589,026	2,019,421	103,759	16,106	11,623

* Won US presidential election.

dominated the state party, and exerted enormous power at the national level. However, the machine lost its clout with the election in 1979 of independent Democrat Jane Byrne as Chicago's first woman mayor, and again in 1983 when Harold Washington became its first black mayor. Although Richard Daley's son, also named Richard Daley, won the mayoralty in 1989, the machine has never recovered the power it once enjoyed.

There is no party registration requirement. As of the November 2000 elections, Republicans held the governorship, Democrats and Republicans split the two US Senate seats, and each party had 10 of the 20 US House seats. In those elections, Democrat Carol Moseley-Braun, the first black woman US Senator, lost to Republican challenger Peter Fitzgerald. The Republicans fared well in the state legislature where they not only retained control of the senate, but also took control of the house.

Photo credit: EPD Photos.

Abraham Lincoln (b.Kentucky, 1809–65), 16th president of the US, is the outstanding figure in Illinois history, having lived and built his political career in the state between 1830 and 1861.

14 LOCAL GOVERNMENT

Illinois has more units of local government (most with property-taxing power) than any other state. In 1997 there were 102 counties, 1,288 municipalities, 1,433 townships, 944 school districts, and 3,068 special districts. Chicago is governed by an elected mayor, clerk, treasurer, and city council composed of 50 aldermen. Other cities may choose either the commission or aldermanic system: most are administered by nonpartisan city managers.

15 JUDICIAL SYSTEM

The state's highest court is the supreme court, consisting of seven justices elected by judicial districts for ten-year terms. The supreme court has appeals jurisdiction generally, and original jurisdiction in certain cases. The chief justice, assisted by an administrative director, has administrative and supervisory authority over all other courts. The appeals court is divided into five districts. Appeals judges hear appeals from the 22 circuit courts, which handle civil and criminal cases.

As of 1998, the crime index in Illinois was 3,714.6 per 100,000 population. Illinois had 44,355 prisoners in 1999.

16 MIGRATION

Immigration from Europe became significant in the 1840s and continued in a heavy stream for about 80 years. Before 1890, most of the new arrivals came from Germany, Ireland, Britain, and Scandinavia. These groups continued to arrive after 1890, but they were soon outnumbered by heavy immigration from southern and eastern Europe. Concern for the welfare of these newcomers led to the establishment by Jane Addams in Chicago of Hull House (1889), which served as a social center, shelter, and advocate for immigrants, and launched the settlement movement in America.

The outbreak of World War I interrupted the flow of European immigrants but also increased the economy's demand for unskilled labor. The migration of blacks from states south of Illinois played an important role in meeting the demand for labor during both world wars. After World War II, the further collapse of the cotton labor market drove hundreds of thousands more blacks to Chicago and other northern cities. The major intrastate migration pattern has been from farms to towns. From 1985 to 1990, the net loss from migration came to 139,360. During 1990–98, the net loss from interstate migration was 516,400, which was offset by a net gain of 336,800 from international migration. In 1998, Illinois admit-

ted 33,163 immigrants, the 6th highest in the nation. In 1996, the federal government estimated that there were 290,000 illegal immigrants living in Illinois. Some 69% of all state residents had been born in Illinois as of 1990.

17 ECONOMY

Since 1950, the importance of manufacturing has declined, but a very strong shift into services—government, medicine, education, law, finance, and business—has underpinned the state's economic vigor. In the 1970s heavy industrial competition from Japan wreaked havoc in the state's steel, television, and automotive industries, while Illinois's high-wage, high-cost business climate encouraged the migration of factories to southern states. Meat-packing, once the most famous industry in Illinois, dwindled after the closing of the Chicago stockyards in 1972.

Chicago remained the nation's chief merchandising center during the early 1980s, and an influx of huge international banks boosted the city's financial strength. Currently, Illinois' major industries include primary and secondary metals; industrial and farm equipment; electric equipment and appliances; electronic components; food processing; and printing equipment. The gross state product in 1998 reached 418 billion, the fourth highest in the nation.

18 INCOME

Illinois is a rich state and has been for the last century. Its $29,853 in per capita (per person) income ranked 8th in 1998. Its 1998 total personal income was $360.3

Photo credit: William Semple.

Chicago waterfront from Olive Park.

billion, 5th in the US. In 1998, 11.1% of the population lived below the poverty level.

19 INDUSTRY

Manufacturing in Illinois, concentrated in but not limited to Chicago, has always been diverse. Of the major industries, food and food products contributed 15%; non-electrical machinery, 14%; chemicals and allied products, 11%; electronics and electronic equipment, 9%; and transportation equipment, 8%. Industrial corporations headquartered in Illinois include Amoco (Chicago), Sara Lee, and Caterpillar Tractor (Peoria). In 1997 there were 39 Fortune 500 companies headquartered in Illinois.

20 LABOR

In mid-1998, the Illinois labor force numbered 6.22 million persons. Some 277,000 were unemployed, for an unemployment rate of 4.5%.

Today, labor unions are powerful in Chicago, but relatively weak downstate. In 1998, 20% of all workers belonged to unions.

21 AGRICULTURE

Total agricultural income in 1999 reached $6.8 billion in Illinois, eighth in the nation. Crops accounted for nearly 78% of the value of farm marketings, with soybeans and corn the leading cash commodities.

The number of farms reached a peak at 264,000 in 1900 and began declining rapidly after World War II, down to 79,000 in 1998. Total acreage in farming was 27.8 million acres (11.3 million hectares) in 1998. The farm population, which averaged 1.2 million persons from 1880 to 1900, declined to 197,000 in 1994.

The major agricultural region is the corn belt, covering all of central and about half of northern Illinois. Among the 50 states, Illinois ranked second only to Iowa in production of corn and soybeans in 1998. The following table shows output of leading field crops in that year:

CROP	VOLUME (MILLION BUSHELS)
Corn for grain	1,473.5
Soybeans	468.6
Hay (million tons)	3.04
Sorghum for grain	7.9
Oats	3.9

22 DOMESTICATED ANIMALS

Livestock is raised almost everywhere in Illinois, but production is concentrated especially in the west-central region. In 1999, Illinois farms had 1.49 million head of cattle, valued at $894 million. Illinois farms had 4.85 million hogs and pigs worth $194 million. Hog production contributes about 11% to the state's annual agricultural receipts; cattle production; 8%; and dairy products, 4%. The dairy belt covers part of northern Illinois, providing milk for several cheese factories. Milk production in 1997 was 2.3 billion pounds (1.1 billion kilograms).

23 FISHING

Commercial fishing is insignificant in Illinois: only 98,000 pounds of fish, valued at $98,000, made up the commercial catch in 1998. Sport fishing is of modest importance in southern Illinois and in Lake Michigan. Some 450 lakes and ponds and 200 streams and rivers are open to the public. The state issued over 420,000 recreational fishing licenses in 1998.

24 FORESTRY

Forestland covering 4.9 million acres (1.9 million hectares) comprises about 12.1% of the state's land area. The majority of Illinois' forests are located in the southern one-third of the state. The Shawnee National Forest encompasses over 260,000 acres (107,000 hectares). In 1995, the value of manufactured shipments from the lumber and wood products industry was $1.27 billion.

25 MINING

The value of nonfuel mineral production for Illinois in 1998 was estimated to be $862 million. The state's five leading nonfuel mineral commodities are crushed stone, portland cement, construction sand and gravel, industrial sand, and clay; the first three commodities accounted for 83% of the 1997 total value.

Illinois is the only state with reported fluorspar production in the United States, and the state continues to lead in the production of tripoli, contributing more than 70% of the tripoli mined in the United

Photo credit: Grant H. Kessler.

Residents enjoy a friendly chat in a small farming community in Fulton County. With three-fourths of the state's land area devoted to farming, Illinois is a major agricultural region.

States. Tripoli, a microcrystalline silicate, is used as an abrasive and as a filler and extender.

26 ENERGY AND POWER

Illinois is one of the nation's leading energy producers and consumers. Electric power production totaled 131.3 billion kilowatt hours (fifth in the US) in 1998. Consumption of energy in 1997 amounted to 3,900 trillion Btu (seventh among the states), of which industry accounted for 36%; residences, 24%; commercial establishments, 18%; and transportation, 22%. Coal-fired plants account for about 54% of the state's power production; nuclear power is also important, particularly for the generation of electricity in the Chicago area.

In 1998, Illinois ranked fourth in natural-gas usage, with 91.9 billion cubic feet delivered to over 3.7 million customers. Petroleum production, though steadily declining, totaled 12.06 million barrels in 1999; reserves were 81 million barrels. Illinois ranked seventh in the US in bituminous coal production in 1998, with 39.7 million tons.

27 COMMERCE

Chicago is the leading wholesaling center of the Midwest. The state's 24,757 wholesale establishments have annual sales of over $285 billion. Chicago is an especially important trade center for furniture, housewares, and apparel. The state's 65,254 retail stores record yearly sales in excess of $112 billion. Leading Illinois-based retailing companies include Sears, Roebuck, with nationwide revenues of $38.2 billion in 1996; Walgreen's, $11.8 billion; McDonald's, $10.7 billion; and Household International, $5 billion. Illinois ranked sixth among the states in total exports with an estimated $29 billion in 1998.

28 PUBLIC FINANCE

Among the larger states, Illinois is known for its low taxes and conservative fiscal policy. Revenues for fiscal year 1997 were $39.04 billion, and expenditures were $35.3 billion. In 1997, the state's debt approached $23.8 billion, or $2,001 per capita (per person).

29 TAXATION

Illinoisans have fiercely resisted the imposition of new and higher taxes. Total state taxes in 1997 were $18.54 billion, or $1,559 per person (the 26th lowest rate). As of 1996, the state personal income tax was a flat 3%. The corporate income tax was 7.3% and the sales tax 6.25%. Excise taxes included charges on cigarettes and on gasoline. The federal government collected $74.4 billion in taxes from Illinois for 1995, and sent back $50.96 billion.

30 HEALTH

Illinois ranks above the national average in deaths due to heart disease and cerebrovascular disease, but below the average in accidents and suicide. In 1995, there were 35.3 breast cancer deaths per 100,000 women, fourth highest among the states.

Chicago serves as a diagnostic and treatment center for patients throughout the Midwest. With 203 facilities (many quite large) and 39,218 beds, Illinois community hospitals recorded over 1.45 million admissions in 1998. In 1996, the state had 31,994 nonfederal physicians and over 98,000 nurses. Over 15% of the state's adults do not have health insurance.

31 HOUSING

In 1999 there were an estimated 4.7 million housing units in Illinois. In 1998, 48,000 new units valued at nearly $5.6 billion were authorized for construction. The median monthly cost for owners with a mortgage in 1990 was $767, and $241 for owners without a mortgage. The same costs in the greater Chicago area of Illinois were $889 and $284, respectively. The median monthly rent in 1990 throughout the state was $445; in the greater Chicago area it was $491.

32 EDUCATION

In 1998, 84.2% of the Illinois adult population held high school diplomas, with nearly 25.8% continuing their education for a bachelor's degree or higher.

In 1995, Illinois had 2,598 public elementary schools, 588 junior high schools, and 639 high schools. Enrollment in public schools for 1997 was 1.99 million. Over 38% of all public school students are ethnic minorities: black, Hispanic, Asian, and Native American. In 1996, the pupilto-teacher ratio was 19.5 in elementary schools and 17.9 in secondary schools. Expenditures for public elementary and secondary schools amounted to $4,950 per student in 1995/96 (35th among the states).

Nonpublic schools, dominated by Chicago's extensive Roman Catholic school system, have shown a slight decrease in enrollment since the early 1980s. In 1997, total nonpublic enrollment in Illinois private schools was 298,620.

Illinois institutions of higher education have always been of the highest caliber, with 183 public and private universities having a total fall 1997 enrollment of 726,199. The state appropriated a $2.6 billion budget for colleges and universities in 1996/97. The largest system, the University of Illinois, operates three major campuses—Champaign-Urbana, Chicago, and Springfield. Illinois maintains a flourishing network of 49 community colleges.

Major private universities include the University of Chicago, Northwestern University (Evanston), Illinois Institute of Technology (Chicago), and Loyola University (Chicago). Each maintains undergraduate and research programs, as well as nationally recognized professional schools.

33 ARTS

Chicago emerged in the late 19th century as the leading arts center of the Midwest, and it continues to hold this premier position.

Architecture is the outstanding art form in Illinois, especially Chicago—where the first skyscrapers were built in the 1880s. Chicago has been a mecca for modern commercial and residential architects ever since the fire of 1871. The Art Institute of Chicago, incorporated in 1879, is the leading art museum in the state. Its French Impressionist collection is especially noteworthy.

Theater groups abound—notably in Chicago, where the Second City comedy troupe and the Steppenwolf Theatre are located. The Chicago Symphony Orchestra boasts world stature. Opera flourished in Chicago in the early 20th century, and was reborn through the founding of the Lyric Opera in 1954. Chicago's most original musical contribution was jazz, imported from the South by black musicians in the 1920s. Such jazz greats as Louis Armstrong, Jelly Roll Morton, and Benny Goodman all worked or learned their craft in the jazz houses of the city's South Side.

The seamy side of Chicago has fascinated writers throughout the 20th century. Among well-known American novels set in Chicago are two muckraking works, Frank Norris's *The Pit* (1903) and Upton Sinclair's *The Jungle* (1906), as well as James T. Farrell's *Studs Lonigan* (1935) and Saul Bellow's *The Adventures of Augie March* (1953). Famous American plays associated with Chicago are *The Front Page* (1928), by Ben Hecht and Charles MacArthur, and *A Raisin in the Sun* (1959), by Lorraine Hansberry.

34 LIBRARIES AND MUSEUMS

Libraries and library science are particularly strong in Illinois. In 2000 there were over 600 public libraries, with a combined book stock of over 40 million. The facilities in Peoria, Oak Park, Evanston, Rockford, Quincy, and the Harold Washington Library Center in Chicago are noteworthy. The outstanding libraries of the University of Illinois (Champaign–Urbana) and the University of Chicago constitute the state's leading research facilities, together with the Newberry Library in Chicago.

Illinois has 277 museums and historic sites. Chicago's Field Museum of Natural History, founded in 1893, has sponsored numerous worldwide expeditions in the course of acquiring some 13 million anthropological, zoological, botanical, and geological specimens. The Museum of Science and Industry, near the University of Chicago, attracts five million visitors a year, mostly children, to see its exhibits of industrial technology.

Just about every town has one or more historic sites authenticated by the state. The most popular is New Salem, near Springfield, where Abraham Lincoln lived from 1831 to 1837. Its reconstruction, begun by press magnate William Randolph Hearst in 1906, includes one original cabin and numerous replicas.

35 COMMUNICATIONS

Illinois has an extensive communications system. In 1999, 91.8% of all households had telephones. Illinois had 125 AM and 294 FM commercial radio stations, when 53 commercial television stations served the state. The National Center for Supercomputing Applications at the University of Illinois (Champaign–Urbana) is involved in software development for the

Internet; there are nearly 260,000 domain names registered in the state.

36 PRESS

As of 1998, Illinois had 24 morning newspapers, 45 evening dailies, and 30 Sunday papers. The Illinois editions of St. Louis newspapers are also widely read. The leading dailies of 1998 and their circulations are the *Chicago Tribune* (673,508); the *Chicago Sun-Times* (485,666); the *Peoria Journal Star* (70,522); and the *Rockford Register Star* (72,434). The most popular magazines published in Chicago are *Playboy* and *Ebony*.

37 TOURISM, TRAVEL, AND RECREATION

The tourist industry is of special importance to Chicago, the nation's leading convention center. The city's chief tourist attractions are its museums, restaurants, and shops. Chicago also boasts the tallest building in the US, the Sears Tower, 110 stories and 1,454 feet (443 meters) high.

For the state as a whole, tourism generated $21 billion in revenue in 1998. There are 42 state parks, 4 state forests, 36,659 campsites, and 25 state recreation places. The Lincoln Home National Historic Site in Springfield is a popular tourist attraction.

Swimming, bicycling, hiking, camping, horseback riding, fishing, and motorboating are the most popular recreational activities. Wildlife observation engages nearly three million Illinoisans annually.

38 SPORTS

Illinois has six major league professional sports teams, all of which play in Chicago: the Cubs and the White Sox of Major League Baseball, the Bears of the National Football League, the Bulls of the National Basketball Association, the Blackhawks of the National Hockey League, and the Fire of Major League Soccer.

The Bulls established a remarkable basketball dynasty fueled by the play of Michael Jordan, perhaps the best athlete in the history of basketball, winning NBA Championships in 1991, 1992, 1993, 1996, 1997, and 1998.

In collegiate sports, the emphasis is on basketball and football. The University of Illinois and Northwestern University compete in the Big Ten Conference. The Depaul University Blue Demons of the Great Midwest Conference consistently rank high among college basketball teams.

Horse racing is also very popular in Illinois. In 1996, thoroughbred horse races drew an attendance of over 1.3 million; trotter horse races; over 904,000.

39 FAMOUS ILLINOISANS

The only Illinois native to be elected president is Ronald Reagan (b.1911), who left the state after graduating from Eureka College to pursue film and political aspirations in California. Abraham Lincoln (b.Kentucky, 1809–65) received his law license in Illinois and established his political and legal careers there. Ulysses S. Grant (b.Ohio, 1822–85), the nation's 18th president, lived in Galena on the eve of the Civil War. Adlai E. Stevenson (b.Kentucky, 1835–1914), founder of a political dynasty, served as US vice-president from 1893 to 1897, but was defeated for the same office in 1900. His grandson, also named Adlai E. Stevenson (b.California, 1900–65), who served as governor of Illinois from 1949 to 1953, was the Democratic presidential nominee in 1952 and 1956, and ended his career as US ambassador to the United Nations. William Jennings Bryan (1860–1925), a leader of the free-silver and Populist movements, was the Democratic presidential nominee in 1896, 1900, and 1908.

US Supreme Court justices associated with Illinois include Chicago-born Arthur Goldberg (1908–90), who also served as secretary of labor and succeeded Stevenson as UN ambassador; Harry A. Blackmun (1908–97); and John Paul Stevens (b.1920). Richard J. Daley (1902–76) was Democratic boss and mayor of Chicago from 1955 to 1976. Jane Byrne (b.1934), a Daley protégé, became the city's first female mayor in 1979; she was succeeded in 1983 by Harold Washington (1922–87), the city's first black mayor. Richard Michael Daley (b. 1942), son of Richard J. Daley, also became mayor.

An outstanding Illinoisan was Jane Addams (1860–1935), founder of Hull House (1889), author, reformer, prohibitionist, and feminist, who shared the Nobel Peace Prize in 1931. Feminist leader Betty Friedan (b. 1921) founded the National Organization for Women in 1966. Winners of the Nobel Prize in physics include Albert Michelson (b.Germany, 1852–1931) and Enrico Fermi (b.Italy, 1901–54). A Nobel award in literature

Photo credit: EPD Photos.

William Jennings Bryan graduated with highest honors from Illinois College in Jacksonville in 1881. The college was founded in 1829.

went to Saul Bellow (b.Canada, 1915), and the economics prize was given to Milton Friedman (b.New York, 1912), leader of the so-called Chicago school of economists. Jerome Friedman (b. 1930) was a 1990 co-recipient of the Nobel Prize for physics, and Harry M. Markowitz (b.1927) won the Nobel prize for economics in 1990.

Some of the most influential Illinoisans have been religious leaders, and many of them also exercised social and political influence. Notable are Mother Frances Xavier Cabrini (b.Italy, 1850–1917), the first American to be canonized as a Catholic saint; Elijah Muhammad (Elijah Poole, b.Georgia, 1897–1975), leader of the Black Muslim movement; and Jesse Jackson (b.North Carolina, 1941), civil rights leader and prominent public speaker.

Outstanding business and professional leaders who lived in Illinois include John Deere (b.Vermont, 1804–86), industrialist and inventor of the steel plow; railroad car inventor George Pullman (b.New York 1831–97); merchant Marshall Field (b.Massachusetts, 1834–1906); sporting-goods manufacturer Albert G. Spalding (1850–1915); breakfast-food manufacturer Charles W. Post (1854–1911); lawyer Clarence Darrow (b.Ohio, 1857–1938); and meat packer Oscar Mayer (1888–1965).

Artists who worked for significant periods in Illinois (usually in Chicago) include architects Frank Lloyd Wright (b.Wisconsin, 1869–1959) and Ludwig Mies van der Rohe (b.Germany, 1886–1969). Important writers include novelists John Dos Passos (1896–1970) and Ernest Hemingway (1899–1961). Poets include Edgar Lee Masters (b.Kansas, 1869–1950); Carl Sandburg (1878–1967); Nicholas Vachel Lindsay (1879–1931); Archibald MacLeish (1892–1982), also Librarian of Congress and assistant secretary of state; Gwendolyn Brooks (b.Kansas, 1917), the first black woman to win a Pulitzer Prize; and Ray Bradbury (b.1920). Robert Butler (b. 1945) was the 1993 winner of the Pulitzer Prize for fiction.

Performing artists connected with the state include opera stars Sherrill Milnes (b.1935); clarinetist Benny Goodman (1909–86); singers Mel Torme (1925-2000) and Grace Slick (b.1939); musicians Ray Charles (b.1918) and Miles Davis (1926–91); comedians Jack Benny (Benjamin Kubelsky, 1894–1974), Bob Newhart (b.1929), and Richard Pryor (b.1940); and a long list of stage and screen stars, including Gloria Swanson (1899–1983), Karl Malden (Malden Sekulovich, b.1913), Jason Robards, Jr. (1922–2000), Charlton Heston (b.1922), Rock Hudson (Roy Fitzgerald, 1925–85), Bruce Dern (b.1936), and Raquel Welch (Raquel Tejeda, b.1942).

Dominant figures in the Illinois sports world include Ernest "Ernie" Banks (b.Texas, 1931) of the Chicago Cubs; Robert "Bobby" Hull (b.Canada, 1939) of the Chicago Black Hawks; owner George Halas (1895–1983) and running back Walter Payton (b.Mississippi, 1954–1999) of the Chicago Bears; and Michael Jordan (b.New York, 1963) of the Chicago Bulls.

40 BIBLIOGRAPHY

Anderson, Kathy. *Illinois*. Minneapolis, Minn.: Lerner, 1993.

Aylesworth, Thomas G. *Western Great Lakes: Illinois, Iowa, Minnesota, Wisconsin*. New York: Chelsea House, 1996.

Brill, Marlene Targ. *Illinois*. New York: Benchmark Books, 1997.

Jensen, Richard J. *Illinois: A Bicentennial History*. New York: Norton, 1978.

McAuliffe, Emily. *Illinois Facts and Symbols*. Mankato, Minn.: Hilltop Books, 1999.

Somervill, Barbara A. *Illinois*. New York: Children's Press, 2001.

Wiley, William. *The Civil War Diary of a Common Soldier: William Wiley of the 77th Illinois Infantry*. Baton Rouge: Louisiana State University Press, 2001.

Wills, Charles. *A Historical Album of Illinois*. Brookfield, Conn.: Millbrook Press, 1994.

Web sites

Enjoy Illinois! [Online] Available http://www.enjoyillinois.com Accessed May 31, 2001.

State of Illinois. Learn Illinois. [Online] Available http://www.state.il.us/kids/learn/ Accessed May 31, 2001.

Glossary

ALPINE: generally refers to the Alps or other mountains; can also refer to a mountainous zone above the timberline.

ANCESTRY: based on how people refer to themselves, and refers to a person's ethnic origin, descent, heritage, or place of birth of the person or the person's parents or ancestors before their arrival in the United States. The Census Bureau accepted "American" as a unique ethnicity if it was given alone, with an unclear response (such as "mixed" or "adopted"), or with names of particular states.

ANTEBELLUM: before the US Civil War.

AQUEDUCT: a large pipe or channel that carries water over a distance, or a raised structure that supports such a channel or pipe.

AQUIFER: an underground layer of porous rock, sand, or gravel that holds water.

BLUE LAWS: laws forbidding certain practices (e.g., conducting business, gaming, drinking liquor), especially on Sundays.

BROILERS: a bird (especially a young chicken) that can be cooked by broiling.

BTU: The amount of heat required to raise one pound of water one degree Fahrenheit.

CAPITAL BUDGET: a financial plan for acquiring and improving buildings or land, paid for by the sale of bonds.

CAPITAL PUNISHMENT: punishment by death.

CIVILIAN LABOR FORCE: all persons 16 years of age or older who are not in the armed forces and who are now holding a job, have been temporarily laid off, are waiting to be reassigned to a new position, or are unemployed but actively looking for work.

CLASS I RAILROAD: a railroad having gross annual revenues of $83.5 million or more in 1983.

COMMERCIAL BANK: a bank that offers to businesses and individuals a variety of banking services, including the right of withdrawal by check.

COMPACT: a formal agreement, covenant, or understanding between two or more parties.

CONSOLIDATED BUDGET: a financial plan that includes the general budget, federal funds, and all special funds.

CONSTANT DOLLARS: money values calculated so as to eliminate the effect of inflation on prices and income.

CONTERMINOUS US: refers to the "lower 48" states of the continental US that are enclosed within a common boundary.

CONTINENTAL CLIMATE: the climate typical of the US interior, having distinct seasons, a wide range of daily and annual temperatures, and dry, sunny summers.

COUNCIL-MANAGER SYSTEM: a system of local government under which a professional administrator is hired by an elected council to carry out its laws and policies.

CREDIT UNION: a cooperative body that raises funds from its members by the sale of shares and makes loans to its members at relatively low interest rates.

CURRENT DOLLARS: money values that reflect prevailing prices, without excluding the effects of inflation.

DEMAND DEPOSIT: a bank deposit that can be withdrawn by the depositor with no advance notice to the bank.

ELECTORAL VOTES: the votes that a state may cast for president, equal to the combined total of its US senators and representatives and nearly always cast entirely on behalf of the candidate who won the most votes in that state on Election Day.

ENDANGERED SPECIES: a type of plant or animal threatened with extinction in all or part of its natural range.

FEDERAL POVERTY LEVEL: a level of money income below which a person or family qualifies for US government aid.

FISCAL YEAR: a 12-month period for accounting purposes.

FOOD STAMPS: coupons issued by the government to low-income persons for food purchases at local stores.

GENERAL BUDGET: a financial plan based on a government's normal revenues and operating expenses, excluding special funds.

GENERAL COASTLINE: a measurement of the general outline of the US seacoast. See also TIDAL SHORELINE.

GREAT AWAKENING: during the mid–18th century, a Protestant religious revival in North America, especially New England.

GROSS STATE PRODUCT: the total value of goods and services produced in the state.

GROWING SEASON: the period between the last 32°F (0°C) temperature in spring and the first

32°F (0°C) temperature in autumn.

HISPANIC: a person who originates from Spain or from Spanish-speaking countries of South and Central America, Mexico, Puerto Rico, and Cuba.

HOME-RULE CHARTER: a document stating how and in what respects a city, town, or county may govern itself.

HUNDREDWEIGHT: a unit of weight that equals 100 pounds in the US and 112 pounds in Britain.

INPATIENT: a patient who is housed and fed—in addition to being treated—in a hospital.

INSTALLED CAPACITY: the maximum possible output of electric power at any given time.

MASSIF: a central mountain mass or the dominant part of a range of mountains.

MAYOR-COUNCIL SYSTEM: a system of local government under which an elected council serves as a legislature and an elected mayor is the chief administrator.

MEDICAID: a federal-state program that helps defray the hospital and medical costs of needy persons.

MEDICARE: a program of hospital and medical insurance for the elderly, administered by the federal government.

METRIC TON: a unit of weight that equals 1,000 kilograms (2,204.62 pounds).

METROPOLITAN AREA: in most cases, a city and its surrounding suburbs.

MONTANE: refers to a zone in mountainous areas in which large coniferous trees, in a cool moist setting, are the main features.

NO-FAULT INSURANCE: an automobile insurance plan that allows an accident victim to receive payment from an insurance company without having to prove who was responsible for the accident.

NONFEDERAL PHYSICIAN: a medical doctor who is not employed by the federal US government.

NORTHERN, NORTH MIDLAND: major US dialect regions.

OMBUDSMAN: a public official empowered to hear and investigate complaints by private citizens about government agencies.

PER CAPITA: per person.

PERSONAL INCOME: refers to the income an individual receives from employment, or to the total incomes that all individuals receive from their employment in a sector of business (such as personal incomes in the retail trade).

PIEDMONT: refers to the base of mountains.

POCKET VETO: a method by which a state governor (or the US president) may kill a bill by taking no action on it before the legislature adjourns.

PROVED RESERVES: the quantity of a recoverable mineral resource (such as oil or natural gas) that is still in the ground.

PUBLIC DEBT: the amount owed by a government.

RELIGIOUS ADHERENTS: the followers of a religious group, including (but not confined to) the full, confirmed, or communicant members of that group.

RETAIL TRADE: the sale of goods directly to the consumer.

REVENUE SHARING: the distribution of federal tax receipts to state and local governments.

RIGHT-TO-WORK LAW: a measure outlawing any attempt to require union membership as a condition of employment.

SAVINGS AND LOAN ASSOCIATION: a bank that invests the savings of depositors primarily in home mortgage loans.

SECESSION: the act of withdrawal, such as a state that withdrew from the Union in the US Civil War.

SERVICE INDUSTRIES: industries that provide services (e.g., health, legal, automotive repair) for individuals, businesses, and others.

SHORT TON: a unit of weight that equals 2,000 pounds.

SOCIAL SECURITY: as commonly understood, the federal system of old age, survivors, and disability insurance.

SOUTHERN, SOUTH MIDLAND: major US dialect regions.

SUBALPINE: generally refers to high mountainous areas just beneath the timberline; can also more specifically refer to the lower slopes of the Alps mountains.

SUNBELT: the southernmost states of the US, extending from Florida to California.

SUPPLEMENTAL SECURITY INCOME: a federally administered program of aid to the aged, blind, and disabled.

TIDAL SHORELINE: a detailed measurement of the US seacoast that includes sounds, bays, other outlets, and offshore islands.

TIME DEPOSIT: a bank deposit that may be withdrawn only at the end of a specified time period or upon advance notice to the bank.

VALUE ADDED BY MANUFACTURE: the difference, measured in dollars, between the value of finished goods and the cost of the materials needed to produce them.

WHOLESALE TRADE: the sale of goods, usually in large quantities, for ultimate resale to consumers.

Abbreviations & Acronyms

AD   Anno Domini
AFDC—aid to families with dependent children
AFL–CIO—American Federation of
   Labor–Congress of Industrial Organizations
AI—American Independent
AM—before noon
AM—amplitude modulation
American Ind.—American Independent Party
Amtrak—National Railroad Passenger Corp.
b.—born
BC—Before Christ
Btu—British thermal unit(s)
bu—bushel(s)
c.—circa (about)
c—Celsius (Centigrade)
CIA—Central Intelligence Agency
cm—centimeter(s)
Co.—company
comp.—compiler
Conrail—Consolidated Rail Corp.
Corp.—corporation
CST—Central Standard Time
cu—cubic
cwt—hundredweight(s)
d.—died
D—Democrat
e—evening
E—east
ed.—edition, editor
e.g.—exempli gratia (for example)
EPA—Environmental Protection Agency
est.—estimated
EST—Eastern Standard Time
et al.—et alii (and others)
etc.—et cetera (and so on)
F—Fahrenheit
FBI—Federal Bureau of Investigation
FCC—Federal Communications Commission
FM—frequency modulation
Ft.—fort
ft—foot, feet
GDP—gross domestic products
gm—gram
GMT—Greenwich Mean Time
GNP—gross national product
GRT—gross registered tons
Hist.—Historic
I—interstate (highway)

i.e.—id est (that is)
in—inch(es)
Inc.—incorporated
Jct.—junction
K—kindergarten
kg—kilogram(s)
km—kilometer(s)
km/hr—kilometers per hour
kw—kilowatt(s)
kwh—kilowatt-hour(s)
lb—pound(s)
m—meter(s); morning
m^3—cubic meter(s)
mi—mile(s)
Mon.—monument
mph—miles per hour
MST—Mountain Standard Time
Mt.—mount
Mtn.—mountain
mw—megawatt(s)
N—north
NA—not available
Natl.—National
NATO—North Atlantic Treaty Organization
NCAA—National Collegiate Athletic Association
n.d.—no date
NEA—National Education Association or National
Endowment for the Arts
N.F.—National Forest
N.W.R.—National Wildlife Refuge
oz—ounce(s)
PM—after noon
PST—Pacific Standard Time
r.—reigned
R—Republican
Ra.—range
Res.—reservoir, reservation
rev. ed.—revised edition
s—south
S—Sunday
Soc.—Socialist
sq—square
St.—saint
SRD—States' Rights Democrat
UN—United Nations
US—United States
USIA—United States Information Agency
w—west

ABBREVIATIONS & ACRONYMS

NAMES OF STATES AND OTHER SELECTED AREAS

	Standard Abbreviation(s)	Postal Abbreviation
Alabama	Ala.	AL
Alaska	*	AK
Arizona	Ariz.	AZ
Arkansas	Ark.	AR
California	Calif.	CA
Colorado	Colo.	CO
Connecticut	Conn.	CN
Delaware	Del.	DE
District of Columbia	D.C.	DC
Florida	Fla.	FL
Georgia	Ga.	GA
Hawaii	*	HI
Idaho	*	ID
Illinois	Ill.	IL
Indiana	Ind.	IN
Iowa	*	IA
Kansas	Kans. (Kan.)	KS
Kentucky	Ky.	KY
Louisiana	La.	LA
Maine	Me.	ME
Maryland	Md.	MD
Massachusetts	Mass.	MA
Michigan	Mich.	MI
Minnesota	Minn.	MN
Mississippi	Miss.	MS
Missouri	Mo.	MO
Montana	Mont.	MT
Nebraska	Nebr. (Neb.)	NE
Nevada	Nev.	NV
New Hampshire	N.H.	NH
New Jersey	N.J.	NJ
New Mexico	N.Mex.(N.M.)	NM
New York	N.Y.	NY
North Carolina	N.C.	NC
North Dakota	N.Dak. (N.D.)	ND
Ohio	*	OH
Oklahoma	Okla.	OK
Oregon	Oreg. (Ore.)	OR
Pennsylvania	Pa.	PA
Puerto Rico	P.R.	PR
Rhode Island	R.I.	RI
South Carolina	S.C.	SC
South Dakota	S.Dak. (S.D.)	SD
Tennessee	Tenn.	TN
Texas	Tex.	TX
Utah	*	UT
Vermont	Vt.	VT
Virginia	Va.	VA
Virgin Islands	V.I.	VI
Washington	Wash.	WA
West Virginia	W.Va.	WV
Wisconsin	Wis.	WI
Wyoming	Wyo.	WY

*No standard abbreviation

Alabama

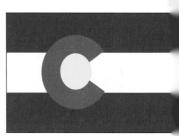

Alaska

Arizona

Arkansas

California

Colorado

Connecticut

Delaware

Florida

Georgia

Hawaii

Idaho

Illinois